Epica Book 15
Europe's Best Advertising

EDITOR
Mark Tungate

ART DIRECTOR
Frédéric Ansermet

EDITORIAL ASSISTANTS
Dara Gannon
Ghenette Haïle-Michaël
Maureen Lynch

COVER DESIGN
Chris Ashworth
Robert Kester
(Getty Images Creative Studio)

COVER IMAGE
John Holden (Stone)

PUBLISHER
AVA Publishing S.A.
sales@avabooks.ch

DISTRIBUTION
North America
Sterling Publishing Co.
www.sterlingpub.com
All other countries
Thames & Hudson Ltd.
sales@thameshudson.co.uk

PRODUCTION
AVA Book Production Pte Ltd.
production@avabooks.com.sg

Printed in Singapore

© COPYRIGHT 2002 EPICA S.A. ALL RIGHTS RESERVED

Under no circumstances can any part of this book be reproduced or copied in any way or form without prior permission of the copyright owners.
EPICA S.A.
65 rue J.J. Rousseau,
92150 Suresnes, France
Tel: 33 (0) 1 42 04 04 32
Fax: 33 (0) 1 45 06 02 88
Internet: www.epica-awards.com
Email: info@epica-awards.com

Epica S.A. has made every effort to publish full and correct credits for each work included in this volume based on the information provided on the Epica entry forms. Epica S.A. and Applied Visual Arts Publishing S.A. (AVA) regret any omissions that may have occurred, but hereby disclaim liability.

Contents

INTRODUCTION
Foreword by Sebastian Turner	5
2001 Winners	6
The Jury	8
Annual Report	10

EPICA D'OR 2001
"Fame At Last" by Lewis Blackwell	12

THE STONE PRIZE
Advertising Photography	16

FOOD & DRINK
Food	26
Confectionery & Snacks	40
Dairy Products	46
Alcoholic Drinks A	54
Alcoholic Drinks B	60
Non-Alcoholic Drinks	68

CONSUMER SERVICES
Transport & Tourism	80
Retail Services	92
Financial Services	110
Public Interest	124
Communication Services	162

THE HOME
Homes, Furnishings & Appliances	176
Household Maintenance	190
Audiovisual Equipment & Accessories	198

HEALTH & BEAUTY
Toiletries & Health Care	204
Beauty Products	212
Prescription Products & Services	216

AUTOMOTIVE
Automobiles	220
Automotive & Accessories	244

BUSINESS TO BUSINESS
Office Equipment	252
Business Services	258
Industrial & Agricultural Equipment	268

FASHION
Clothing & Fabrics	272
Footwear & Personal Accessories	282

MISCELLANEOUS
Media	292
Recreation & Leisure	310

TECHNIQUES
Interactive	324
New Media	336
Direct Marketing	346
Publications	358
Packaging Design	366
Illustration & Graphics	372

Sebastian Turner, CEO, Scholz & Friends AG.

Photo: Sava Hlavacek

Ideas sell best

Recall values in advertising are pretty down-to-earth. According to various estimates, 50 to 75% of all advertising makes no impact at all. However, these figures are challenged by a new study in which an amazing 87% of the commercials covered by the report achieved or even exceeded their targets. The advertisements in question? The 400 commercials which did best at creative competitions.

So, can we conclude that creative advertisements always succeed? Big flops prove the contrary: lots of campaigns have been praised for their creativity while totally failing in the marketplace. On the other hand, the list of advertising campaigns that have succeeded despite their lack of creativity is pretty long, meaning that creativity does not necessarily affect the outcome of a campaign. So what does this tell us?

Looking at the situation from the consumer's point of view provides some useful insights. Consumer interest in advertising is extremely low and continues to decrease. An international study of advertising recall values has shown that in 1960, 40% of commercial TV viewers could remember one specific spot, whereas today only 8% are able to do so. Even if consumers had nothing better to do than study advertising messages all day, they could not absorb, let alone retain, all the information that is imposed on them by ads.

Of course, the number of ads has exploded over the past few years. How can an advertisement reach its target under such circumstances? One method might be to use a few TV commercials or print ads over a comparatively long period of time. They might thus gain high popularity, but not necessarily become widely accepted – or even create sympathy for a brand. At least one adverse side-effect is the tiring effect of new TV commercials on the target group, provided people are watching in the first place.

The advertising industry seems to be trapped in a vicious cycle: the more monotonous and bland TV commercials become, the less widely accepted they are. Alternatively, high-impact commercials have to be repeated more often in order to increase the pressure and get the desired attention – otherwise monotony sets in and interest levels fall. Consumer surveys show that the final result of these methods is the same: most consumers have had enough of advertising and try to avoid it.

Yet if the majority of advertising is considered annoying by consumers, is it possible that 61% of them would miss ads if they did not exist? This is the result of a survey conducted in Great Britain. However, as we all know, the British are famous for producing the most creative advertising in the world.

Does this mean that the effectiveness of creative advertising varies from country to country? Interestingly enough, the German market provides a good indication. Two brands have achieved success as a result of the outstanding creative quality of their advertising over the past few years, namely Audi and Mercedes-Benz. Internal studies comparing advertising expenditure with recall values demonstrate this correlation. Both brands show a steep increase in popularity compared to the amount of budget spent. None of their numerous rival marques can demonstrate an equally favourable equation. And both brands offer – in addition to a precisely defined brand core – entertaining advertisements.

A recent joint study by the German Society for Consumer Research and the Gesamtverbandes Werbeagenturen (German Association of Advertising Agencies) measured both advertising pressure – that's to say, the clients' budgets – and the quality of the advertising concerned. High quality ads were deemed to achieve "by far the best results" and led to the conclusion that "the most innovative rather than the biggest [spenders] will make it".

A comparison between the two most important advertising competitions in Germany and Switzerland provides further insights. Every year, the Art Directors Club (ADC) rewards the most creative advertising campaign, as chosen by its jury. Only a very small percentage of all print, poster and commercials have a chance to win these awards. If creativity had only a little influence on the success of advertising, the ADC winners would make a negligible showing in competitions based on effectiveness. However, this is far from the case! In fact, of the campaigns that received Effie (advertising effectiveness) awards from Germany's advertising agencies association in the 1990s, a high percentage were also recognised by the ADC for their creative quality.

Finally, practical experience supports the assumption that creative advertising sells better. An investigation of 480 more-than-usually effective campaigns from all over the world concludes that "the most successful campaigns are clearly more creative than average campaigns". The authors of the study are former Procter & Gamble marketing managers, and thus above any suspicion of praising creativity for their own benefit. In fact, they are supported by the equally objective Nestlé boss Helmut Maucher, who observes: "There are plenty of examples where, rather than an extremely high budget, the idea, the creativity and the intelligent positioning of an advertising campaign have guaranteed success."

Sebastian Turner, CEO, Scholz & Friends AG.

Winners

Epica d'Or

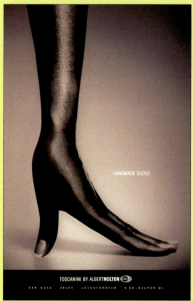
The Stone Prize

EPICA WINNERS 2001

Category	Agency	Client/Campaign
EPICA D'OR	MOTHER (LONDON)	QTV MUSIC CHANNEL "THE DANSTER" CAMPAIGN
THE STONE PRIZE (PHOTOGRAPHY)	EDO KARS for YOKYOR (AMSTERDAM)	ALBERT NOLTEN FOOTWEAR "HANDMADE SHOES"

PRINT WINNERS

Category	Agency	Client
FOOD	SCHOLZ & FRIENDS (HAMBURG)	CHIO CHIPS
CONFECTIONERY & SNACKS	D'ARCY MASIUS BENTON & BOWLES (HAMBURG)	MARS MINIATURES
DAIRY PRODUCTS	CLM/BBDO (PARIS)	BOUNTY ICE CREAM
ALCOHOLIC DRINKS (A)	GREY (WARSAW)	LUKSUSOWA POTATO VODKA
ALCOHOLIC DRINKS (B)	VVL/BBDO (BRUSSELS)	CARLSBERG BEER
NON-ALCOHOLIC DRINKS	CLM/BBDO (PARIS)	PEPSI COLA
TRANSPORT & TOURISM	LEO BURNETT (OSLO)	SAS AIRLINES
RETAIL SERVICES	SCHOLZ & FRIENDS (BERLIN)	FIONA BENNETT HATS
FINANCIAL SERVICES	PUBLICIS (ZÜRICH)	DIE MOBILIAR INSURANCE
PUBLIC INTEREST	SPRINGER & JACOBY (HAMBURG)	UNICEF
COMMUNICATION SERVICES	SPRINGER & JACOBY (HAMBURG)	DEUTSCHE TELEKOM T-DSL
HOMES, FURNISHINGS & APPLIANCES	CALLEGARI BERVILLE GREY (PARIS)	LIGNE ROSET FURNITURE
HOUSEHOLD MAINTENANCE	ADVICO YOUNG & RUBICAM (ZÜRICH)	TELA PAPER TABLE WARE
AUDIOVISUAL EQUIPMENT & ACCESSORIES	JERLOV & KÖRBERG (GOTHENBURG)	FENDER GUITARS
TOILETRIES & HEALTH CARE	MICHAEL CONRAD & LEO BURNETT (FRANKFURT)	LADY SHAVER
PRESCRIPTION PRODUCTS	SPRINGER & JACOBY (BARCELONA)	SAETIL PAIN RELIEVER
AUTOMOBILES	DDB (BRUSSELS)	VOLKSWAGEN TDI
AUTOMOTIVE & ACCESSORIES	SCHOLZ & FRIENDS (BERLIN)	MERCEDES-BENZ TRUCKS
OFFICE EQUIPMENT	BDDP & FILS (PARIS)	MICROSOFT OFFICE
BUSINESS SERVICES	LAMTAR (PARIS)	MEDIAMETRIE AUDIENCE MEASUREMENT
INDUSTRIAL & AGRICULTURAL EQUIPMENT	CREATIVE CENTER CARDEA (SARAJEVO)	ISKRAEMECO ELECTRIC METERS
CLOTHING & FABRICS	PARADISET DDB (STOCKHOLM)	DIESEL JEANS & WORKWEAR
FOOTWEAR & PERSONAL ACCESSORIES	YOKYOR (AMSTERDAM)	ALBERT NOLTEN FOOTWEAR
MEDIA	PUBLICIS (MADRID)	MARCA SPORTS NEWSPAPER
RECREATION & LEISURE	HASAN & PARTNERS (HELSINKI)	KANSALLIS NATIONAL MUSEUM
INTERACTIVE: CD ROMS	SCHOLZ & VOLKMER (WIESBADEN)	MERCEDES-BENZ A CLASS
INTERACTIVE: WEBSITES	FRAMFAB (DENMARK)	NIKE FREESTYLE
INTERACTIVE: BANNERS	FORSMAN & BODENFORS (GOTHENBURG)	LIBERO UP&GO DIAPERS
NEW MEDIA	PUBLICIS (AMSTELVEEN)	BONZO DOG FOOD
DIRECT MARKETING	HARRISON TROUGHTON WUNDERMAN (LONDON)	AA ROADSIDE ASSISTANCE
PUBLICATIONS	JUNG VON MATT (HAMBURG)	MINI COOPER/MINI ONE CUBE
PACKAGING DESIGN	INTELLECTA CORPORATE (STOCKHOLM)	BARSQUARE WINE LABELS
ILLUSTRATION & GRAPHICS	ROSE DESIGN ASSOCIATES (LONDON)	ROYAL MAIL MILLINERY STAMPS

FILM WINNERS

Category	Agency	Client
FOOD	LOWE BRINDFORS (STOCKHOLM)	KF ORGANIC FOODS, "RESTAURANT"
CONFECTIONERY & SNACKS	FHV/BBDO (AMSTELVEEN)	SNICKERS, "CHIMPANZEE"
DAIRY PRODUCTS	OUTSIDER (LONDON) for AMV BBDO (LONDON)	UTTERLY BUTTERLY, "DESIGNER"
ALCOHOLIC DRINKS (A)	McCANN-ERICKSON (BRUSSELS)	WILLIAM LAWSON'S, "THE HAKA"
ALCOHOLIC DRINKS (B)	GORGEOUS ENTERPRISES (LONDON) for LOWE LINTAS (LONDON)	HEINEKEN, "BLACKMAIL" CAMPAIGN
NON-ALCOHOLIC DRINKS	MOTHER (LONDON)	DR PEPPER, "EMERGENCY"
TRANSPORT & TOURISM	2AM FILMS (LONDON) for IRISH INTERNATIONAL (DUBLIN)	AER LINGUS CAMPAIGN
RETAIL SERVICES	ROBERT/BOISEN & LIKE MINDED (COPENHAGEN)	INTERFLORA, "FORMULA 1"
FINANCIAL SERVICES	COLLABORATE (STOCKHOLM)	LÄNSFÖRSÄKRINGAR INSURANCE, "PRISON"
PUBLIC INTEREST	SAATCHI & SAATCHI (MILAN)	MTV DEATH PENALTY, "MISTAKE"
COMMUNICATION SERVICES	BDDP & FILS (PARIS)	LA POSTE, "VIRTUAL WORLD"
HOMES, FURNISHINGS & APPLIANCES	LEAGAS DELANEY PARIS CENTRE (PARIS)	IKEA, "TIDY UP" CAMPAIGN
AUDIOVISUAL EQUIPMENT	OGILVY & MATHER (FRANKFURT)	KODAK, "CHAMELEON"
TOILETRIES & HEALTH CARE	McCANN-ERICKSON (MANCHESTER)	DUREX CONDOMS, "SQUARE"
BEAUTY PRODUCTS	MOTHER (LONDON)	ORGANICS SHAMPOO, CAMPAIGN
AUTOMOBILES (2 WINNERS)	ELASTICA (LISBON)	AUDI, "PUDDLE"
	SAATCHI & SAATCHI (FRANKFURT)	AUDI MULTITRONIC, "THE FAN"
AUTOMOTIVE & ACCESSORIES	JUNG VON MATT (MUNICH)	BMW C1 MOTORBIKE, "MAGIC CAR"
OFFICE EQUIPMENT	OGILVY & MATHER (PARIS)	IBM EUROPE, "CHEESEWARS"
BUSINESS SERVICES	McCANN-ERICKSON (ZÜRICH)	RANDSTAD, "HITCHHIKER"
INDUSTRIAL & AGRICULTURAL PRODUCTS	EURO RSCG CORPORATE (PARIS)	AIRBUS INDUSTRY, "THE MAGMA"
CLOTHING & FABRICS	GORGEOUS ENTERPRISES (LONDON) for LOWE LINTAS (LONDON)	REEBOK, "SOFA"
FOOTWEAR & PERSONAL ACCESSORIES	KOLLE REBBE WERBEAGENTUR (HAMBURG)	GAULOISES, "RENDEZVOUS"
MEDIA	MOTHER (LONDON)	QTV MUSIC CHANNEL CAMPAIGN
RECREATION & LEISURE	LOWE LINTAS & PARTNERS (COPENHAGEN)	DANISH LOTTERY, "DREAMING"
INTERACTIVE: WEB COMMERCIALS	THE LEITH AGENCY (EDINBURGH)	THE LEITH AGENCY XMAS CARD

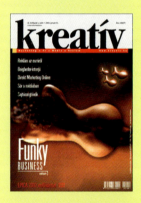   

  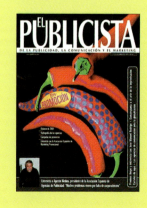 

   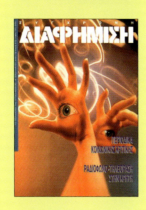      

The Jury

The Epica jury is made up of representatives from Europe's leading advertising magazines.

AUSTRIA
Extra Dienst

BELGIUM
Pub

CZECH REPUBLIC
Strategie

DENMARK
Markedsføring

FINLAND
Markkinointi & Mainonta

FRANCE
CB News

GERMANY
Lürzer's International Archive
Werben und Verkaufen

GREAT BRITAIN
Creative Review
Marketing Week
The Drum

GREECE
Advertising Today

HUNGARY
Kreatív

IRELAND
IMJ

ITALY
Pubblicitá Italia
Pubblico
Strategia

NETHERLANDS
Adformatie
Nieuws Tribune

NORWAY
Kampanje

POLAND
Media i Marketing Polska

PORTUGAL
Prisma

RUSSIA
Advertising Ideas
Kreativ.Creativity

SLOVAKIA
Stratégie

SLOVENIA
MM

SPAIN
El Publicista

SWEDEN
Resumé

SWITZERLAND
Werbe Woche

TURKEY
Marketing Türkiye

Photos: Hara Mahlerová (Strategie)

Annual Report

The awards ceremony took place in January 2002 at Prague's famous Národní dům na Smichove (National House), near the Vlata River. The event was hosted by Strategie, the Czech Republic's leading weekly advertising and marketing magazine, in partnership with its sister publication from Slovakia.

Results

Epica celebrated its 15th anniversary in 2001 with 5283 entries from 643 agencies, studios and production companies.

There were a total of 62 winners, up on the previous year's 58. Of these, 28 were film winners, including the Epica d'Or, while 34 were for print entries and other disciplines (including interactive, direct marketing and packaging design). There were also 273 finalists (entries that did not win in their categories but achieved scores high enough to qualify as winners).

Work from 38 countries was entered for the competition, with 25 countries reaching the final list of winners and finalists. For the first time, Germany was the most successful country, with 13 winners and no less than 66 finalists. France moved up from 4th to 2nd place, while Great Britain maintained its position at the number three slot. Sweden slipped to 4th place. A special mention must go to Bosnia, which got its first ever Epica winner in 2001.

	Entrants	Entries	Winners	Finalists
AUSTRIA	25	249	0	2
BELARUS	1	5	0	0
BELGIUM	22	196	3	3
BOSNIA	1	3	1	0
BULGARIA	1	2	0	0
CROATIA	3	19	0	1
CZECH REPUBLIC	8	49	0	4
DENMARK	25	228	3	9
FINLAND	20	137	1	6
FRANCE	34	264	9	39
GEORGIA	2	17	0	0
GERMANY	117	1234	13	66
GREAT BRITAIN	53	402	12	28
GREECE	11	58	0	0
HOLLAND	39	273	4	11
HUNGARY	9	50	0	0
ICELAND	2	16	0	2
IRELAND	5	35	1	2
ISRAEL	9	56	0	0
ITALY	41	401	1	10
LEBANON	2	9	0	1
LITHUANIA	2	8	0	0
LUXEMBOURG	1	2	0	0
NORWAY	13	84	1	11
POLAND	13	77	1	3
PORTUGAL	17	115	1	7
ROMANIA	5	31	0	0
RUSSIA	13	75	0	2
SAUDI ARABIA	1	1	0	0
SLOVAKIA	4	26	0	1
SLOVENIA	16	103	0	6
SPAIN	22	157	2	15
SWEDEN	76	703	6	32
SWITZERLAND	17	117	3	11
TURKEY	6	49	0	0
U.A.E.	2	7	0	1
UKRAINE	4	24	0	0
YUGOSLAVIA	1	1	0	0
TOTAL	643	5283	62	273

Epica d'Or: The 15th Epica d'Or was won by Mother, London, for the QTV campaign, "The Danster", featuring a wannabe rock star. The films were produced by Talkback, London and directed by Graham Linehan (see p.12 & 293).

Stone Prize: The Stone Prize for European advertising photography was won by Edo Kars for the "Handmade Shoes" print ad for Albert Noten shoes, art-directed by Mart Groen of YokYor, Amsterdam (p. 16).

Internet Sites: For more information, visit *www.epica-awards.com* and *www.adforum.com* where the 2001 film winners can be viewed in real-time. Visit *www.gettyimages.com/stone* for more information on Stone.

"I dedicate the following act of destruction to the memory of Kurt Cobain"

"If it wasn't for music I'd either be dead or in prison – know what I mean?"

"I do live a dangerous life... sorry if it offends people, but I am a rock & roller"

"Be honest, don't you think I might be just a little bit black?"

"Feedback is my evil mistress"

Fame at last
by Lewis Blackwell

There are few instantly recognisable characters in commercials – but The Danster, star of this year's Epica d'Or winner, is one of them. Male viewers will secretly identify with this rock star wannabe, while women will be reminded of partners who have begged them not to throw out their vinyl record collection, or spent whole evenings rearranging their CDs in chronological order.

When London agency Mother was asked by EMAP Digital to launch QTV (a cable television version of its successful music magazine Q) "to the right audience", it was obvious which creatives should handle the job. Jim Thornton and Ben Mooge are both writers. Mooge, the younger by ten years, is an English graduate who arrived at Mother as a tea boy but soon discovered he was better at writing ads ("I was rubbish at making tea", he confides). He found himself sitting next to Thornton and the pair immediately established a rapport based on their obsession with popular music in all its forms.

Dan "The Danster" Danielson is their creation, and they had no difficulty in fleshing him out, right down to his trainers. Within two weeks of receiving the brief, Thornton and Mooge had put together a blueprint for their character, including his Oasis-style jacket and unbranded baseball cap – which signals his determination to resist global branding while cunningly concealing his receding hairline.

To this character sketch they added about half a dozen one-line gags, and took the outline to the man who was their first choice for bringing it to life, Graham Linehan. The Irish writer-director is best known for Father Ted, a hugely popular and somewhat surreal British TV comedy series. Depicting the chaotic rural household of three eccentric Irish priests, the series was an unexpected mainstream success. Linehan is also the name behind Big Train, a zany and sardonic sketch show. He had never directed a commercial before but, as a former music journalist, he recognised the potential of The Danster and agreed immediately.

Despite the campaign's subsequent success Linehan admits that he is not a natural commercials director. "The QTV ads were enjoyable to do, and Mother are a great company, but I'm not a huge fan of directing advertisements in general. I hate the meetings, for one thing. And I hate the fact that the ads can be re-cut without your permission, as I really think that comedy happens in the editing suite."

Linehan attributes much of the campaign's success to the actor who filled The Danster's training shoes. "We wouldn't have done nearly so well if we'd cast anyone other than Martin Freeman. He's an incredibly talented actor, and his sense of humour is such that I didn't have to tell him the point of any joke more than once. That made it easier to come up with things on the day, as I knew that he could handle any ideas I threw at him."

Only six spots had been scheduled at the original brief, but these were each shot in one take, and were in the can well before the end of the schedule. By then there was no stopping the crew, as more ideas came thick and fast from the creatives, the director, the cameraman ("a star in his own firmament", according to Thornton and Mooge) and The Danster himself, Martin Freeman. A self-confessed music

THOUSANDS WHO'VE MADE IT

FOR THE MILLIONS WHO HAVEN'T

"Listen to this delay, it's way too long"

"I got tendonitis from playing the guitar"

"I bought this... I don't know what it is"

"My music's sort of Lennon & McCartney meets Motorhead"

nerd, Freeman not only understood but could actually envisage himself as the character. While filming in a guitar shop, for example, he began to ad-lib spontaneously. In the resulting spot, he returns a piece of electronic equipment, confessing: "I bought this last week." Pause. "I don't know what it is."

Crew members stepped in to play additional characters. Mooge appears as a music shop assistant, for instance, and in the hilarious café commercial, members of the crew play the waitress and The Danster's girlfriend. When The Danster is presented with the bill, he signs his autograph instead of paying it. In another spot, he pathetically importunes his partner: "Do you not think I might be just a little bit black?"

The girlfriend was put in the script at the suggestion of the client, to avoid making The Danster look like a complete and utter loser. Not surprisingly, she makes an early exit. As the pair stroll through a shopping centre, she ducks into a store while he complains about the disappearance of the word "The" from pop music. "Oasis, Moby, Blur...what's wrong with the word 'The'? It was all right for The Beatles. It was all right for The Stones. It was even all right for The The..."

Thanks to a combination of enthusiasm and efficiency, for a surprisingly small budget of £110,000, the team produced eleven 30-second commercials and twelve 10-second "break bumpers". And each one contains a priceless Danster moment, whether he's proclaiming: "Feedback is my evil mistress!", or failing to smash a guitar after announcing: "This act of destruction is dedicated to the memory of Kurt Cobain." Taxi drivers seem to particularly suffer at The Danster's hands. In one spot, he drones on about his musical influences instead of providing directions, while in another he outlines the hazards of his dangerous rock and roll lifestyle – before realising that his seatbelt isn't fastened and flying into a panic. Even a passing elderly woman gets the Danster treatment, when he tells her: "If it wasn't for my music, I'd probably be either dead or in prison, know what I mean?"

The adoption of The Danster as a cult figure among the music TV-watching generation is remarkable, given that the spots were only ever seen by the relatively small group of subscribers to EMAP cable television channels. Yet while most of The Danster's audience don't share his sad lack of self-awareness, most of them have indulged in his fantasy rock star life for at least a few moments. The series' tag-line says it all: "QTV. Thousands who've made it...for the millions who haven't."

Thornton and Mooge are surprised by the success of their creation, imagining that honours such as the Epica d'Or are only handed out to "slick surfing commercials" for high-profile clients. But they are especially pleased that audiences have found the campaign entertaining, admitting that they would much rather entertain people than sell products.

The ad-hoc Danster shoot is typical of the organic approach that characterises their work, and the agency's approach in general. At Mother, individual creatives are free to develop their own campaigns, as well as other enterprises, and Thornton and Mooge both get involved in separate projects. With a Norwegian colleague, Mooge recently directed a video for a disc that went to number one in Norway. It's the sort of statistic The Danster would love – and he is not alone. Hence his popularity with a huge audience – even if half of them are laughing at him with a tinge of embarrassment.

Lewis Blackwell is the creative director of Getty Images, the world's leading provider of images. For many years he was the editor-in-chief and publisher of the magazine Creative Review, and now contributes columns to several titles worldwide. As a writer he is also known for several critically acclaimed books on communication, including the bestselling creative title The End Of Print. His most recent book is Soon: Brands of Tomorrow.

"Many of the target audience were frustrated musicians and even frustrated music journalists. Perversely, they had done nothing to realise their ambitions."
is dead (Q research)

Q

It should have been me.

The Danster concept: as presented to the client.

Icon in the making: Mother's blueprint for the Danster character.

PLEASE ALLOW ME TO INTRODUCE MYSELF......... DAN 'THE DANSTER' DANIELSON

- **Unbranded baseball hat** ("I haven't sold out man") cunningly concealing his impending loss of hair. However Moby's recent success is making him seriously consider using baldness as a style statement.

- **On the road stubble.** "I'm a working musician. Shaving's for boybands. I'm too busy creating to be shaving."

- **The hand that once touched the hem of Joe Strummer's garment.** Well, leather jacket anyway.

- **Anorak.** River Island copy of hirsute Oasis frontman's jacket, circa '96. Plus it's bloody cold in the Plymouth Arndale Centre.

- **Cargo Pants:** 60/40 polyester cotton mix, £38.99 from The Gap (Branches nationwide).

- **Specially reinforced Caterpillars** to cope with his rigorous touring commitments. Around Plymouth. Prefers Assyrian open-toed sandals when composing "You can't beat that African vibe".

- **Ear.** Routinely syringed for improved pitch perception.

- Having once shone as an alto at school, sadly puberty exacted a fearsome revenge on these poor vocal chords.

- **Smiths' Meat is Murder t-shirt** hidden beneath original Levis jacket (no front pockets) on account of him finding a bacon buttie too hard to resist.

- **Fingers of left hand** horribly calloused due to years of frenetic fretwork. Showing increasing signs of evolving a plectrum between thumb and forefinger.

- **Acute tendonitis** caused by overuse of wah-wah pedal.

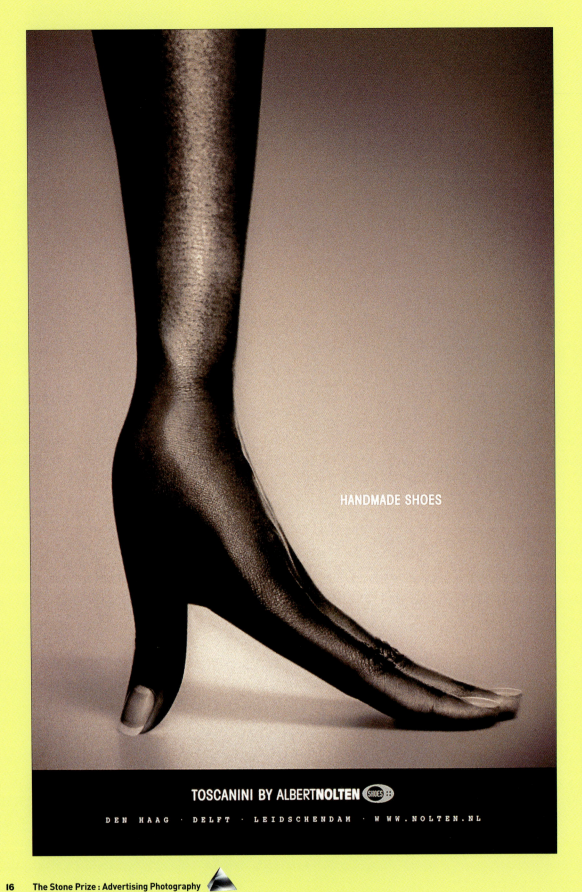

16   The Stone Prize : Advertising Photography

Photographer:	Edo Kars
Creative Directors:	Mart Groen
	Ralph Wilmes
Agency:	YokYor, Amsterdam
Client:	Albert Nolten Shoes

The Stone Prize : Advertising Photography   17

Photographers:	Alfred Seiland
	Helmut Newton
Creative Director:	Sebastian Turner
Art Directors:	Julia Schmidt
	Petra Reichenbach
Agency:	Scholz & Friends, Berlin
Client:	Frankfurter Allgemeine Zeitung

18 The Stone Prize : Advertising Photography

Photographer:	Dominik Mentzos	**Photographer:**	Rankin
Creative Directors:	Dr. Stephan Vogel Thomas Hofbeck	**Creative Director:** **Copywriter:**	Anne de Maupeou Olivier Dermaux
Copywriter:	Philipp Bnttcher	**Art Director:**	Mathieu Vinciguerra
Art Director:	Marco Weber	**Agency:**	CLM/BBDO, Paris
Agency:	Ogilvy & Mather, Frankfurt	**Client:**	Kookaï
Client:	IBM		

The Stone Prize : Advertising Photography

Photographer: Marc Gouby
Art Director: Damien Bellon
Agency: BDDP & Fils, Paris
Client: Clan Campbell

20 The Stone Prize : Advertising Photography

Photographer:	Nicholas Moore
Creative Directors:	Antoine Barthuel
	Daniel Forh
Copywriter:	Etienne Turquet
Art Directors:	Aurélie Scalabre
	Patrick Samot
Agency:	BETC Euro RSCG, Paris
Client:	Air France

The Stone Prize : Advertising Photography

Photographer: Raimundas Svilpa	**Photographer:** Christian Kettiger
Art Director: Raimundas Svilpa	**Creative Director:** Pierre Berville
Agency: RF, Klaipeda	**Art Director:** Patrice Jean Baptiste
Client: Klaipeda Cultural Center	**Agency:** Callegari Berville Grey, Paris
	Client: Ligne Roset Furnishings

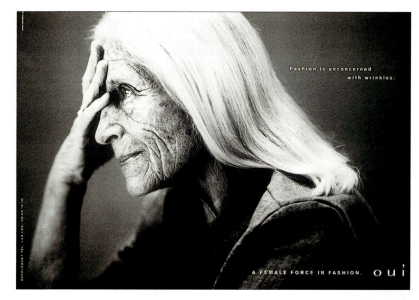

22 The Stone Prize : Advertising Photography

Photographer:	Giblin & James	**Photographer:**	Anatol Kotte
Creative Director:	Billy Mawhinney	**Creative Directors:**	Claudia Hammerschmidt
Copywriter:	Pete Bastiman		Susanne Ahlers
Art Director:	Steve Mawhinney	**Copywriter:**	Carlos Obers
Agency:	Faulds Advertising, Edinburgh	**Art Director:**	Susanne Ahlers
Client:	Key 103 FM	**Agency:**	RG Wiesmeier, Munich
		Client:	Oui Ladies Fashions

Photographer:	Jean-Pierre Khazem
Art Directors:	Erik Kessels
	Karen Heuter
Agency:	KesselsKramer,
	Amsterdam
Client:	Diesel

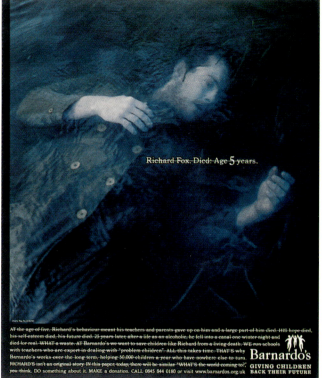

The Stone Prize : Advertising Photography

Photographer:	Nadav Kander	Photographer:	Hans Kroeskamp
Art Director:	Adrian Rossi	Creative Director:	André Rysman
Agency:	Bartle Bogle Hegarty, London	Copywriter:	Frank Marinus
Client:	Barnardos	Art Director:	Jan Macken
		Agency:	TBWA\Brussels
		Client:	Samsonite

The Stone Prize : Advertising Photography 25

Photographer:	Alex Georgiou	Photographer:	Frank Uyttenhove
Creative Director:	Aliki Anagnostara	Creative Director:	André Rysman
Copywriter:	Anastasia Georgopoulos	Copywriter:	Frank Marinus
Art Director:	Nikos Kotoulas	Art Director:	Jan Macken
Agency:	TBWA\Athens	Agency:	TBWA\Brussels
Client:	Freestyle Hairdressers	Client:	Levis Paints

Agency:	Scholz & Friends, Hamburg
Creative Director:	Stefan Setzkorn
Copywriter:	Stephanie Völzow
Art Director:	Stefanie Zimmermann
Photographer:	Frank Evers
Client:	Chio Chips Website

We're looking for more organic farmers.

KF

Agency:	Lowe Brindfors, Stockholm	A couple are dining in an expensive restaurant when one of the waiters sprays their food with some kind of chemical. When the male diner asks what it is, the waiter replies: "Poison." But he goes on to explain that most of the food we eat is sprayed with the same stuff. A neighbouring diner nods in agreement. Reassured, the couple accept a couple of squirts of the liquid and continue with their meal. KF Organic Foods, on the other hand, offer chemical-free products, with no unexpected ingredients.
Creative Director:	Johan Nilsson	
Copywriter:	Staffan Ryberg	
Art Director:	Mitte Blomqvist	
Production:	EFTI	
Director:	Felix Herngren	
Producers:	Cornelia Opitz	
	Francy Suntinger	
Photographer:	Göran Hallberg	
Client:	KF Änglamark Organic Foods, "The Restaurant"	

Food

Agency:	Lowe Brindfors, Stockholm
Creative Director:	Johan Nilsson
Copywriter:	Björn Persson
Art Director:	Kristofer Mårtensson
Production:	Acne
Directors:	Tomas Skoging
	Adam Springfeldt
Producers:	Maria Tamander
	David Olsson
	Mark Baughen
Client:	KF Signum Foods, "Scarecrow"

The Italian sun shines through a window on a man laying in bed, his arms splayed out in the shape of a cross. As he gets up, it's clear that he is stuck in this position. Walking down a lane, he is joined by other men with the same malady. When they stand in a field, the situation becomes clear – they are human scarecrows. The man explains that they are tomato farmers who care about their product so much that they don't trust ordinary scarecrows. KF Signum chooses its tomatoes with care.

Agency:	Lowe Brindfors, Stockholm
Creative Director:	Johan Nilsson
Copywriter:	Staffan Ryberg
Art Director:	Mitte Blomquist
Photographer:	Fredrik Lieberath
Client:	KF Änglamark Organic Foods

Agency:	Ogilvy & Mather, Frankfurt	Agency:	Leo Burnett, Paris
Art Director:	Minh Khai Doan	Creative Directors:	Christophe Coffre
Photographer:	Thomas Strogalski		Nicolas Taubes
Client:	Kraft Tomato Ketchup	Copywriters:	Axel Orliac
			Laurent Dravet
		Art Director:	Pascal Hirsch
		Photographer:	Pascal Hirsch
		Client:	Heinz Tomato Ketchup

30 Food

Agency:	Forsman & Bodenfors, Gothenburg
Copywriter:	Martin Ringqvist
Art Director:	Johan Eghammer
Production:	Atmosfär, Stockholm
Director:	Jörgen Lööf
Producers:	Berit Tilly Charlotte Most
Client:	Abba Seafood Sandwich Spread, "Early Morning"

A young woman comes down for breakfast, squeezes the last of the sandwich spread onto her bread, and chucks the tube into the bin. Her flatmate appears, and without comment rescues the tube. She squeezes it in the door to force out what appears to be a final squirt. But then a third flatmate arrives, takes the tube, puts her boots on and goes to the launderette nearby. She uses an electric clothes press to squeeze out the very last piece of paste. People will do anything to use up all of their Abba seafood spread.

Agency:	Paltemaa Huttunen Santala TBWA, Helsinki
Copywriter:	Markku Rönkkö
Art Director:	Jyrki Reinikka
Production:	Vulcan Films
Director:	Marko Antila
Producers:	Mika Sylvin Marja Vattulainen
Client:	Vaasan Bread, "Harp"

We're back in medieval times, and a knight and his damsel are about to start a picnic in a countryside setting. Gentle harp music accompanies the scene. But there's a problem – the bread isn't sliced, and the knight's sword has been broken in battle. The solution? The knight grabs the bread, marches a few metres to the spot where the harpist is sitting, and uses the instrument's fine strings to slice the loaf. Vaasan Pre-Sliced Bread, traditional yet modern, would have saved him the effort.

Food 31

Agency:	McCann-Erickson, Prague	**Agency:**	Leo Burnett, Amsterdam
Creative Directors:	Jo Johansen Lars Killi	**Creative Directors:**	Martijn van Sonsbeek Ewald Theunisse
Copywriter:	Juraj Janiš	**Copywriters:**	Elise de Jong Ewald Theunisse
Art Director:	Tereza Víznerová	**Art Director:**	Robert van den Heuvel
Photographer:	Nikola Tačevski	**Photographer:**	Bert Teunissen
Client:	Rama Margarine	**Client:**	John West Canned Fish

Food

Agency:	Leo Burnett, Paris	
Creative Directors:	Christophe Coffre	
	Nicolas Taubes	
Copywriter:	Christophe Coffre	
Art Director:	Nicolas Taubes	
Production:	1/33 Productions	
Director:	Neil Harris	
Producers:	Audrey Chaouat	
	Catherine Guiol	
Client:	Charal Meat,	
	"The Bedroom"	

A married couple are sleeping soundly in their bed. Suddenly, the woman wakes up with a scream. She is shocked when she realises that her own husband has bitten her – and not in an erotic way. "Look what you've done!" she says, examining the damage in a full-length mirror. "What's the matter with you?" In fact, he was craving flesh. "How long is it since you've given meat to your husband?" asks the tagline.

Agency:	Leo Burnett, Paris	
Creative Directors:	Christophe Coffre	
	Nicolas Taubes	
Copywriter:	Christophe Coffre	
Art Director:	Nicolas Taubes	
Production:	1/33 Productions	
Director:	Neil Harris	
Producers:	Audrey Chaouat	
	Catherine Guiol	
Client:	Charal Meat,	
	"The Lift"	

A man with a small dog enters an apartment building. As he gets into the lift, he takes the family pet into his arms. The doors close and they disappear from view – but a second later we hear the dog whine in distress. When they emerge from the lift, the dog scurries into the apartment, where the man's wife is horrified to notice "there's a piece of him missing"! The man explains: "We ran into a Doberman." But we know the truth. "How long is it since you've given meat to your husband?"

Agency:	Euro RSCG, Helsinki	Agency:	Bates Norway, Oslo
Creative Director:	Jussi Mansukoski	Creative Director:	Thorbjørn Naug
Copywriter:	Jussi Mansukoski	Copywriter:	Henrik Hagelsteen
Art Director:	Minna Lavola	Art Director:	Thorbjørn Naug
Photographer:	Kalle Valpas	Photographer:	Albert Boullet
Client:	Kariniemi Free Range Chicken	Client:	Mills Havbris, Fish Products

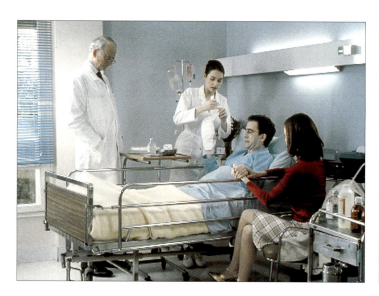    

Agency:	Leo Burnett, Paris	
Creative Directors:	Christophe Coffre	
	Nicolas Taubes	
Copywriter:	Mathieu Villoutreix	
Art Director:	Roland de Pierrefeu	
Production:	Quad	
Director:	Alexandre Coffre	
Producer:	Catherine Guiol	
Client:	Heinz Tomato Ketchup, "The Finger"	

A woman is comforting her husband in hospital after what has clearly been a painful operation. When the bandages come off, however, we see that he has merely had cosmetic surgery – to elongate his finger. His wife looks delighted, especially when she takes him home and sees that his enhanced digit enables him to reach the last blob of Heinz Ketchup in the bottle. More disappointingly, he keeps the delicious morsel for himself.

Agency:	Mother, London	
Creative Directors:	Robert Saville	
	Mark Waites	
Copywriters:	Carlos Bayala	
	Gabriela Scardaccione	
Client:	Supernoodles Vindaloo, "Chariots of Fire"	

Two men face each other at the start of a hallway in a suburban home. They turn and begin running, in slow motion, to a soundtrack of Vangelis' music from the film Chariots of Fire. It's clear the men are racing towards an urgent goal – but what? As one of the men stumbles, the other reaches the door at the end of the hall, wrenches it open, and throws himself inside...the toilet. The men have been eating Supernoodles Vindaloo, and their bowels have been unable to withstand the fiery snack. The screams from behind the door say it all.

Agency:	Michael Conrad & Leo Burnett, Frankfurt	Agency:	D'Arcy Masius Benton & Bowles, Hamburg
Creative Director:	Manfred Wappenschmidt	Creative Directors:	Deborah Hanusa Andre Klein
Copywriter:	Caroline Trebeljahr	Copywriter:	Susanne Latour
Art Director:	Daniela Skwrna	Art Director:	Kai Grützmacher
Photographer:	Reinhard Hunger	Photographer:	Sebastian Engel
Client:	Heinz Condiment Sauces	Client:	Trill Bird Food

Agency:	Mother, London
Creative Directors:	Robert Saville
	Mark Waites
Copywriter:	Yan Elliot
Art Director:	Luke Williamson
Client:	Supernoodles, "Face Off" & "Car"

"I think the ladies have had enough." We're in a pub, and a slender man wearing a T-shirt with the word 'salad' on it is picking a fight with a stocky guy whose shirt reads 'Supernoodles'. The pair are surrounded by their gangs – the salad crew wear shirts reading 'brown rice' and 'rocket', while the Supernoodles mob favour 'fried eggs' and 'sausages'. As the gangs burst out of the pub, the conflict becomes a West Side Story-style musical number. When the cops arrive, only the salad gang are fit enough to flee. Supernoodles are delicious, but unfortunately, "You are what you eat".

Our seedy but loveable Supernoodles gang are out driving their old car. When they stop at a junction, a posh convertible swishes up alongside them, containing a trio whose shirts read 'caviar', 'pheasant' and 'paté'. The snobby driver asks: "Did you paint that car yourself?", while his companion adds: "Don't fancy yours much!" The Supernoodles mob stare vacantly, and it looks as if violence might erupt. But when the convertible roars away, they remain transfixed – by the sight of two grasshoppers mating on a branch across the street.

Food 37

Agency:	CLM/BBDO, Paris	A young Chinese man is walking along a line of cars waiting at traffic lights, handing out flyers to the drivers. When he hands one to a woman, she takes one look at him, grabs him, and begins violently hauling him through the car window, intent on abducting him. "Fancy Chinese?" asks the tagline. Then you won't be able to resist Luang Chinese food.	In another execution, a Chinese man is leaving a newspaper kiosk, scrutinising his morning paper. Suddenly his eyes widen in shock as a woman locks him in an embrace, kissing him so passionately that they fall back against a rack of magazines. "Fancy Chinese?" You'll love Luang Chinese food.	**Agency:** Lowe Lintas & Partners, Brussels
Creative Directors:	Bernard Naville Vincent Behaeghel			**Creative Director:** Georges LaFleur
Copywriters:	Agathe Marsilly			**Copywriter:** Eric Maerschalck
Art Directors:	Chrystel Bonneau			**Art Director:** Herlinde Cornelis
Production:	1/33 Productions			**Photographer:** Hans Hansen
Director:	David Charhon			**Client:** Hak Vegetables "We Don't Eat Enough Vegetables"
Producers:	Richard Jacobs Pierre Marcus France Monnet			
Client:	Luang Chinese Foods, "Flyers" & "Kiosk"			

Agency:	McCann-Erickson, Prague
Creative Directors:	Jo Johansen
	Lars Killi
Copywriter:	Janek Růžička
Art Director:	Tereza Víznerová
Production:	Mini Max Films
Director:	Erik Poppe
Producers:	Tibor Hutter
	Roxana Pfeffermannová
Client:	Disko Biscuits, "Newcomer", "Mock-up" & "Etude"

David arrives at an Alcoholics Anonymous-type class which helps people learn how to share. Encouraged by the group's tutor, he recounts that he was with his daughter when he opened his first packet of new Disko biscuits. Of course, he gave her one. Then he cracks, and the truth comes out. "No – you're right, I lied! I didn't give her anything!" David sobs, comforted by the rest of the group. Disko biscuits are hard to share.

It's lesson two, and David seems to be making progress, cheerfully handing out Disko biscuits to the group. "Now let's try with the real packet," says the group leader, revealing that David has been working with a mock-up. As soon as he gets his hands on the real Diskos, David is up to his old tricks, hugging the packet tightly to his chest, and eventually running away.

Time for some role-play. David is installed behind a door with a packet of Diskos, pretending to be at home. Another male member of the group is selected to play Stanja, his girlfriend, and dons a wig. But when she knocks, David refuses to open up. "I know you're in there," Stanja cries, "I can hear you nibbling!" But David won't budge. Diskos are still too hard to share.

Agency:	Grey & Trace, Barcelona	Agency:	Grey & Trace, Barcelona
Creative Directors:	Jürgen Krieger	Creative Directors:	Jürgen Krieger
	Agustín Vaquero		Agustín Vaquero
	Jose Miguel Tortajada		Jose Miguel Tortajada
	Joan Mas		Joan Mas
Copywriters:	Lidia González	Copywriters:	Lidia González
	Isahac Oliver		Isahac Oliver
Art Directors:	Andrés Borisenko	Art Director:	Andrés Borisenko
	Eduardo Miravalles	Client:	Ortiz Tuna
Client:	Maheso Frozen Foods		

What are those lying on the desk? 🍬 Mmmh, not bad. 🍬 Well, there's so many of them, she'll never notice. 🍬 Anyway, eating on your own makes you fat. 🍬 And she shouldn't leave them lying around if she doesn't want anyone to take them. 🍬 One more. 🍬 And another – gotta keep up the old blood sugar! 🍬 And one more, to sustain me on the long trip back to my desk. 🍬 Oh, are they all gone?

I think one is permissible. 🍬 Well, one is nothing really. 🍬 Just one more, then that's it. 🍬 It's not really the time of year for wearing my bikini. 🍬 They're so small, I don't think another one will make any difference. 🍬 One more, but that really is the last one. 🍬 I'll go to aerobics tomorrow – guide's honour! 🍬 But first I'll just have another. 🍬 Oh, there aren't any! 🍬 Now, where am I going to hide the empty bag?

I might try one. 🍬 One more. 🍬 Then common sense must prevail. 🍬 Okay, just one more of these naughty little devils. 🍬 Eh? How did that get in my mouth? 🍬 This really is the last one. 🍬 Even though I did run the escalator this morning. 🍬 And yesterday as well. 🍬 And I suppose I could always run down this evening too. 🍬 That's it. 🍬 I'll save the leftovers for later. 🍬 Leftovers? 🍬 What leftovers?

Confectionery & Snacks

Agency:	D'Arcy Masius Benton & Bowles, Hamburg
Creative Directors:	Andre Klein Deborah Hanusa
Copywriters:	Andre Klein Nicole Steffen
Art Director:	Bettina Busch
Client:	Mars Miniatures

Confectionery & Snacks 41

Agency:	FHV/BBDO Creative Marketing Agency, Amstelveen
Creative Directors:	John Toth Bart-Jan Horrée
Production:	M-80 Films, Santa Monica
Director:	Tenney Fairchild
Producers:	Glenn Rudolph Ilaria St. Florian
Client:	Snickers, "Chimpanzee"

In a sweltering shack deep in the African jungle, a scientist is carrying out a series of behavioural tests on a chimpanzee called Maggie. Talking into a tape recorder, he notes that when she reaches into a jar of peanuts, Maggie is unable to get her hand out – because unclenching her fist would mean letting go of the food. With a sigh, the scientist reaches into the pocket of his lab coat for his Snickers bar. But his hand gets stuck. As he struggles, Maggie looks on, the roles reversed.

42 **Confectionery & Snacks**

Agency:	TBWA\España, Barcelona
Creative Director:	Kike Fernández
Copywriters:	Kike Fernández
	Jordi Giralt
Art Director:	Marielo Gil
Photographers:	Vicens San Nicolás
	Dani Valenciano
Client:	Fresk Mints

Agency:	CLM/BBDO, Paris
Creative Director:	France Bizot
Copywriter:	Benoît Sahores
Art Director:	Cédric Haroutiounian
Photographer:	Rad-ish
Client:	Bounty

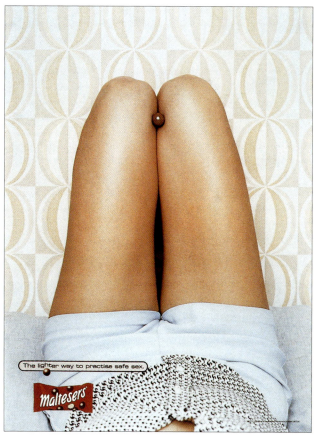

Agency:	D'Arcy, London	Agency:	Springer & Jacoby, Hamburg
Creative Director:	Nick Hastings	Creative Director:	Thomas Walmrath
Copywriter:	Trevor Webb	Art Director:	Nina Rühmkorf
Art Director:	Steve Campbell	Photographer:	Björn Ole Frank
Photographer:	Alexandra Klever	Client:	Fisherman's Friend
Client:	Maltesers		

44   Confectionery & Snacks

Agency:	Jean & Montmarin, Paris
Creative Director:	Gérard Jean
Copywriter:	Sidonie Jean
Art Director:	Hervé Barussaud
Production:	Big Production
Director:	Les Zoo
Producers:	Christophe Arnaud
	Nicole Le Goff
Client:	Lutti Crypto Chocolates, "The Princess"

A princess is in her castle doing some needlework when the door crashes open – and a hairy, axe-wielding Viking stands before her. Realising that Vikings have only one thing on their minds, the princess lifts her dress to reveal a solid-looking chastity belt. The Viking counters with a packet of Crypto sweets. The Princess hands him the key – which turns out to be attached to a whole bunch. As the Viking wastes his time trying to pick her lock, the Princess indulges herself by scoffing the sweets.

Agency:	Lowe Lintas, Amsterdam
Creative Directors:	Aad Kuijper
	Pieter van Velsen
Copywriter:	Aad Kuijper
Art Director:	Pieter van Velsen
Production:	25 FPS
Director:	Maarten Treurniet
Producers:	Bas Pinkse
	Hanneke Kramer
	Violet van der Straaten
Client:	Yes Chocolate Cake, "The New Rilana"

A man is watching TV, his new Rilana car just visible through the window behind him. Coincidentally, the TV is showing a review of the Rilana – "an ideal car for the Dutch market". It goes on to say that the car leans dangerously in the wind, has dodgy brakes and won't start in the cold. The man's wife enters, handing him a coffee and a Yes chocolate bar. The man grumbles: "Well, that's nice, isn't it!" His wife agrees, thinking he's referring to the snack. The message is clear: at least some things in life are reliable.

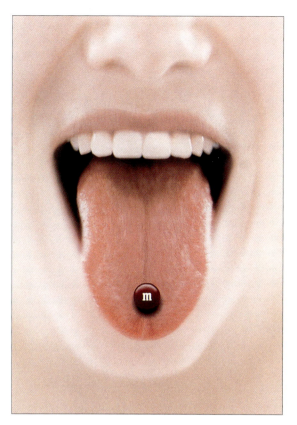

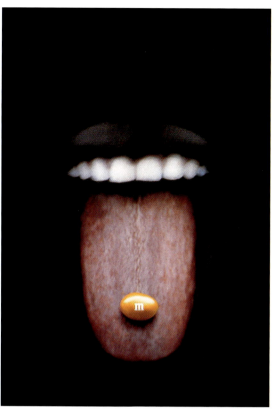

Sweet new dress

Confectionery & Snacks

Agency:	BBDO, Düsseldorf	Agency:	Leo Burnett, Budapest
Creative Director:	Marco Pupella	Creative Director:	Robert Lovy
Copywriter:	Peter Menzel	Copywriters:	Nagy Dezsö
Art Director:	Katja Luckas		Csákvári Dániel
Photographers:	Rene Shenouda	Art Directors:	Laurent Lacorre
	Jost Hiller		Csákvári Dániel
Client:	M&M's	Photographer:	Mészáros László
		Client:	Gold Fischli

46 Dairy Products

Agency:	CLM/BBDO, Paris
Creative Directors:	France Bizot
	Neil Bishrey
Copywriter:	Neil Bishrey
Art Director:	France Bizot
Photographer:	Giblin & James
Client:	Bounty Ice Cream

 Dairy Products 47

Agency:	AMV/BBDO, London	In a pretentious documentary featuring a hand-held camera, fast editing and tricky visual effects, a trendy Scandinavian furniture designer is explaining where he gets his inspiration. "Everywhere!" he claims. But the interviewer has noticed an oval packet of Utterly Butterly Scandinavian Style spread on the designer's desk, and that all his work appears to be oval too. "I don't understand the question," says the designer, trying to cover up the fact that the spread has had an influence on his work. "Have you gone utterly Scandinavian?" asks the tagline.
Copywriter:	Tony Strong	
Art Director:	Mike Durban	
Production:	Outsider	
Director:	David Lodge	
Producers:	Benji Howell	
	Toby Courlander	
	Simon Monhemius	
Client:	Utterly Butterly, "Designer"	

48 Dairy Products

Agency:	Lowe Brindfors, Stockholm	
Creative Director:	Johan Nilsson	
Copywriter:	Johan Nilsson	
Art Director:	Patrick Waters	
Production:	Pinguin Film	
Director:	Fredrik Edfeldt	
Producers:	Anders Stjernström, William Hicks	
Client:	Arla Yoggi Yalla Yoghurt, "Moped"	

A pretty girl is standing in an empty parking lot drinking her Yoggi Yalla yoghurt, while her potential boyfriend shows off on his moped. Finally, he comes to a halt in front of her. "Do you like me?" asks the girl, waiting for the obvious response. But the boy is completely dense and tongue-tied. Instead of turning on the charm, he mumbles incoherently. Luckily for the girl, her yoghurt is "not nearly as thick."

Agency:	Edson, FCB, Lisbon
Creative Director:	Edson Athayde
Copywriter:	Sandro Porto
Art Director:	Liliana Dantas
Production:	Show Off
Director:	Alexandre Montenegro
Producers:	Raul Nunes, César Monteiro
Client:	Parmalat Milk, "Straw"

A simple shot of a glass of milk, with a bent straw in it. A finger comes into frame, and moves the straw gently from side to side, using the implement's tiny hinge. Drinking Parmalat Milk helps your joints remain equally supple.

Dairy Products

Agency:	Euro RSCG MRT, Lisbon
Creative Director:	Jorge Teixeira
Copywriter:	Mário Nascimento
Art Director:	Paulo Ramalho
Client:	Mimosa Dairy Products

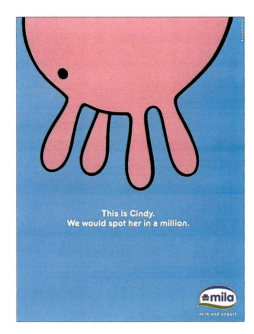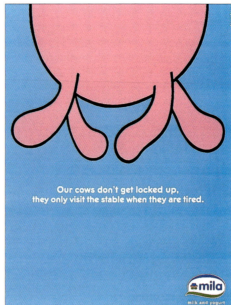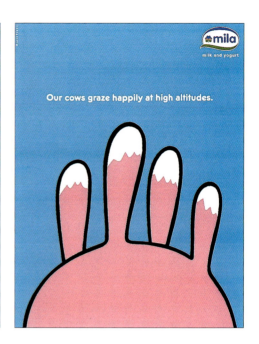

50 Dairy Products

Agency:	Black Pencil, Milan	Agency:	Jean & Montmarin, Paris	Panier de Yoplait with cream; it's quite a change from fuel oil.
Creative Director:	Sergio Rodriguez	Creative Director:	Gérard Jean	
Copywriter:	Carlo Cavallone	Copywriter:	Sidonie Jean	
Art Director:	Michele Bedeschi	Art Director:	Hervé Barussaud	
Illustrator:	Libero Gozzini	Photographer:	Paul Goirand	
Client:	Mila Dairy Products	Client:	Panier de Yoplait	

Dairy Products

Agency:	Advico Young & Rubicam, Zürich	Agency:	Advico Young & Rubicam, Zürich
Creative Directors:	Martin Spillmann Hansjoerg Zuercher	Creative Directors:	Martin Spillmann Hansjoerg Zuercher
Copywriter:	Peter Broennimann	Copywriter:	Peter Broennimann
Art Directors:	Dana Wirz Mathias Babst	Art Director:	Mathias Babst
Photographer:	Julien Vonier	Photographer:	Julien Vonier
Client:	Swiss Milk Producers	Client:	Swiss Milk Producers

52 **Dairy Products**

Agency:	Rönnberg McCann, Stockholm	**Agency:**	The White House, Reykjavik
Copywriter:	Kalle Widgren	**Creative Director:**	Sverrir Bjornsson
Art Director:	Alexander Fredlund	**Copywriters:**	Erling I. Saevarsson
Photographer:	Sesse Lind		Anna Agustsdottir
Client:	Yoplait Petits Filous	**Art Directors:**	Erling I. Saevarsson
			Kristin Thora Gudbjartsdottir
		Illustrators:	Erling I. Saevarsson
			Kristin Thora Gudbjartsdottir
		Client:	Osta-og Smjorsalan, Icelandic Cheese

Dairy Products

Agency:	Saatchi & Saatchi, Madrid
Executive Director:	Cesar Garcia
Creative Director:	Miguel Roig
Copywriter:	Samuel Vazquez
Art Director:	Amabel Minchan
Photographer:	Alfonso Perez
Client:	Mini Babybel

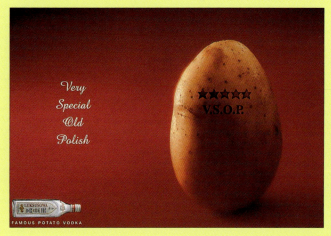
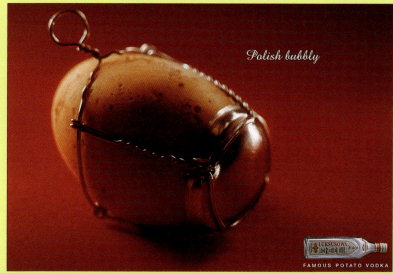

54 Alcoholic Drinks A

Agency:	Grey, Warsaw
Creative Director:	David Millingen
Copywriters:	David Millingen
	Kasia Sosnierz
Art Directors:	Grzegorz Waliczek
	David Millingen
Photographer:	Jacek Wokowski
Client:	Lucsusowa Vodka

 Alcoholic Drinks A 55

Agency:	McCann-Erickson, Brussels
Creative Director:	Jean-Luc Walraff
Copywriters:	Jean-Luc Walraff
	Philippe Thito
Art Director:	Michel Derèse
Production:	Pix & Motion
Director:	Olivier Venturini
Producers:	Kato Maes
	Brigitte Baudine
	Anne Gasia
Client:	William Lawson's, "The Haka"

A rugby match is about to begin between fierce foes Scotland and New Zealand. There's a sense of expectation as the teams file onto the pitch. Right away, the New Zealanders commence their pre-match ritual: the Maori Haka war-dance, designed to turn their opponents' knees to jelly. But the Scots remain curiously unimpressed – and reply in their own inimitable way.

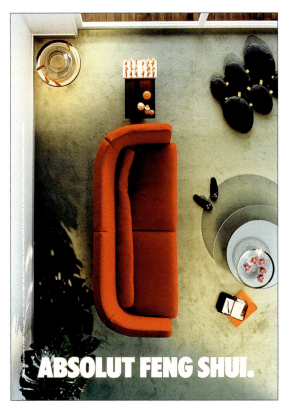

56 Alcoholic Drinks A

Agency:	TBWA\España Madrid
Creative Director:	Angel Iglesias Guillermo Ginés
Copywriter:	Guillermo Ginés
Art Director:	Angel Iglesias
Client:	Absolut Vodka

NB: Copito is the only white gorilla in captivity – and a well-known 'character' in Barcelona.

Agency:	TBWA\Paris
Copywriters:	Sophie Guyon Jean-Marie Boillot
Art Directors:	Sophie Guyon Pascal Etchebarne
Photographers:	Joe Magrean Michel Dubois
Client:	Absolut Vodka

Alcoholic Drinks A

Agency:	D'Adda, Lorenzini, Vigorelli, BBDO, Milan	Agency:	Jung von Matt, Hamburg
Creative Directors:	Pino Rozzi Roberto Battaglia	Creative Directors:	Jan Rexhausen Oliver Kapusta
Copywriter:	Pino Rozzi	Copywriters:	Dirk Silz Alex Ball
Art Director:	Roberto Battaglia	Art Directors:	Stefan Wurster Oliver Grandt Christer Andersson
Photographer:	David Ferrua	Photographer:	Michael Schnabel
Client:	Cinzano	Client:	Ballantine's Scotch Whisky

Agency: The Bridge, Glasgow	**Agency:** McCann-Erickson, Amstelveen
Creative Director: Jonathan D'Aguilar	**Creative Director:** Kees Rijken
Copywriter: Chris Watson	**Copywriters:** Kees Rijken
Art Director: Alex Donald	Evelien Oosterveld
Client: Bulleit Bourbon	Miranda Bijl
	Art Directors: Leendert van der Plas
	Ron Gessel
	Linda Boonman
	Photographers: Anne van Gelder
	Bianca Pillet
	Client: Bacardi Breezer

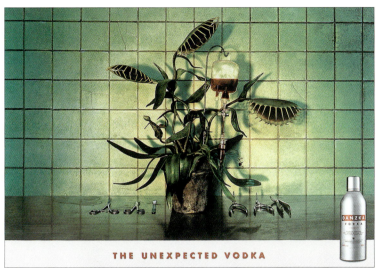
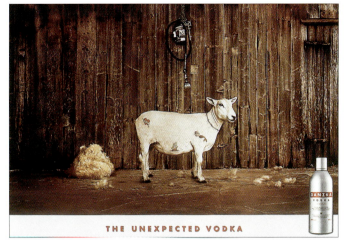

Alcoholic Drinks A   59

Agency:	Young & Rubicam, Copenhagen
Creative Director:	Peder Schack
Art Director:	Peder Schack
Photographer:	Steen Larsen
Client:	Danzka Vodka

60 Alcoholic Drinks B

Agency:	WL/BBDO, Brussels
Creative Director:	Willy Coppens
Copywriter:	Angelo Di Berardino
Art Director:	Frank van de Vijver
Photographer:	Hans Kroeskamp
Client:	Carlsberg Beer

Agency:	Lowe Lintas, London
Creative Director:	Charles Inge
Copywriter:	Tony Barry
Art Director:	Damon Collins
Production:	Gorgeous Enterprises
Director:	Chris Palmer
Producers:	Suza Horvat
	Charles Crisp
Client:	Heineken, "Blackmail", "We Mean It", "Nearly There" & "Threat"

Four films, one campaign. Sales of Heineken are not high enough, so the makers of the ad have an excruciating punishment in store – magician Paul Daniels and his wife Debbie singing a syrupy duet, off-key, on a kitsch set. "Buy a pint of Heineken or we'll keep running this commercial," threatens the tagline. In the second film, the pair are joined by two equally tuneless celebrities, familiar to British viewers. And by the third version, nearly every TV star who has never managed to hold a note is visible on screen, in a tour-de-force of tastelessness. Finally, in the fourth execution (literally), sales of Heineken have risen...so two lions are sent on stage to devour the performers. "How refreshing. How Heineken."

Alcoholic Drinks B

Agency:	Leo Burnett Advertising, Prague
Creative Director:	Věra Česenková
Copywriter:	Joe Gallo
Art Director:	Fady Salameh
Production:	Dawson
Director:	Martin Krejčí
Producers:	Monika Kristlová, Nikola Lapáčková
Client:	Radegast Beer, "Bodycheck"

In the Czech Republic, a man is standing at a bar, about to pick up his pint of Radegast beer. As he reaches for it, a woman swerves in from nowhere and knocks him to the floor. The woman takes a swig of his Radegast and rubs the crick in her neck. She has executed a 'body check', a move familiar to ice hockey fans. Radegast is the official sponsor of Czech hockey.

Agency:	The Leith Agency, Edinburgh
Creative Director:	Gerry Farrell
Copywriters:	Chris & Lee
Art Directors:	Chris & Lee
Production:	Stark Films, London
Director:	Colin Gregg
Producers:	Greig Jordan, Les Watt
Client:	Carling Beer, "Cracking"

After a plane crash, a man finds himself on a desert island with nobody but a crab for company. By an incredible coincidence, he finds that a fridge stocked with Carling lager has survived the wreck. But there's no electricity, so the beer is unacceptably warm. Our hero teams up with the friendly crab, who helps him construct a generator, and even gets it going by running on a treadmill. By sunset, the man is sipping a can of cold beer...and cracking a leg of freshly grilled crab.

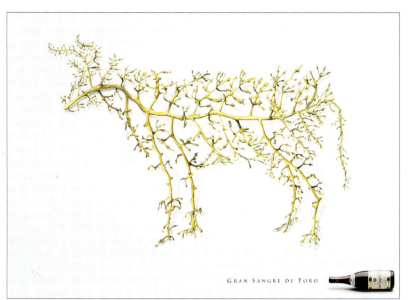

Agency:	Tandem Campmany Guasch DDB, Barcelona
Creative Directors:	David Guimaraes Fernando Macia
Copywriters:	Xavier Valero Jordi Mitjans
Art Director:	Paco Marco
Client:	Bodegas Miguel Torres Wine

64 Alcoholic Drinks B

Agency:	Lowe Lintas GGK, Warsaw
Creative Director:	Lechoslaw Kwiatkowski
Copywriter:	Pawel Heinze
Art Director:	Krzysztof Iwiński
Production:	Hell Productions
Director:	Johan Gulbranson
Producers:	Magda Wolosz, Maciek Strzeszewski
Client:	Krolewskie Beer, "Hairdresser"

Three Polish friends gather in the street. "For the hairdresser," says one, and holds out his cap. His friends donate their change. At dinner, the man gives the money to his wife. "For the hairdresser," he says, affectionately. The following day, his wife is at the hairdresser, waiting for her perm to set. Meanwhile, our 'generous' friend has invited his mates over, so they can drink Krolewskie Beer and watch the match in peace. In this house, at least, Krolewskie Beer rules!

Agency:	Lowe Lintas, London
Creative Director:	Charles Inge
Copywriter:	Paul Silburn
Art Director:	Vince Squibb
Production:	Gorgeous Enterprises
Director:	Frank Budgen
Producers:	Paul Rothwell, Sarah Hallett
Client:	Stella Artois, "Hero's Return"

Two French soldiers return to their village after the First World War. One of them has a bandaged arm. They are greeted effusively by the villagers – including the wounded man's father, who owns the local café. At the bar, the wounded man recounts how his friend Henri saved his life. Delighted, the father uncorks some wine. But the son asks for Stella Artois beer instead. The father reluctantly complies. When Henri asks for Stella too, the father pretends he's run out. Stella Artois is too precious to give away, even to your son's saviour.

Alcoholic Drinks B   65

Agency:	Tandem Campmany Guasch DDB, Barcelona	Agency:	Springer & Jacoby, London
Creative Director:	Danny Ilario	Creative Directors:	Kurt Georg Dieckert Stefan Schmidt
Copywriter:	Xavier Valero	Copywriters:	Heiko Freiland Johannes Hofmann
Art Director:	Xavier Sole	Art Directors:	Stein Lundberg Johannes Hofmann
Client:	Estrella Damm Beer	Photographers:	Alan Mahon Simon Hawes
		Client:	Madaboutwine.com

Alcoholic Drinks B

Agency:	Lowe Lintas Digitel, Zagreb	Agency:	Wiktor/Leo Burnett, Bratislava
Creative Director:	Goran Štimac	Creative Director:	Raffo Tatarko
Copywriter:	Tvrtko Kurbaša	Copywriters:	Vlado Slivka
Art Director:	Goran Štimac		Igor Brossmann
Client:	Heineken	Art Directors:	Rast'o Záležák
			Peter Kačenka
		Photographer:	Martin Fridner
		Client:	Hubert Sparkling Wine

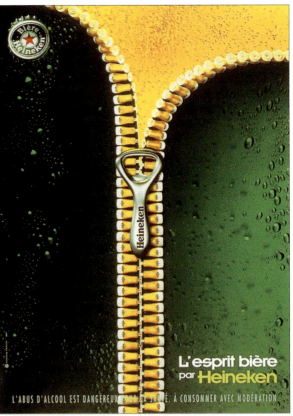

Agency:	Publicis Conseil, Paris
Creative Director:	Olivier Georgeon
Art Director:	Pierre Pénicaud
Photographer:	Andy Barter
Client:	Heineken

The spirit of beer by Heineken.

Alcoholic Drinks B   67

68 Non-Alcoholic Drinks

Agency:	CLM/BBDO, Paris
Creative Directors:	fred&farid
Copywriters:	Mathieu Degryse
	Yves-Eric Deboey
Art Directors:	Mathieu Degryse
	Yves-Eric Deboey
Photographers:	Mathieu Degryse
	Yves-Eric Deboey
Client:	Pepsi

Non-Alcoholic Drinks

Agency:	Mother, London
Creative Directors:	Robert Saville
	Mark Waites
Copywriters:	Yan Elliot
	Mark Waites
Art Directors:	Luke Williamson
	Kim Gehrig
	Caroline Pay
Client:	Dr. Pepper, "Emergency"

A teenage boy is browsing through racks of drinks at the supermarket. The choice leaves him uninspired, until he spots something he's never tried – Dr. Pepper. "What's the worst that could happen?" he muses, opening the fridge door. Suddenly, he is buried under an avalanche of cans and boxes. Seconds later the fire brigade arrives. The fire chief says that to pull the boy free, they must remove his underwear. Borne aloft and butt naked through the city streets, he attracts crowds, TV crews, even a helicopter. Dr. Pepper – what's the worst that could happen?

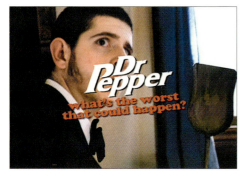

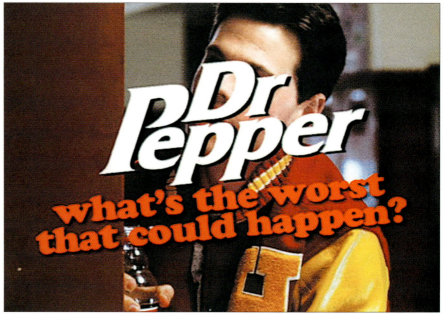

Non-Alcoholic Drinks

Agency:	Mother, London
Creative Directors:	Robert Saville
	Mark Waites
Copywriters:	Yan Elliot
	Mark Waites
Art Directors:	Luke Williamson
	Kim Gehrig
	Caroline Pay
Client:	Dr. Pepper, "Over-Friendly Father" & "Tissue"

It's the occasion every young man dreads – meeting a girlfriend's father. Our hero arrives at the house to pick up his date for the prom. Dad shows him in, and offers him a Dr. Pepper: "What's the worst that could happen?" Emerging from the kitchen with the bottle, the father suggests they fight for it. Then he abruptly wrestles the boy to the floor, forcing the shocked teenager to retaliate. By the time the girlfriend appears on the stairs, in a glamorous gown, her boyfriend is standing over the prone father, apparently about to hit him with a fire iron.

In a corridor at high school, an athletic-looking guy is approached by a stunning blonde with a curvaceous figure. She offers him a sip of her Dr. Pepper. "Come on – what's the worst that could happen?" Gratefully, he takes a swig – but then begins coughing and spilling the stuff down his chin. Panicking, he snatches at a piece of tissue emerging from her tight-fitting top, and finds himself unravelling the contents of her padded bra. She slaps him and runs off, humiliated. He looks sheepish, having blown his chance with the prettiest girl in school.

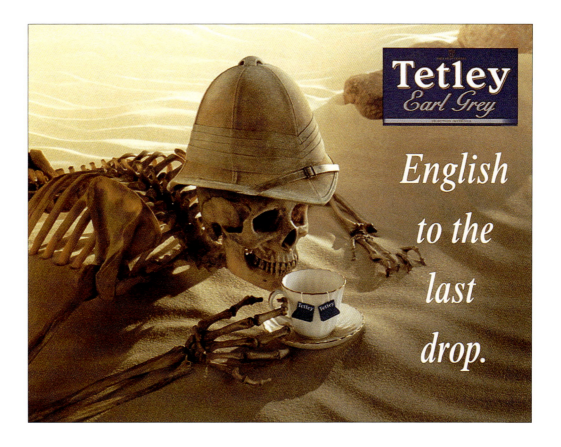

Agency:	D'Arcy, Paris	Agency:	BETC Euro RSCG, Paris
Creative Director:	André Paradis	Creative Directors:	Antoine Barthuel
Copywriter:	Christophe Corsand		Daniel Fohr
Art Director:	Marc Collombet	Copywriter:	Caroline Cornu
Photographer:	Richard Mummery	Art Director:	Sophie Deiss
Client:	Tetley Earl Grey Tea	Photographer:	Christophe Meimoom
		Client:	Evian Mineral Water

Non-Alcoholic Drinks

Agency:	Forsman & Bodenfors, Gothenburg	Agency:	Impact/BBDO, Beirut
Copywriter:	Jonas Enghage, Oscar Askelöf	Creative Director:	Dani Richa
Art Directors:	Andreas Malm, Mikko Timonen	Art Director:	Alexandre Shoukair
Photographer:	Henrik Halvarsson	Photographer:	Cédric Ghoussoub
Client:	Mer Fruit Drink	Client:	Pepsi

"There's nothing better than Irn-Bru when you've just been laid."

www.irn-bru.co.uk

Agency:	The Leith Agency, Edinburgh	A boy and his dad are sitting in front of the TV when a good-looking woman walks past in a bathrobe. The boy immediately scurries outside, where his mates are waiting in a line. They each pay him a can of Irn-Bru to peer through the bathroom window at the naked woman under the shower. Finally, she screams, and the boy's pals run off. The woman sticks her head out of the window. "How did we do, son?" "Not bad, mum," he replies, handing her one of the many tins of free Irn-Bru. "Not bad."	**Agency:**	The Leith Agency, Edinburgh
Creative Director:	Gerry Farrell		**Creative Director:**	Gerry Farrell
Copywriter:	Tony Durston		**Copywriters:**	Chris & Lee
Art Director:	Ash Ward		**Art Directors:**	Chris & Lee
Production:	Mallinson Television Productions, Glasgow		**Photographer:**	Euan Myles
Director:	Martin Wedderburn		**Client:**	Irn-Bru
Producers:	Simon Mallinson Claire Signy			
Client:	Irn-Bru, "Shower"			

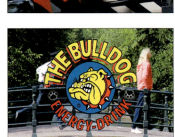

74   Non-Alcoholic Drinks

Agency:	McCann-Erickson, Amstelveen
Creative Directors:	Peter van der Helm, Robin Stam
Copywriter:	Robin Stam
Art Director:	Peter van der Helm
Production:	Ijswater Commercials, Amsterdam
Director:	Hanro Smitsman
Producer:	Koert Bary
Client:	Bulldog Energy Drink, "Energy"

A scruffy, overweight guy is standing on an Amsterdam street, taking a piss against a tree while swigging from a can of Bulldog energy drink. As the lyrical music suggests, he is blissfully happy with the fine weather and this simple but satisfying act. Zipping himself up, he spots two policemen, who have come to admonish him for his lack of decorum. Unconcerned, he ambles away. They sprint after him, but appear to be stuck in slow motion, while he outdistances them at strolling pace. Clearly, Bulldog energy drink has magical properties.

Agency:	Futura DDB, Ljubljana
Creative Directors:	Zoran Gabrijan, Benjamin Ivancic
Copywriter:	Zoran Gabrijan
Art Director:	Benjamin Ivancic
Production:	Gustaf Film
Director:	Grega Vesel
Client:	Ace Soft Drink, "Shake Before Use"

A customer enters a trendy café and points to the bottle of Ace behind the bar. The barman nods and opens a refrigerator. Inside is a half-naked man, frost in his hair, shaking uncontrollably in the cold. He is holding a bottle of Ace. The barman takes it from his hand and gives it to the customer. But he notices that the customer shakes the bottle anyway, so he goes back to the fridge – and turns the dial to an even colder setting. The bar has found a way of ensuring that every bottle of Ace is shaken before use.

Agency:	Ogilvy & Mather, Paris Global cooling.
Creative Director:	Bernard Bureau
Copywriter:	Bernard Bureau
Art Director:	Thierry Chiumino
Photographer:	Vincent Dixon
Client:	Perrier Mineral Water

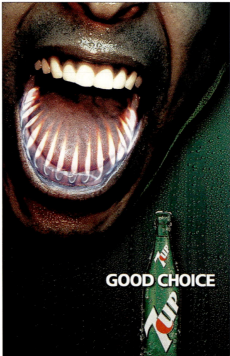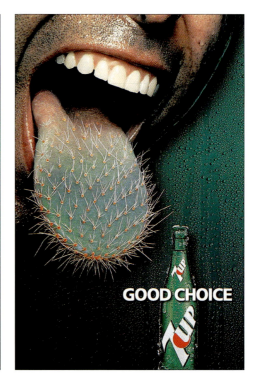

Non-Alcoholic Drinks

Agency:	claydonheeleyjonesmason, London	
Creative Directors:	Pete Harle	
	Dave Woods	
Art Directors:	Simon Hazelhurst	
	Eric Ronshaugen	
Photographer:	George Logan	
Client:	7 UP	

Agency:	Jean & Montmarin, Paris
Creative Director:	Gérard Jean
Copywriter:	Benoît Schmider
Art Director:	Thierry Chantier
Photographers:	Billy & Hells
Client:	Gini

How long since your last Gini? The hottest of cool drinks.

Agency:	Publicis Conseil, Paris	Water that follows you everywhere.
Creative Director:	Olivier Georgeon	
Copywriter:	Olivier Georgeon	
Art Directors:	Frédéric Clavière	
	Caroline Picard	
Photographer:	Cédric Porchez	
Client:	Vittel Mineral Water	

Non-Alcoholic Drinks

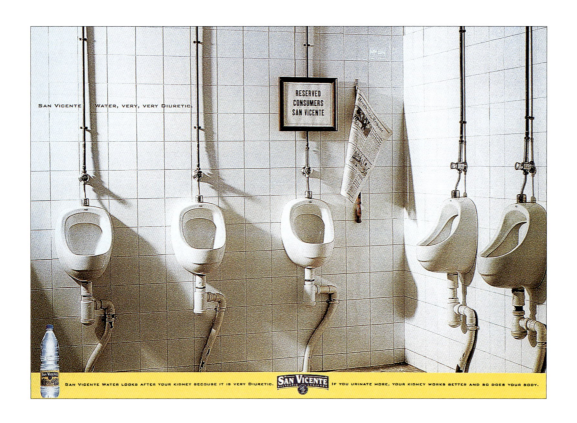

78 Non-Alcoholic Drinks

Agency:	TBWA\España, Barcelona	Agency:	Paradiset DDB, Stockholm
Creative Director:	Ramón Sala	Copywriter:	Anders Lidzell
Copywriters:	Ramón Sala	Art Director:	Kjell Doktorow
	Guillermo Ramírez	Photographer:	Bisse Bengtsson
	Carles Riau	Client:	Mariestads Beer
Art Directors:	Jordi Sebastià		
	Meritxell Horts		
Photographer:	Rafael Juvé		
Client:	San Vicente Water		

Non-Alcoholic Drinks 79

Agency:	The Leith Agency, Edinburgh
Creative Director:	Gerry Farrell
Copywriters:	Chris & Lee
Art Directors:	Chris & Lee
Photographer:	Nick Meek
Client:	Orangina

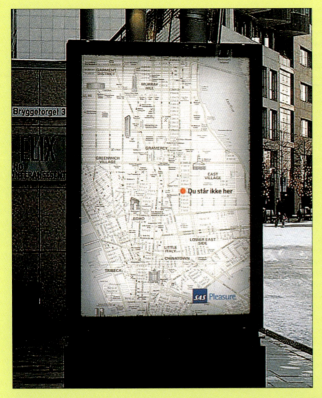

Transport & Tourism

Agency:	Leo Burnett, Oslo	You are not here.
Copywriters:	Morten Kristiansen	
	Katrine Bervell	
Art Directors:	Morten Kristiansen	
	Katrine Bervell	
Client:	SAS Airlines,	
	Pleasure Winter Breaks	

Transport & Tourism

Agency:	Irish International Group, Dublin
Creative Director:	Mal Stevenson
Copywriter:	Adrian Cosgrove
Art Director:	Kevin Leahy
Production:	2am Films, London
Director:	Paul Goldman
Producers:	Helen Hayden
	Noel Byrne
Client:	Aer Lingus Airlines, "Child Psychologist", "Manwatcher" & "Tailor"

The three films feature professionals who take themselves far too seriously, but learn a thing or two from Aer Lingus staff. In the first of the three, a child psychologist tells an off-screen interviewer that she has an instinctive understanding of young minds. Yet she is driven to distraction by her own noisy children on a plane. The Aer Lingus stewardess quietens them instantly with a magic trick, a kind word and some sweets.

In the second film, a 'manwatcher' explains that "57% of all human communication" is through body language – which he is an expert at deciphering. When a woman winks at him on a plane, he thinks she is attracted to him. He is embarrassed when an Aer Lingus steward rushes up with a tissue – she merely had something in her eye.

The third film features a tailor who claims to have an excellent eye for the details of clothing – until he picks up the wrong overcoat in the Aer Lingus executive lounge. Luckily, a member of staff has spotted the error.

82 Transport & Tourism

Agency:	Leo Burnett, Oslo	**Agency:**	Jung von Matt, Hamburg
Creative Director:	Erik Heisholt	**Creative Directors:**	Jan Rexhausen
Copywriter:	Erik Hersoug		Oliver Kapusta
Art Director:	Morten Kristiansen	**Production:**	Markenfilm, Wedel
Production:	4½	**Director:**	Marc Schoelermann
Director:	Harald Zwart	**Producers:**	Sandra Eichhoefer
Producers:	Espen Horn		Burak Heplevent
	Vigdis Roset		Mark Rotá
Client:	Airport Express Train, "Mon Amour"		Yvonne Crzib
		Client:	Sixt Online Services, "Hotel"

Nicole is waiting at an airport in the south of France. While the other people in the arrivals area greet their relatives and loved ones, she is left standing alone. The voiceover reveals that Nicole was waiting for her rather plain Norwegian pen-friend, who missed his flight because of bad traffic. Things end happily for Nicole, who meets a childhood sweetheart – the plane's pilot – at the airport. But her pen-friend remains stuck in a shack in Norway with his dogs. If only he'd taken the Airport Express Train...

Still clad in her white gown, a bride walks around a luxurious hotel room in a daze, running her fingers through the sparkling chandelier and flopping onto the huge bed. Then she goes into the bathroom, where her new husband is washing his face. "Darling, it must have been really expensive..." she says. "No, I booked it with e-Sixt." Furious, the bride bashes his head against the basin. If you want to impress, don't say you booked online with e-Sixt – it's dangerously cheap.

Transport & Tourism

Agency:	Publicis, Zürich
Creative Director:	Jean Etienne Aebi
Copywriter:	Daniel Krieg
Art Director:	Lori Fischer
Photographers:	Stefan Minder
	Felix Schregenberger
Client:	ZVV Verkehrsverbund, Zürich Public Transport

84 Transport & Tourism

Agency:	Van Walbeek Etcetera, Amsterdam	**Agency:**	TBWA\Paris, France
Creative Director:	Willem van Harrewijen	**Creative Director:**	Jean-Pierre Barbou
Copywriter:	Antoine Houtsma	**Copywriter:**	Jean-François Bouchet
Art Director:	Ferdinand Fransen	**Art Director:**	Jessica Gerard-Huet
Photographer:	Jan Holtslag	**Photographer:**	Kevin Griffin
Client:	Thalys Nederland, High-Speed Train	**Client:**	TGV, High-Speed Train

Agency:	BETC Euro RSCG, Paris
Creative Directors:	Antoine Barthuel Daniel Fohr
Copywriter:	Etienne Turquet
Art Director:	Aurélie Scalabre
Photographer:	Lis Collins
Client:	Air France

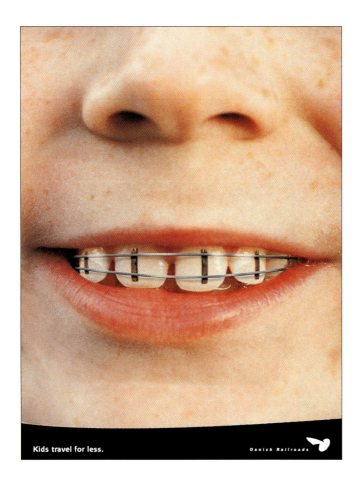

86 Transport & Tourism

Agency: Umwelt, Copenhagen	**Agency:** Grey & Trace, Madrid	Iguazu Falls, 9 days from 199,000 ptas.
Photographer: Jesper Skovboolling	**Creative Directors:** Carmen Veiguela	
Client: Danish Railroads, Child Discount	Guillermo Pérez-Agua	Scuba Diving at the Great Barrier Reef, 9 days from 250,000 ptas.
	Agustín Vaquero	
	Montserrat González	
	Copywriter: Aline Bastida	
	Art Director: Montserrat González	
	Photographers: Gonzalo Puertas	
	Nahuel Berger	
	Client: Travelprice, Online Travel Agency	

Agency:	TBWA\Paris, France	You miss London.
Creative Directors:	Eric Holden	
	Rémi Noel	
Copywriter:	Cécile Guais	
Art Director:	Laurent Bodson	
Photographer:	Bruno Comtesse	
Client:	Eurostar	

Transport & Tourism 87

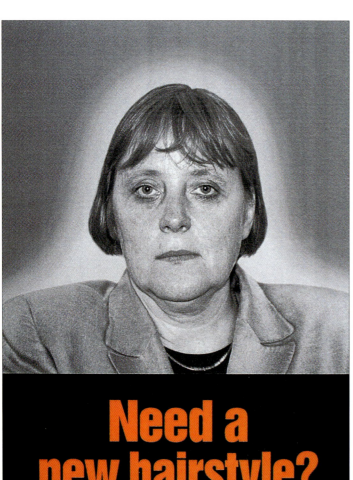

Transport & Tourism

Agency:	Ogilvy Canaveral, Paris	How is he going to take it?
Creative Director:	Anne Bessaguet	
Copywriters:	François d'Epenoux	At his own rhythm.
	Xavier Martel	
Art Director:	Cécile Boulet	
Photographers:	Tim Flach	
	James Cotier	
	Eric Dreyer	
Client:	Thalys, High Speed Train	

Agency:	Jung von Matt, Munich	NB: The ad shows top German politician Angela Merkel who is well known for always having the same boring hairstyle.
Creative Director:	Bernhard Lukas	
Copywriter:	Eva Goede	
Art Directors:	Tomas Tulinius	
	Markus Maczey	
Photographer:	André Mühling	
Client:	Sixt Car Rental	

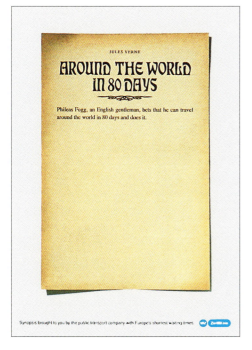
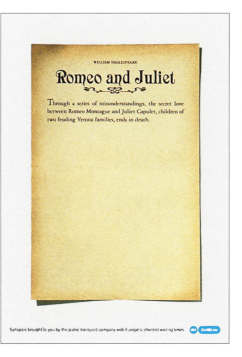
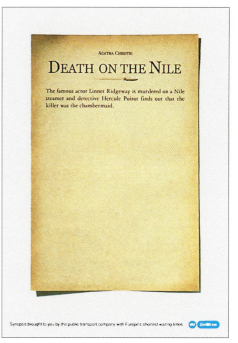

Agency:	Advico Young & Rubicam, Zürich	Synopsis brought to you by the public transport company with Europe's shortest waiting times.	**Agency:**	1576 Advertising, Edinburgh
Creative Director:	Peter Broennimann		**Creative Directors:**	David Reid
Copywriters:	Margrit Brunswick			Adrian Jeffery
	Juerg Brechbuehl		**Copywriter:**	Adrian Jeffery
	Stefan Ehrler		**Art Director:**	Rufus Wedderburn
Art Directors:	Dana Wirz		**Client:**	Visit Scotland
	Patrik Rohner			
Photographer:	Julien Vonier			
Client:	VBZ Public Transport			

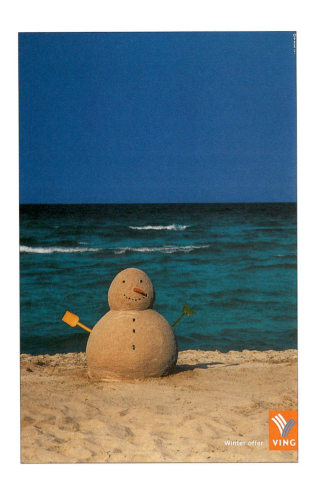

90 Transport & Tourism

Agency:	JBR McCann, Oslo
Creative Director:	Eivind Solberg
Copywriters:	Bjørnar Olsen
	Espen Lie Andersen
Art Director:	Eivind Solberg
Photographer:	Thomas Brun
Client:	Ving Travel Agency

Agency:	Jung von Matt, Hamburg
Creative Directors:	Constantin Kaloff
	Ove Gley
Copywriter:	Ove Gley
Art Director:	Katja Winterhalder
Client:	Deutsch Bahn, German Railways

Agency:	1576 Advertising, Edinburgh	A couple are eating a meal at a beachside restaurant, comparing the taste of their food. "This fish is gorgeous," says the woman, "try it, darling." But then she passes her fork to a short red-haired stranger, who tries the fish and agrees with her before passing it on to her husband. The same thing happens when the husband passes her a bite of his steak. A voiceover explains that you don't want a middleman with you on holiday, so why have one when you book? By dispensing with travel agents, Direct Holidays cut out the middleman.
Creative Directors:	David Reid, Adrian Jeffery	
Copywriter:	Adrian Jeffery	
Art Director:	David Reid	
Production:	Stark Films, London	
Director:	Wayne Holloway	
Producers:	Cressida Luxton, Kiri Jones	
Client:	Direct Holidays, "Steak"	

Agency: Publicis, Zürich
Creative Directors: Daniel Krieg, Uwe Schlupp
Copywriter: Daniel Krieg
Art Director: Raul Serrat
Client: SF Snowboard School

92 Retail Services

Agency:	Scholz & Friends, Berlin
Creative Directors:	Joachim Schoepfer Martin Pross
Art Directors:	Marco Fusz Maik Heindorf
Photographer:	Matthias Koslik
Client:	Fiona Bennett Hats

Agency:	Robert/Boisen & Like Minded, Copenhagen
Creative Director:	Michael Robert
Copywriter:	Joachim Nielsen
Art Director:	Michael Robert
Production:	Bullet
Director:	Kasper Wedendahl
Producers:	Rikke Katborg
	Dorte Tellerup
Client:	Interflora, "Formula 1"

A man is sprawled on a sofa watching the motor racing. He notices that his beer glass is empty, but obviously can't be bothered to get up and pour another one. His wife walks past, notices the empty glass, and takes it. Then she brings a fresh glass, full of beer, and hands it to him with an indulgent smile. He is obviously in her good books. It's Interflora – the power of flowers.

94 Retail Services

Agency:	Robert/Boisen & Like Minded, Copenhagen
Creative Director:	Michael Robert
Copywriter:	Joachim Nielsen
Art Director:	Michael Robert
Production:	Bullet
Director:	Kasper Wedendahl
Producers:	Rikke Katborg
	Dorte Tellerup
Client:	Interflora, "Tool Shop" "Meatballs" & "Football Trophy"

Three more spots demonstrating the power of flowers. We're in a tool shop, and a customer can't decide between a normal, reasonably-sized drill and a massive, far more macho version, which is no doubt incredibly expensive. His wife appears, takes the small drill from him and puts it back on the shelf. To his astonishment, she encourages him to buy the DIY fanatics' dream tool.

In another spot, a woman is ladling out meatballs for her family. But while the father and older brother are given just one, she piles her youngest son's plate high with food. Could he have used Interflora recently?

And finally, a couple are unpacking crates after moving into their new home. The woman unearths a football trophy, at first looking at it with distaste. But after noticing her partner's pleading expression, she gives it pride of place on a shelf. Interflora – the power of flowers.

Agency:	Xynias, Wetzel, Von Büren, Munich
Creative Director:	Matthias Wetzel
Art Director:	Chris Mayrhofer
Client:	Prinz Myshkin Vegetarian Restaurant

96 Retail Services

Agency:	Leo Burnett, Oslo
Copywriter:	Janne Brenda Lysø
Art Director:	Stian Johansen
Production:	EPA International, Stockholm
Director:	Axel Laubscher
Producers:	Annelie Lindstrøm
	Richard Patterson
Client:	McDonald's, "Toothfairy"

A small boy is staying with his grandfather. To his delight, the boy discovers that he has a loose tooth – which he pulls out and puts in a water glass beside his bed. When he wakes up, a shiny coin has appeared in its place. The pair go and spend the money at McDonald's. That evening, the boy walks into his slumbering grandfather's bedroom, and spots a set of false teeth in a glass. In the morning, grandfather discovers his dentures have been taken and replaced by coins. The boy grins at him...time for another trip to McDonald's?

Agency:	Republica, Albertslund
Creative Director:	Joachim Rosenstand
Copywriter:	Christian Grau
Art Director:	Hans Troldahl
Production:	Nordisk Film Commercial
Director:	Anders Holm
Producers:	Stig Lauritsen
	François Grandjean
Client:	Coop Prix Supermarket, "Dog"

A large, loveable dog is ushered into a basket in the hall as his owner leaves for the supermarket. As soon as the door slams, the dog scampers to the window and looks out, making sure the coast is clear. Then he jumps joyously onto the sofa and starts throwing the cushions around with his teeth, an activity which is clearly banned. But his master returns and catches him in the act. The hound looks crestfallen. Not everyone appreciates the fast service at Coop Prix Supermarket.

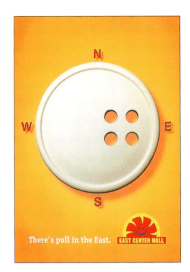
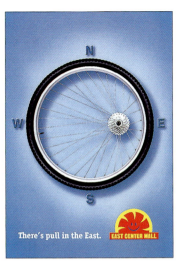
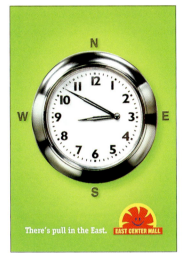
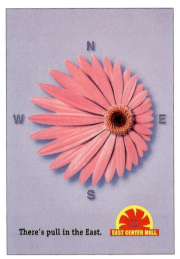
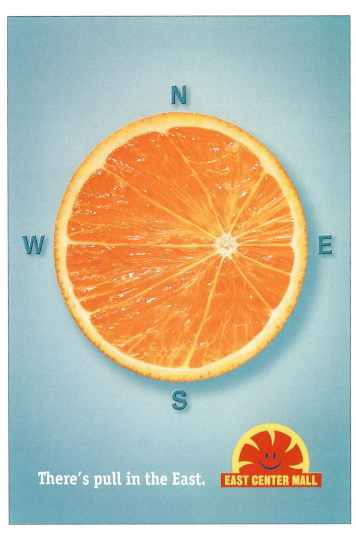

Agency:	hasan & partners, Helsinki	Agency:	Publicis, Zürich
Copywriter:	Jussi Turhala	Creative Directors:	Markus Gut Markus Ruf
Art Director:	Kimmo Kivilahti	Copywriter:	Markus Ruf
Photographer:	Pekka Potka	Art Director:	Markus Gut
Client:	East Center Mall	Client:	Sportplausch Wider Racing Bikes

Retail Services 97

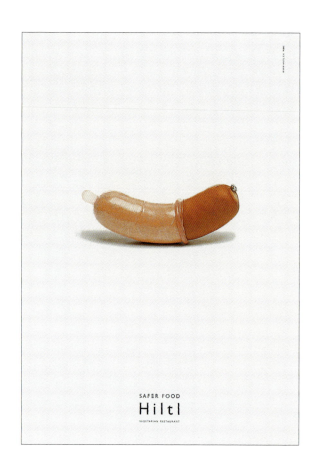

Retail Services

Agency:	Wirz Werbung, Zürich	**Agency:**	Jean & Montmarin, Paris
Creative Director:	Matthias Freuler	**Creative Director:**	Gérard Jean
Copywriters:	Regula Geiser	**Copywriter:**	Christophe Trouvé-Dugény
	Daniel Mueller	**Art Director:**	Thierry Meunier
Art Director:	Barbara Hartmann	**Photographer:**	Richard Dangerfield
Photographer:	Hans Ruedi Rohrer	**Client:**	Houra.fr Cybermarket
Client:	Hiltl Vegetarian Restaurant		

Petit-Suisse as seen by a lazy woman.

Q-Tip as seen by a lazy man.
Yes, it's laziness and so what!

Agency:	BDDP & Fils, Paris	A delivery boy parks his moped on a dark street. Holding a package of takeaway food, he walks up to a gracious but Gothic-looking house. He rings the bell. The door opens, and an imposing figure steps out of the shadows. We see malevolent eyes, a scowl – and a hockey mask. It's Hannibal Lecter. Before the boy can react, the notorious cannibal has grabbed him, hauled him inside and slammed the door. With S Comme Services, you can have your favourite meal delivered to your home...	**Agency:**	Scholz & Friends, Hamburg
Creative Director:	Olivier Altmann		**Creative Director:**	Günther Schneider
Copywriter:	Olivier Couradjut		**Copywriter:**	Ian Scott Paterson
Art Director:	Rémy Tricot		**Art Director:**	Christian Binder
Production:	Hamster Publicité		**Photographer:**	Michaela Rein
Director:	Eric Valette		**Client:**	Carow & Wrono, Garden Center For Carnivorous Plants
Producer:	Christine Bouffort			
Client:	S Comme Services Cybermarket, "The Delivery"			

100 Retail Services

Agency:	Grey, Århus
Copywriter:	Lone Tvedergaard Bach
Art Director:	Thomas Hoffmann
Production:	B&W Film, Copenhagen
Director:	Niels Gråbøl
Producers:	Berglund & Weiss
	Hans Jan Pedersen
Client:	Fakta Supermarket,
	"Grab a Customer",
	"Flasher" &
	"The Tampax Trick"

Shopping at Fakta Supermarket only takes five minutes, but the staff would love it if you'd stay a bit longer. That's why they've come up with three ways of making their customers linger. In the first film, staff prevent customers from leaving by holding tightly onto their legs.

In execution number two, a buxom redheaded member of staff walks past a customer – and briefly opens her coat, flashing her body. He looks astonished as she walks innocently away.

In the third spot, a woman attempts to take a box of sanitary towels from a shelf, only to find it is attached to a piece of elastic, and simply bounces back into place. Shopping in Fakta only takes five minutes, but "we do wish you'd stay a little longer".

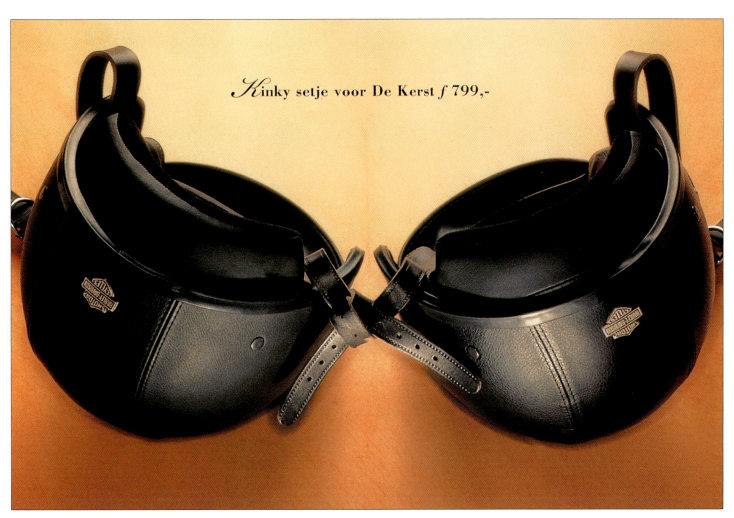

Agency:	Grey, Århus	Four ads broadcast during a single evening. A shot of a milk carton. The narrator announces bargain prices at Fakta. "One carton of milk, five crowns. Two cartons of milk, ten crowns." There are no fancy promotions at this supermarket – things are always cheap. Later that evening: "17 cartons of milk, 85 crowns", etc. By the time the evening is wearing to a close, the narrator has reached 346,517 cartons of milk, at 1,732,595 crowns. But then comes a correction – in fact the price is 1,732,585 crowns. But it's not a bargain, just an error. Prices stay fixed at Fakta.
Copywriter:	Lone Tvedergaard Bach	
Art Director:	Thomas Hoffmann	
Production:	B&W Film, Copenhagen	
Director:	Niels Gråbøl	
Producers:	Berglund & Weiss	
	Hans Jan Pedersen	
Client:	Fakta Supermarket, "Bargain Prices"	

Agency:	De Amsterdamse School, Amsterdam	A kinky pair for Christmas.
Creative Director:	Frans Pootjes	
Copywriter:	Frans Pootjes	
Art Director:	Peter Tromp	
Photographer:	Diederik Kratz	
Client:	Harley Davidson	

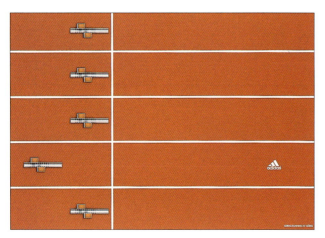
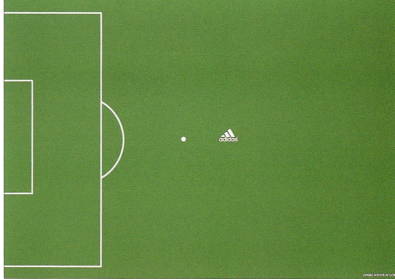

102 Retail Services

Agency:	Springer & Jacoby, Hamburg
Creative Directors:	Florian Grimm, Amir Kassaei
Art Director:	Gerrit Zinke
Illustrator:	Gerrit Zinke
Client:	Ludwig Görtz, Adidas Shoes

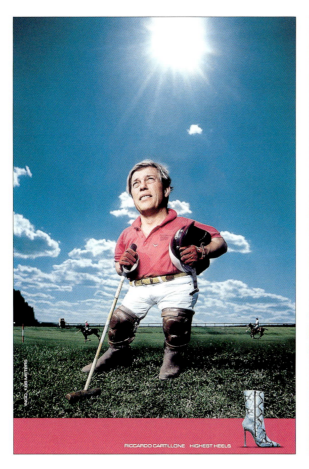

Agency:	Scholz & Friends, Berlin	Ingo: 1.95 meters	**Agency:**	Scholz & Friends, Berlin
Creative Directors:	Sebastian Turner Johannes Krempl	Dag: 1.94 meters Riccardo Cartillone. Highest heels.	**Creative Director:** **Art Director:**	Sebastian Turner Bjoern Ruehmann
Art Director:	Bjoern Ruehmann		**Photographer:**	Sven Ulrich Glage
Photographer:	Sven Ulrich Glage		**Client:**	Riccardo Cartillone Shoes
Client:	Riccardo Cartillone Shoes			

104 Retail Services

Agency:	Leo Burnett, Oslo
Creative Director:	Erik Heisholt
Copywriters:	Odd Einar Hennøy
	Erik Heisholt
Art Director:	Paul Westum
Production:	Moland Film
Director:	Hans Petter Moland
Producers:	Carl Christian Hvoslet
	Vigdis Roset
Client:	Rimi Grocery Stores, "Devoted Fan"

A middle-aged man and his wife turn up at a football pitch in the middle of nowhere. The stands are empty, and there's an air of desolation. The players appear. They are hopeless – particularly the team in green. Then, by pure chance, the green team score. The man is ecstatic, as if this were a World Cup Final. The woman hands him a toilet roll, which he hurls onto the pitch in joyous celebration. Then another. Then yet another. But he can afford it, because a six-pack of toilet paper costs next to nothing at Rimi.

Agency:	GKM Werbeagentur, Berlin
Creative Director:	Werner Gerhard
Copywriter:	Astrid Uhle
Art Director:	Kai Fatheuer
Production:	blm Filmproduktion, Hamburg
Director:	Frank Papenbrook
Producers:	Sandra Dahnke
	Marcel Rose
Client:	KD Kaiser's Drugstore, "The Police Station"

A criminal with a shaven head sits on a stool in a police station, getting his photo taken for the files. Left profile. Right profile. Straight ahead. But as he gets up, the photographer – who remains off-screen – takes another snap. Then he takes some more, encouraging the criminal to adopt increasingly seductive poses. "Look at the camera! Yeah, baby!" By the end, the criminal-turned-supermodel is sporting a red feather boa. Getting pictures developed at KD Kaiser's is so cheap that you can take as many photos as you like.

Agency:	Leo Burnett, Warsaw
Creative Director:	Darek Zatorski
Copywriters:	Magdalena Kamoy
	Teresa Biernacka
Art Director:	Ksenia Kononenko
Photographer:	Makar Gippenreiter
Client:	Ikea

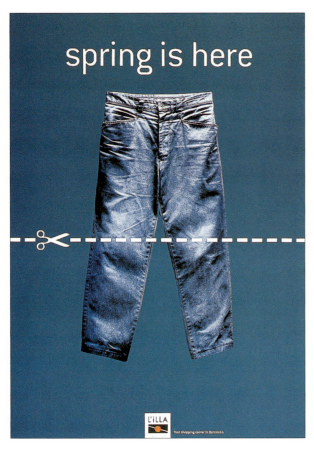

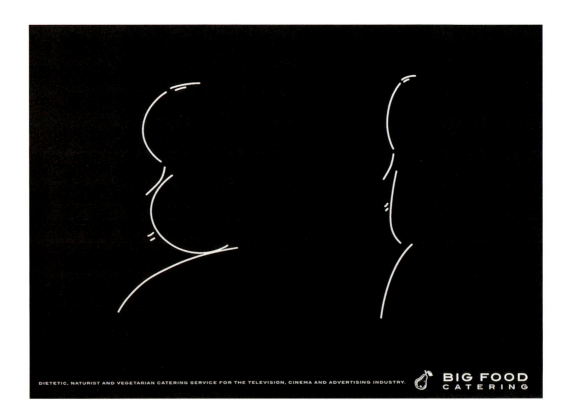

106 Retail Services

Agency:	Tandem Campmany Guasch DDB, Barcelona	**Agency:**	TBWA\España, Barcelona
Creative Director:	Jose Maria Roca de Viñals	**Creative Director:**	Xavi Munill
Copywriter:	Sergi Zapater	**Copywriters:**	Xavi Munill
			Miquel Sales
Art Directors:	Juan Ramon Alfaro	**Art Directors:**	Tomás Descals
	Emma Carrau		Alex Martín
Client:	L'Illa Diagonal Shopping Center	**Client:**	Big Food Catering

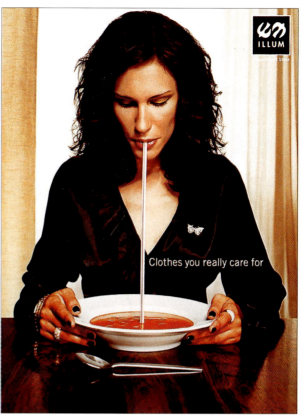

Retail Services 107

Agency:	Robert/Boisen & Like Minded, Copenhagen
Creative Director:	Michael Robert
Copywriters:	Joachim Nielsen
	Kristel Krøjer
Art Directors:	Jesper Schmidt
	Michael Robert
Photographers:	Henrik Büllow
	Anna & Petra
Client:	Illum
	Department Store

108   Retail Services

Agency:	Romson Seidefors, Stockholm	Waistcoat from Paul Smith with details in fake fur.	**Agency:**	BBDO, Düsseldorf	
Copywriter:	Jacob Nelson		**Creative Director:**	Jan van Meel	
Art Director:	Patrik Bruckner		**Copywriter:**	Gerrit Kleinfeld	
Photographer:	Lasse Karkkainen		**Art Director:**	Sebastian Druschel	
Client:	Nordiska Kompaniet Department Store		**Photographer:**	Robin Merkisch	
			Client:	Beates Hundesalon, Dog Grooming Parlor	

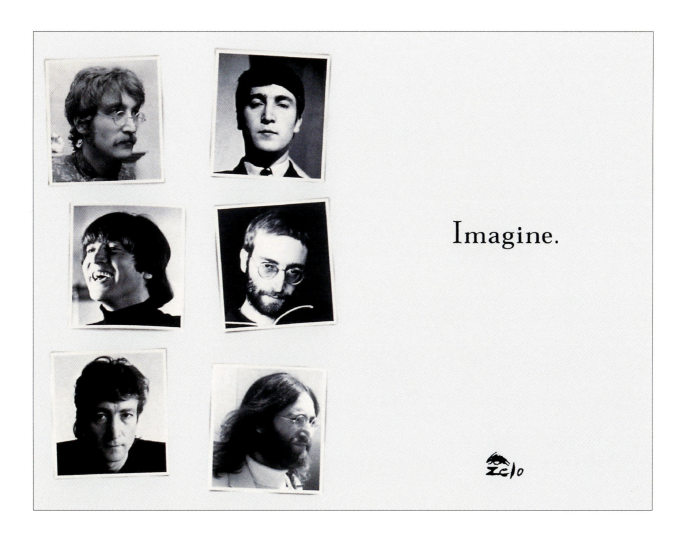

Agency:	Jung von Matt, Zürich	
Creative Directors:	Daniel Meier	
	Alexander Jaggy	
Copywriter:	Dominik Imseng	
Art Director:	Felix Dammann	
Client:	Zelo Hairdressers	
Agency:	TSM-Palmares, Brussels	Top brands unveil their summer collections.
Creative Director:	Paul-Henri Guilmin	
Copywriters:	Stephane Daniel	
	Genevieve Pochet	600 top brands announce the spring.
Art Directors:	Hugo Battistel	
	Luc Pieltain	
Photographers:	Xavier Harcq	600 top brands unveil their autumn-winter collections.
	Bertrand Castay	
Client:	Inno Department Store	

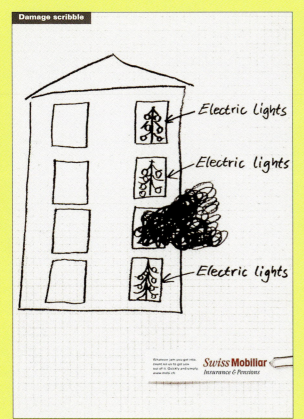
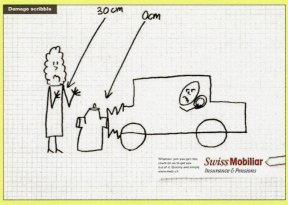
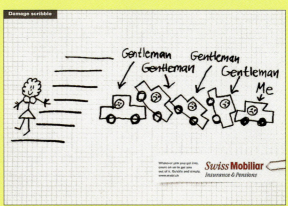
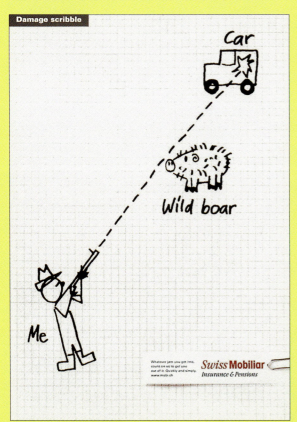
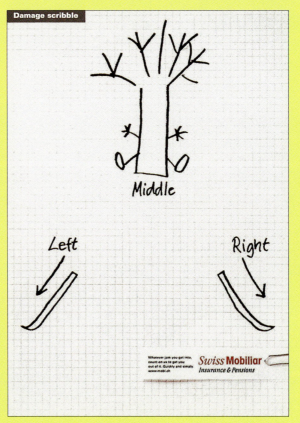

Financial Services

Agency: Publicis, Zürich
Creative Directors: Uwe Schlupp
Jean Etienne Aebi
Copywriter: Markus Tränkle
Client: Die Mobiliar Insurance

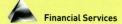 **Financial Services**

Agency:	Collaborate, Stockholm
Creative Director:	Bo Rönnberg
Copywriter:	Totte Stub
Art Director:	Arvid Svanvik
Production:	Acne
Director:	Lukas Hammar
Producer:	David Olsson
Client:	Länsförsäkringar Insurance, "Prison"

Two prison guards are slumped in front of their closed-circuit TV screens when they hear one of the prisoners – "the new guy" – hollering. When one of the guards goes to check, the prisoner complains that his cell is cold, because of a draught coming from behind the washbasin. The guard lifts the basin aside, to discover a large hole in the wall. "Didn't you notice anything?" the prisoner asks his cell mate, who is lying on a bunk glaring at him. "I mean, you've been lying there for four years!" Sometimes, life insurance is a good idea.

Financial Services

Agency:	DDB, Brussels
Creative Director:	Michel De Lauw
Copywriter:	Benoît Pirson
Art Director:	Georges Amerlynck
Production:	Pix & Motion
Director:	Anne-Marie Vandeputte
Producers:	Kato Maes
	Brigitte Verduyckt
Client:	Wecover Car Insurance, "Coconut"

A driver painstakingly manoeuvres his new car into a parking space between two palm trees. As he gets out and closes the door, it is obvious that the vehicle is his pride and joy. After a last fond look, he walks away. But then he winces as he hears a coconut fall onto the car's bonnet. He turns and howls in anger, kicking another coconut in his frustration. It hits the palm tree, and coconuts begin crashing down on his car. He should have been insured with Wecover.

Agency:	TBWA\Paris
Creative Director:	Jean-Pierre Barbou
Copywriter:	Alain Picard
Art Director:	Robin de Lestrade
Production:	Première Heure
Director:	Frédéric Planchon
Producers:	Ghislaine Byramjee
	Evelyne Luverdis
Client:	Axa Insurance, "Reincarnation"

During a colourful tour of India, we meet some of the animals that make up the country's wildlife. And according to the subtitles, they all have names: tigers called John and Sonali, Pablo the bull, Doug the rat, even a mosquito named Marcello – who comes to a sticky end when he lands on the shoulder of a man in Benares. In fact, these were the creatures' identities before they were reincarnated. Some people believe that after our present life, we live many others...but Axa believes we live many lives during this one, and adapts its insurance products accordingly.

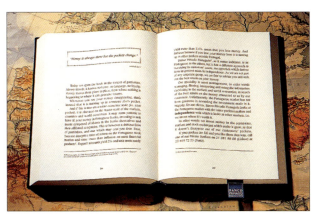

Financial Services

Agency:	BBDO Portugal, Lisbon
Creative Director:	Pedro Bidarra
Copywriter:	Pedro Bidarra
Art Directors:	José Heitor
	José Bomtempo
	Marco Dias
	Rogério Serrasqueiro
Photographer:	Alexander Koch
Client:	Banco Privado Portugues

"Friendship is like money. Easier made than kept." (Samuel Butler)

"A billion here, a billion there, pretty soon it's real money." (Everett Dirksen)

"I don't like money but the truth is it calms the nerves." (Joe Louis)

"From birth to age 18, a girl needs good parents, from 18 to 25 she needs good friends, from 35 to 55 she needs a good personality and from 55 on she needs cash." (Sophia Tucker)

"Money is always there but the pockets change." (Gertrude Stein)

"How did you go bankrupt?" asked Bill. "Two different ways," replied Mike. "Gradually and then suddenly." (Ernest Hemingway)

"Bah!" said Scrooge. "Humbug!" (Charles Dickens)

"Money isn't everything - but it ranks right up there with oxygen." (Rita Davenport)

Financial Services

Agency:	Lowe Brindfors, Stockholm
Creative Director:	Johan Nilsson
Copywriter:	Björn Hjalmar
Art Director:	Patrick Waters
Production:	Acne
Director:	Fredrik Edfeldt
Producers:	David Olsson, Mark Baughen
Client:	Swedbank, "Cuckoo Clock"

An elderly couple are sitting quietly at a table, finishing their meal. All is tranquil, until the cuckoo clock chimes – and the bird falls straight off its perch, into the butter dish. A last feeble chime, and the clock's spring follows. Unexpected expenses? Be prepared with a savings account at Swedbank.

Agency:	Duval Guillaume, Brussels
Creative Director:	Jens Mortier
Copywriter:	Jens Mortier
Art Director:	Philippe De Ceuster
Production:	Pix & Motion
Director:	Raf Wattion
Producers:	Kato Maes, Andreas Hasle
Client:	Axion Bank, "Respect"

A teenage girl washes her face and pats it dry with a towel in front of the mirror. But then she notices something – she has had a terrible acne breakout. And what's more, the pimples are singing the Aretha Franklin soul number, "Respect". The girl watches hypnotised for a second, and then pops one of the zits onto the mirror – where it goes right on singing. Being a teen is tough, but Axion Bank respects youth.

Agency:	Young & Rubicam, Copenhagen	Agency:	Van Walbeek Etcetera, Amsterdam
Creative Directors:	Peder Schack Tom Olsen	Creative Director: Copywriters:	Willem van Harrewijen Antoine Houtsma
Art Director:	Peder Schack		Dick van der Lecq
Photographer:	Christian Gravesen	Art Director:	Raymond van Schaik
Illustrator:	Martin Moos	Photographer:	Jan Holtslag
Client:	Nykredit Østifterne Forsikring Insurance	Client:	Yarden Funeral Insurance

116 Financial Services

Agency:	The Leith Agency, Edinburgh
Creative Director:	Gerry Farrell
Copywriter:	Dougal Wilson
Art Director:	Gareth Howells
Production:	MTP
Director:	Tony Smith
Producers:	Simon Mallinson, Les Watt
Client:	BFI & Accenture, "Some Like It Hot" & "Don't Look Now"

In a Hollywood office, a couple of young mavericks are telling a producer why he should remake the classic movie Some Like It Hot. The film features Jack Lemmon and Tony Curtis, as jazz musicians on the run from gangsters, who disguise themselves as women and join an all-female band, headed by Marilyn Monroe. "Nobody listens to jazz," complains the producer. "How about rock? Instead of Monroe, we get Meatloaf. He already has the hair…" To avert this nightmare scenario, Accenture and BFI are bringing the original back to the big screen.

This time we're in a London restaurant, and an English hopeful is pitching his idea to a Hollywood producer – a remake of Don't Look Now. In "the scariest film ever" a couple are grief-stricken when their daughter drowns. A year later, in Venice, they meet a psychic who claims she can contact the dead child…The producer isn't happy. "Does she have to drown? Can't she just break her leg?" He also sees Whoopi Goldberg in the role of the psychic. Fortunately for us, Accenture and BFI are bringing the original back to the big screen.

Financial Services

Agency:	&Co., Copenhagen
Art Director:	Thomas Hoffmann
Photographer:	Noam Griegst
Client:	Danske Bank, Youth Campaign

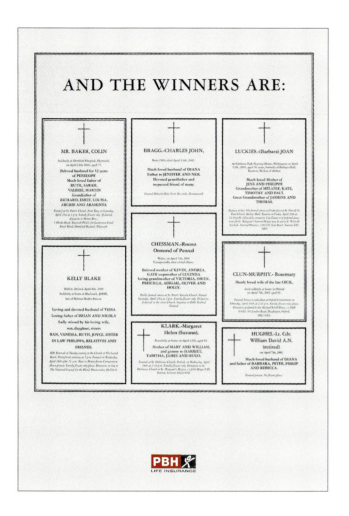
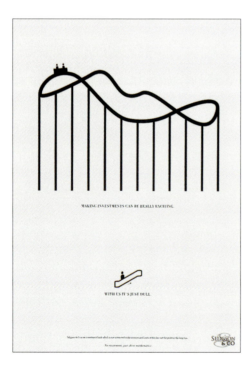

Financial Services

Agency:	Duval Guillaume, Brussels	Agency:	Skandaali, Helsinki
Creative Director:	Jens Mortier	Copywriters:	Sari Mikkonen-Mannila, Markku Haapalehto
Copywriter:	Jens Mortier	Art Directors:	Vesa Siirilä, Erkki Mikola
Art Director:	Philippe De Ceuster	Illustrator:	Vesa Siirilä
Illustrator:	Philippe De Ceuster	Client:	Seligson & Co. Investment Bank
Client:	PBH Life Insurance		

Financial Services	**119**
Agency:	Zapping, Madrid
Creative Directors:	Uschi Henkes
	Urs Frick
	David Palacios
Copywriter:	David Palacios
Art Directors:	Marcos Fernandez
	Uschi Henkes
Client:	MAAF Car Insurance

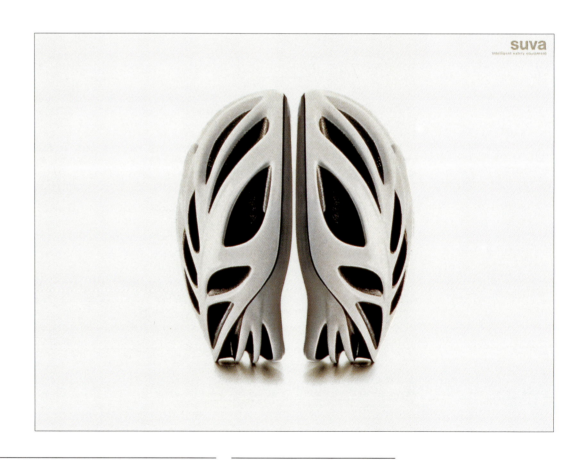

Financial Services

Agency:	Demner, Merlicek & Bergmann, Vienna	A father is in a restaurant with his little boy, who is eating an enormous chocolate cake. Dad asks if he can have a piece, but the kid refuses. Dad then tries every trick in the book to try to get some cake – funny expressions, walking his fingers across the table, opening his mouth wide. But the boy won't budge, and eats all the cake himself. Do you really want to be dependent on your children's generosity? Better start saving for a decent pension.	**Agency:**	McCann-Erickson, Zürich
Creative Director:	Johannes Krammer		**Creative Director:**	Claude Catsky
Copywriter:	Johannes Krammer		**Copywriter:**	Claude Catsky
Art Director:	Elisabeth Sauter		**Art Director:**	Alvaro Maggini
Production:	Filmhaus Wien		**Photographers:**	Stefan Minder
Director:	Trevor Melvin			Felix Schregenberger
Producers:	Dr. Wolfgang Ramml, Maresi McNab		**Client:**	Suva Insurance, Accident Prevention
Client:	Wiener Städtische, "Cake"			

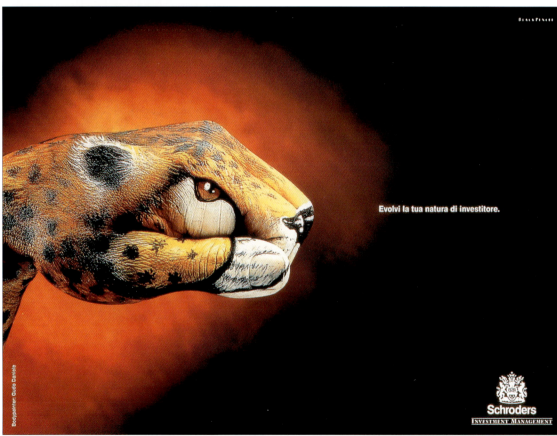

Agency:	Black Pencil, Milan	Develop your investing instincts.
Creative Director:	Sergio Rodriguez	
Copywriter:	Carlo Cavallone	
Art Director:	Michele Bedeschi	
Client:	Schroders Investment Management	

Financial Services

Financial Services

Agency:	Demner, Merlicek & Bergmann, Vienna
Creative Director:	Johannes Krammer
Copywriters:	Johannes Krammer
	Monika Prelec
Art Director:	Kerstin Heymach
Photographer:	Volker Möhrke
Client:	Creditanstalt, CA-Investments

Financial Services

Agency:	McCann-Erickson, Zürich
Creative Director:	Claude Catsky
Copywriter:	Claude Catsky
Art Director:	Alvaro Maggini
Photographers:	Stefan Minder
	Felix Schregenberger
Client:	Suva Insurance, Accident Prevention

124　Public Interest

Agency:	Springer & Jacoby, Hamburg	Life is beautiful. When you don't look too closely. It's so easy to overlook things...
Creative Directors:	Timm Weber Uli Gürtler Bettina Olf	...like the fact that throughout the world 300,000 children are used as soldiers.
Copywriter:	Sven Keitel	.. like the fact that throughout the world
Art Director:	Claudia Tödt	250 million children are forced to work.
Illustrator:	Helga Nandorf	
Client:	UNICEF	.. like the fact that throughout the world 100 million children are living on the street.

Public Interest

Agency:	Saatchi & Saatchi, Milan
Creative Directors:	Guido Cornara Agostino Toscana
Copywriters:	Guido Cornara Agostino Toscana
Production:	BRW
Director:	Agostino Toscana
Producers:	Federico Turchetti Mario Camerini Daniela Gasparotto
Client:	MTV Anti-Death Penalty Initiative, "Mistake"

We see a man leaning on a shovel. In a voiceover, Leonel Herrera describes how in 1981 he was accused of shooting dead a policeman – and wounding another officer – in Los Fresnos, Texas. The wounded cop accused Leonel, who was picked up on the street, drunk. "This became proof of my guilt." Leonel was sentenced to death. Years later, new evidence revealed that Leonel's brother, Raul, committed the crime. But it was too late. A last shot shows us Leonel's grave. The man with the shovel is the cemetery caretaker. The death penalty is the only injustice that can't be put right.

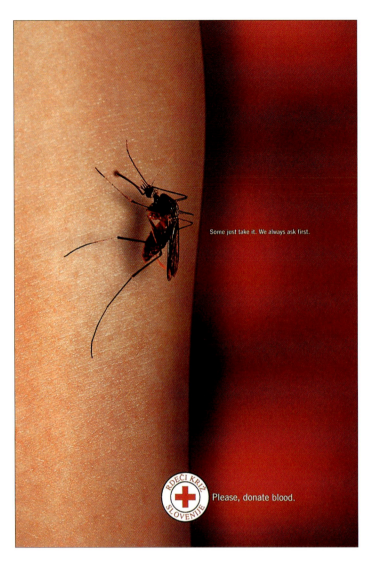

Some just take it. We always ask first.

Please, donate blood.

Some just take it.
We always ask first.

Please donate blood.

Public Interest

Agency:	Pristop, Ljubljana
Creative Director:	Mateja D. Zavrl
Copywriter:	Simona Kepic
Art Director:	Saša Leskovar
Client:	Slovenian Red Cross, Blood Donations

Agency:	Pristop, Ljubljana
Creative Director:	Mateja D. Zavrl
Copywriter:	Simona Kepic
Art Director:	Sasa Leskovar
Client:	Slovenian Red Cross, Blood Donations, "Vampire"

A grainy, classic black and white horror film, with Bela Lugosi as Count Dracula. A young woman is hypnotised by terror as he approaches, then faints as he enfolds her in his cloak and sinks his fangs into her neck. "Some just take it," observes the narrator. "We always ask first." The Red Cross is looking for blood donors.

Agency:	Ogilvy & Mather, Frankfurt	A snowy moonlit landscape, with pine trees and tiny Alpine huts against a backdrop of mountains. On the soundtrack, children sing a Christmas carol. Sleigh bells chime, and we see a point of light streaking through the sky, leaving a trail of twinkling dust. It can only be Santa Claus. Suddenly, from the bottom of the screen, two anti-aircraft guns appear – and blast Santa's sleigh out of the sky. There is no peace on earth, the ad reminds us. In many countries, there is war. That's why the German Red Cross urgently needs donations.	**Agency:**	McCann-Erickson, Milan
Creative Directors:	Thomas Hofbeck, Dr. Stephan Vogel		**Creative Directors:**	Stefano Campora, Alessandro Canale, Stefano Colombo, Dario Neglia
Copywriter:	Dr. Stephan Vogel		**Copywriter:**	Davide Rossi
Art Directors:	Thomas Hofbeck, Jens Frank		**Art Director:**	Matteo Civaschi
Production:	Das Werk		**Client:**	Worldwide Fund for Nature
Director:	Thomas Hofbeck			
Client:	German Red Cross, "Peace"			Protected national park.

Agency:	Euro RSCG Switzerland, Zürich	
Creative Director:	Frank Bodin	
Copywriter:	Jürg Waeber	
Art Director:	Urs Hartmann	
Photographer:	Stefan Minder	
Client:	GSTF, Free Tibet	

Agency:	Euro RSCG Switzerland, Zürich
Creative Director:	Frank Bodin
Copywriter:	Jürg Waeber
Art Director:	Urs Hartmann
Production:	Blood, Sweat & Tears Ltd.
Director:	Frank J. Estermann
Producers:	Fredy Messmer, Yves Spink
Client:	GSTF, Free Tibet, "The Games of Beijing With Tibet"

A blank wall. A gunshot, and a bullet hole appears. Then another, and then three in quick succession. Finally, it becomes apparent that the pattern of holes resembles the Olympic logo. The ad is a political protest against the Olympics in China, and the country's human rights record. "The games of Beijing," says the tagline. "With Tibet."

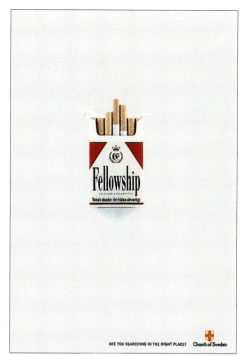

Public Interest	**129**
Agency:	Paradiset DDB, Stockholm
Copywriter:	Anders Lidzell
Art Director:	Paola Pellettieri
Photographer:	Lasse Kärkkainen
Illustrator:	Lena Berglund
Client:	The Church of Sweden

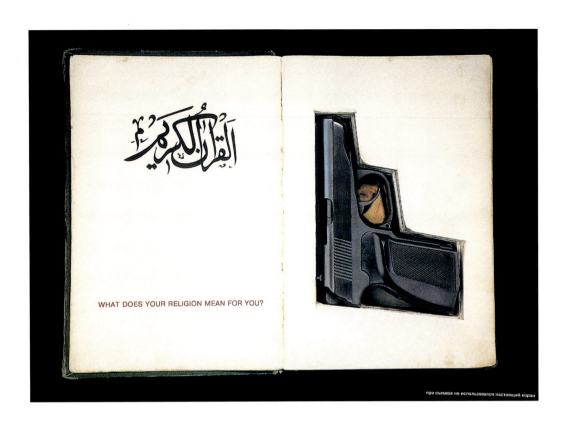

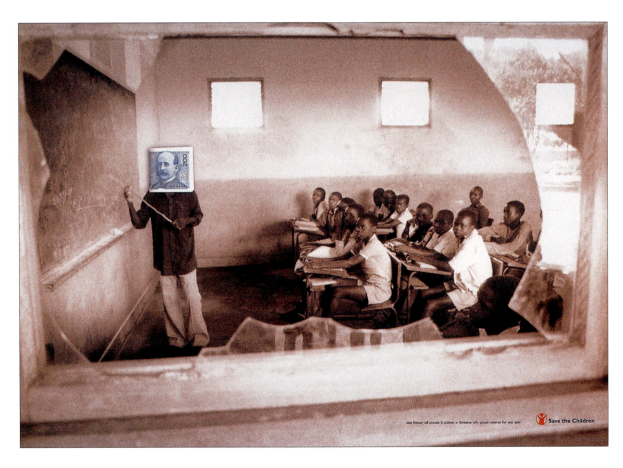

130 Public Interest

Agency:	Belaya Karona, Minsk	Agency:	Leo Burnett, Oslo
Creative Director:	Oleg Ustinovich	Creative Director:	Erik Heisholt
Copywriter:	Oleg Ustinovich	Copywriter:	Erik Heisholt
Art Director:	Oleg Ustinovich	Art Directors:	Jan Bjørkløf
Photographer:	Gregory Livshits		Øivind Eide
Client:	Belaya Karona, Religious Freedom Initiative	Client:	Save the Children Foundation

100 kroner will provide five children with school material for one year.

Agency:	McCann-Erickson Portugal, Lisbon
Photographers:	Jean Guany
	James Nachtey
	Paula Bronstein
Client:	Sindicato dos Jornalistas

Public Interest

Agency:	Kaisaniemen Dynamo, Helsinki	
Copywriter:	Vesa Kujala	
Art Director:	Henna Aapola	
Photographer:	Lauri Eriksson	
Client:	TV Licence Inspection	

Agency:	Ogilvy & Mather, Frankfurt
Creative Directors:	Thomas Hofbeck, Dr. Stephan Vogel
Copywriter:	Philipp Böttcher
Art Director:	Marco Weber
Production:	Neue Sentimental Film
Director:	Claus Dowie
Producer:	Alexander Hess
Client:	SWR TV, Anti-TV Violence Initiative, "Bad Dreams"

A child's bedroom at night. The camera pans in on the bed, where a little girl is tossing and turning in her sleep. The soundtrack takes us inside her head, which is filled with screams, shout, impacts, gunshots...Her hair is soaked with perspiration, and her eyes move rapidly under the closed lids, seeing who knows what ghastly, disturbing images. Suddenly, with a shout, she snaps opens her eyes...which have become TV screens. Parents have a responsibility to protect their children from TV violence.

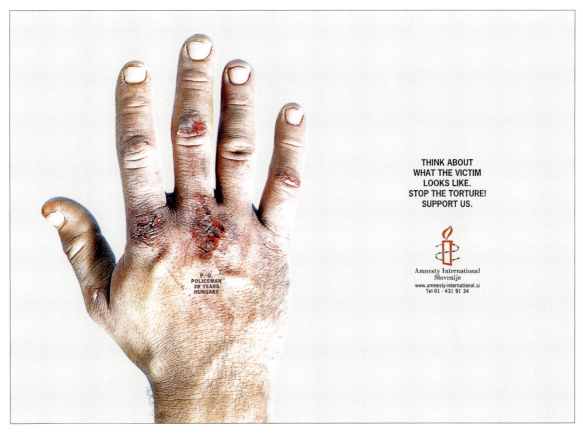

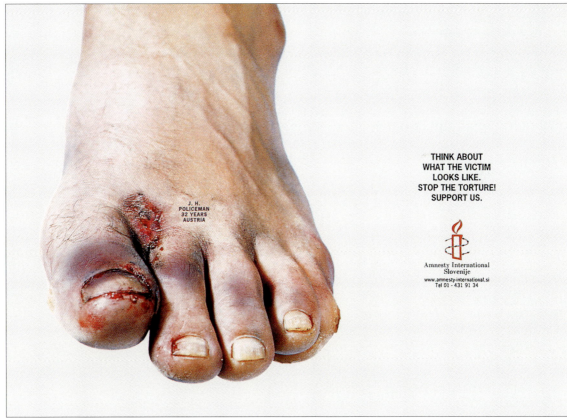

Public Interest 133

Agency:	Futura DDB, Ljubljana
Creative Directors:	Zoran Gabrijan
	Benjamin Ivancic
Copywriter:	Zoran Gabrijan
Art Director:	Benjamin Ivancic
Photographer:	Franci Virant
Client:	Amnesty International

Public Interest

Agency:	Garbergs Annonsbyrå, Stockholm
Copywriter:	Lotta Lundgren
Art Director:	Paola Pellettieri
Photographer:	Lasse Kärkkäinen
Client:	Amnesty International

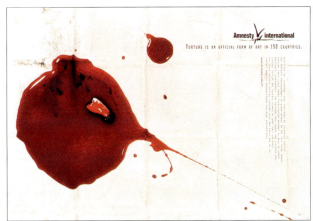
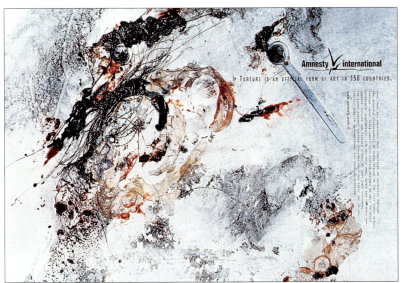

Agency:	Bates, Paris
Creative Director:	Franck Rey
Copywriter:	Franck Rey
Art Director:	Aude Commissaire
Photographer:	Mickaël Baumgarten
Client:	Amnesty International

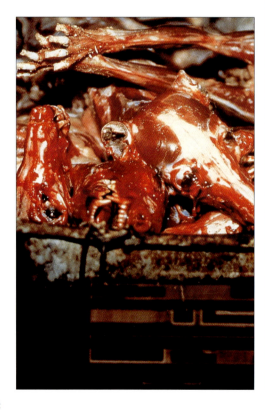

136 **Public Interest**

Agency:	Ogilvy & Mather, Frankfurt	Agency:	Jung von Matt, Hamburg
Creative Directors:	Thomas Hofbeck	Creative Directors:	Goetz Ulmer
	Dr. Stephan Vogel		Thomas Wildberger
Copywriters:	Dr. Stephan Vogel	Copywriter:	Antonio Lopez
	Philipp Böttcher	Art Director:	Corinna Falusi
Art Director:	Marco Weber	Client:	NOAH, Animal Rights
Photographer:	Pascal Günter		
Client:	Worldwide Fund For Nature		

Agency:	McCann Erickson Portugal, Lisbon
Photographer:	Carlos Martins
Client:	Observatório do Ambiente, Environmental Protection

Public Interest

Agency:	Cole, Russell & Pryce, Stockholm
Copywriters:	Håkan Engler Olle Sjödén
Art Director:	Mick Born
Production:	Forsberg & Co.
Director:	Alex Brügge
Client:	Förbundet Djurens Rätt, Animal Rights, "Experiments on Animals"

As a beautiful woman sashays onto a minimalist set, it appears that we are in yet another glossy cosmetics commercial. This seems to be confirmed when the woman explains that her hair and skin are very important to her, which is why her company's products are tested very carefully. "Every year we torture and kill 35,000 animals in Europe," she adds cheerfully. "Because I'm worth it!" Most cosmetic companies test their products on animals, the ad explains. To find out which don't, go to the Animal Rights website, www.djurensratt.org.

Agency:	Jung von Matt, Hamburg
Creative Directors:	Goetz Ulmer Thomas Wildberger
Copywriter:	Antonio Lopez
Art Director:	Gabriella Uenal
Client:	NOAH, Animal Rights

Public Interest 139

Agency: Scholz & Friends, Berlin
Creative Directors: Martin Krapp
Lutz Pluemecke
Copywriter: Oliver Handlos
Art Director: Raphael Puettmann
Client: Berlin Society for the Protection of Animals

Too small? Yet every year childabusers still manage to poke inside again and again and again and again...

140 Public Interest

Agency:	Jung von Matt, Hamburg	**Agency:**	Kolle Rebbe Werbeagentur, Hamburg
Creative Director:	Hermann Waterkamp	**Creative Directors:**	Bernd Huesmann
Copywriter:	Willy Kaussen		Erik Hart
Art Director:	Regina Wysny	**Copywriter:**	Deborah Nohke
Client:	Dunkelziffer, Organisation For Sexually Abused Children	**Art Director:**	Katharina Heyn
		Photographer:	Marcus Wendler
		Client:	ZornRot, Organisation For Sexually Abused Children

Agency:	The White House, Reykjavik	NB: During the day, the family portrait appeared normal - but at night when the sign was back-lit, bruises and other marks of violence appeared on the woman and the child, and the text changed.	Agency:	JBR McCann, Oslo
Creative Director:	Sverrir Bjornsson		Creative Director:	Paal Tarjeii Aasheim
Copywriter:	Anna Agustsdottir		Copywriter:	Paal Tarjeii Aasheim
Art Directors:	Sigrun Gylfadottir		Art Director:	Geir Florhaug
	Kristin Thora Gudbjartsdottir		Photographer:	Collin Eick
Photographer:	Fridrik Orn Hjaltested		Client:	Red Cross Child Relief
Illustrator:	Sigrun Gylfadottir			
Client:	Stigamot, Against Domestic Violence			

142   Public Interest

Agency:	McCann-Erickson Polska, Warsaw
Creative Directors:	Jaroslaw Wiewiórski, Józef Dutkiewicz, Agnieszka Dymecka
Copywriters:	Iwona Kluszczyńska, Malgorzata Wlodarska
Production:	ITI Film Studio
Director:	Slawomir Fabicki
Producers:	Andrzey Poleč, Tomasz Lukasiewicz
Client:	PARPA, "Childhood Without Violence"

A little girl is trying to feed her teddy bear in what seems like a harmless childhood game. But when she spills some food, things take a sinister turn. "Look what you've done!" she shouts at the mute creature. "Don't look at me like that!" She viciously twists the bear's ear, ranting and raving – and with horror we realise that she has learned this behaviour from her parents. Finally she breaks down in tears. "I don't love you!" And the bear is abandoned in a cupboard. PARPA is working to protect Polish children from domestic violence.

Agency:	Leo Burnett, Milan
Executive Director:	Enrico Dorizza
Copywriter:	Mauro Manieri
Art Director:	Filippo Magri
Production:	Nemo Productions
Director:	VA-H
Producers:	Luca Fanfani, Anna Paula Avetti, Antonello Filosa
Client:	ENPA, Animal Protection Organisation, "Unattended Dogs"

A dog is tied to a traffic sign beside a busy highway. A boy strokes the animal, obviously unwilling to leave it behind, but his father pulls him into a parked car. They drive off. Have they abandoned the family pet? Apparently not, because a second later the car reverses, the father gets out and rescues the dog. A couple of seconds later, a truck driver arrives with a plate of food for the missing animal – which clearly belonged to him. But as he left it in such an unsuitable place, is he fit to own a pet?

Agency:	Euro RSCG, Helsinki	**Agency:**	Publicis Werbeagentur, Frankfurt	Fire Department seeks volunteers.
Creative Director:	Jussi Mansukoski	**Creative Directors:**	Claus-Steffen Braun	
Copywriter:	Maija Mansukoski		Michael Koecher	
Art Director:	Jani Ekonen	**Art Director:**	Guenter Schlicht	
Illustrator:	Teemu Tuohimaa	**Photographer:**	Jan Steinhilber	
Client:	Finnish Federation of Visually Impaired	**Client:**	Landesfeuerwehr-Verband Hessen	

144 Public Interest

Agency:	Springer & Jacoby, Hamburg	NB: The campaign used famous brands whose packaging features children's faces, but with the faces removed to emphasise the plight of missing kids.
Creative Directors:	Timm Weber Bettina Olf	
Copywriter:	Sven Keitel	
Art Director:	Claudia Tödt	
Client:	Parental Initiative For Missing Children	

Public Interest　145

Agency:	Springer & Jacoby, Hamburg	We're looking at a tacky set familiar to anyone who has ever tuned in to a TV shopping channel. But instead of the latest gadget for peeling potatoes or removing stains, the product on offer is a small child, looking totally baffled as he revolves on a tiny podium. "Our kids are available in many colours," says the bland presenter. "Oops! We just heard that white is sold out already." It may seem like an unlikely scenario – but in some countries, children really are bought and sold like products. UNICEF is fighting child trafficking.	**Agency:**	Springer & Jacoby, Hamburg
Creative Directors:	Timm Weber, Bettina Olf		**Creative Directors:**	Andreas Geyer, Ulrich Zünkeler, Thomas Walmrath
Copywriter:	Sven Keitel		**Copywriters:**	Oliver Heidorn, Hinnerk Landmann
Art Director:	Claudia Tödt		**Art Directors:**	Nina Rühmkorf, Silke Baltruschat
Production:	Markenfilm, Wedel		**Illustrator:**	Nina Rühmkorf
Director:	Sebastian Strasser		**Client:**	Pro Familia Marriage Counselling
Producers:	Uli Scheper, Fabian Barz, Jassna Sroka			
Client:	UNICEF, "Child"			

Public Interest

Agency:	McCann-Erickson, Madrid
Creative Directors:	Nicolás Hollander, Marcos García, Juan Nonzioli
Production:	Tesauro
Director:	Sébastien Grousset
Producer:	Luis Felipe Moreno
Client:	Bancos De Alimentos, "Naked Woman"

Astonished bystanders look on as a naked woman rummages through rubbish bins on a busy city street. Are they shocked by her behaviour, or the fact that she has no clothes on? Perhaps they should be more concerned about the fact that she is obviously desperate for something to eat. The Bancos De Alimentos – the Food Bank – reminds us that even in the 21st century, thousands of people are starving not far from our homes.

Agency:	McCann-Erickson, Madrid
Creative Directors:	Nicolás Hollander, Juan Nonzioli
Production:	Puente Aéreo, Barcelona
Director:	José Luis López
Producer:	Luis Felipe Moreno
Client:	Bancos De Alimentos, "Boy"

On a concrete sports pitch, a boy is deftly keeping a football in the air by flipping it from foot to foot, among other tricky manoeuvres. He explains that he is trying to break a world record by keeping the ball off the ground for 72 hours. The voiceover suggests that as he seems to have plenty of time on his hands, he might find something more rewarding to do. Like become a volunteer at the Bancos De Alimentos – the Food Bank.

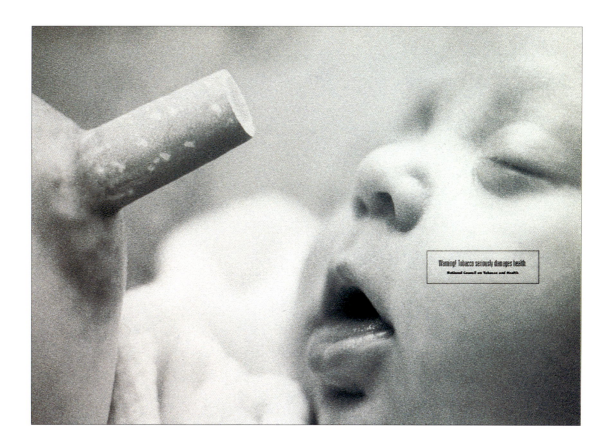

Public Interest 147

Agency:	JBR McCann, Oslo	Agency:	Bates Portugal, Lisbon
Creative Director:	Eivind Solberg	Creative Directors:	Judite Mota
Copywriter:	Petter Gulli		Pedro Ferreira
Art Director:	Joachim A. Haug	Copywriter:	António Páscoa
Photographers:	Anne Rippy	Art Director:	Nuno Tristão
	Nick Dolding	Photographer:	Alexander Koch
Client:	National Council On Tobacco & Health	Client:	Instituto Nacional De Cardiologia Preventiva, Heart Disease Prevention

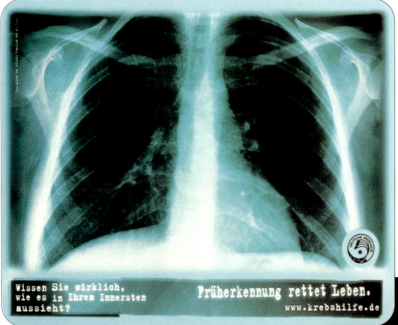
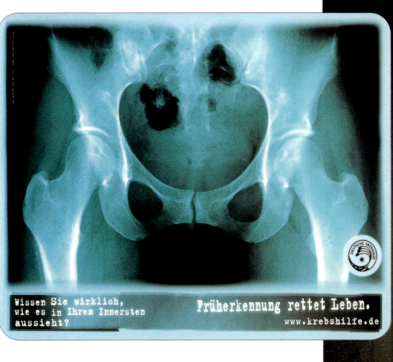
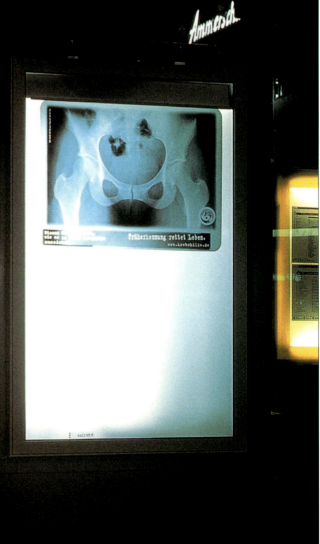

148 Public Interest

Agency:	Publicis Werbeagentur, Frankfurt
Creative Directors:	Michael Boebel
	Dirk Bugdahn
	Hadi Geiser
Copywriter:	Hadi Geiser
Art Directors:	Dirk Bugdahn
	Denise Overkamp
Client:	Deutsche Krebshilfe, German Cancer Society

Do you really know how things look deep inside you? Early diagnosis saves lives.

NB: The campaign featured genuine X-ray photographs, which were clamped to the outside of a Citylight display, imitating the way a physician uses an illuminator to view X-rays

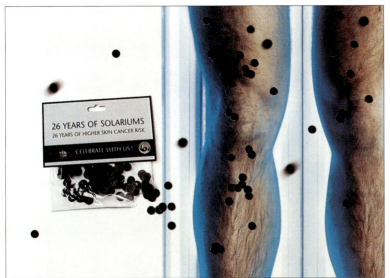
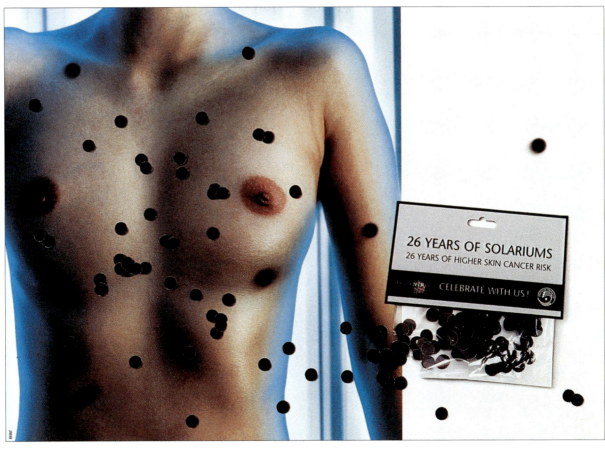

Agency:	Heimat Werbeagentur, Berlin
Creative Directors:	Guido Heffels
	Jürgen Vossen
Copywriter:	Andreas Manthey
Art Directors:	Tim Schneider
	Anna Kiefer
Photographer:	Jens Boldt
Client:	ADP, Skin Cancer Prevention

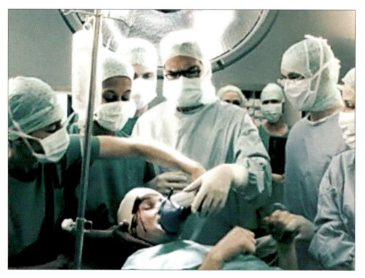 

Public Interest

Agency:	Markku Rönkkö, Helsinki	
Creative Director:	Markku Rönkkö	
Production:	Woodpecker Film	
Director:	Jappe Päivinen	
Producer:	Merja Metsävaara-Mildh	
Client:	City of Helsinki, European City of Culture, "Like Father Like Son"	

A woman opens the inner front door of her apartment to pick up the morning paper. Her teenage son slumps into the room, dead to the world, an empty beer bottle rolling from his grip. He must have passed out there last night. As the woman walks through the living room, she passes her husband, snoring on the sofa where he has crashed out in front of dozens of empty bottles. She slaps him irritably with the paper. Helsinki may be the European city of culture, but it needs to wake up to its alcohol problems.

Agency:	McCann-Erickson, Zürich
Creative Director:	Claude Catsky
Copywriter:	Claude Catsky
Art Director:	Claude Catsky
Production:	Wirz & Fraefel Productions
Director:	Ernst Wirz
Producer:	Stefan Fraefel
Client:	Alcoholics Anonymous, "The Hooligan"

A football hooligan is being wheeled quickly down a hospital corridor on a stretcher, bleeding from a nasty head wound. He's still drunk, singing and shouting and making grabs for the nurses' skirts. They get him to the operating theatre, where he is surrounded by surgeons. One of them has suspiciously shaky hands. He lowers his surgical mask, and begins burbling incoherently, just as drunk as his patient. The hooligan looks worried, but the anaesthetic has already begun to take hold...Alcoholism can affect anyone.

Agency:	Forsman & Bodenfors, Gothenburg
Copywriter:	Martin Ringqvist
Art Directors:	Staffan Forsman
	Staffan Håkanson
Client:	Salvation Army

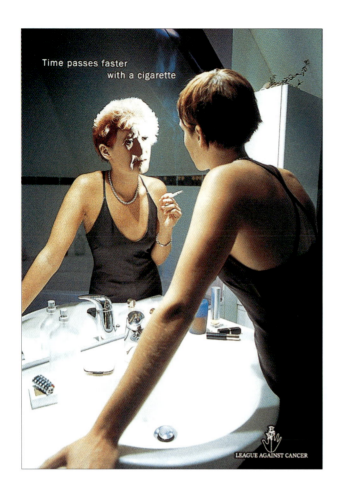
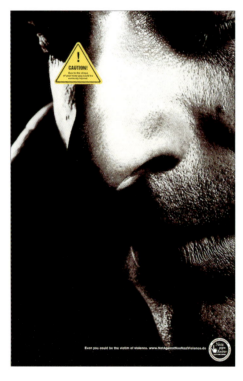
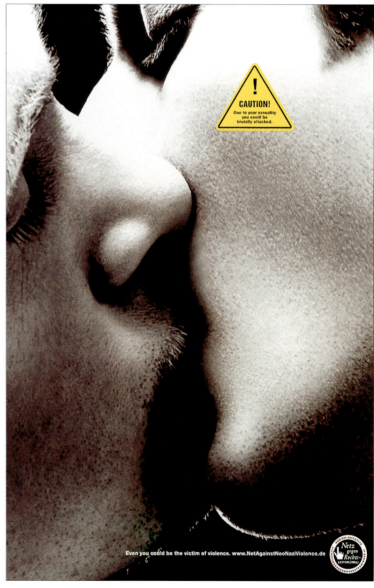

Public Interest

Agency:	Soria & Grey, Bratislava	**Agency:**	Springer & Jacoby, Hamburg	Due to the shape of your nose you could be seriously injured.
Creative Director:	Boris Ondreička	**Creative Directors:**	Thomas Walmrath Andreas Geyer Ulrich Zünkeler	
Copywriter:	Oliver Lippo			Due to your sexuality you could be brutally attacked.
Art Director:	Marián Mihálik	**Copywriters:**	Ulrich Zünkeler Thomas Walmrath	
Photographer:	Táňa Hojčová	**Art Director:**	Nina Rühmkorf	
Client:	Liga Proti Rakovine, Anti-Smoking	**Photographer:**	Carsten Witte	
		Client:	Net Against Neo-Nazi Violence	

Agency:	Scholz & Friends, Berlin	I am proud to be a German.	**Agency:**	Kolle Rebbe, Hamburg
Creative Directors:	Sebastian Turner, Lutz Pluemecke, Martin Krapp		**Creative Directors:**	Bernd Huesmann, Erik Hart
Copywriter:	Oliver Handlos		**Copywriter:**	Alexander Baron
Art Director:	Raphael Puettmann		**Art Director:**	Florian Scherzer
Photographer:	Matthias Koslik		**Photographer:**	Andreas Gehrke
Client:	Initiative Against Neo-Nazi Violence		**Client:**	Initiative Against Neo-Nazi Violence

Public Interest

Agency:	TBWA\Paris
Creative Director:	Eric Galmard
Copywriter:	Vincent Lobelle
Art Director:	Stephen Cafiero
Client:	AIDES, Anti-Aids Association, "The Meeting"

"Sorry I'm late," says a young office worker, hurrying into a boardroom where his colleagues await him. He starts to unbutton his shirt. On cue, everyone stands up and begins undressing in a brisk, businesslike fashion. Is this a strange experiment, or some kind of orgy? One of the women provides the answer. "And as usual," she instructs her companions, "no condoms." They agree. Of course, this is not a typical office scenario – which is why, in normal circumstances, it is perfectly safe to work with an HIV Positive person.

Agency:	Leo Burnett Advertising, Prague
Creative Director:	Bill Stone
Copywriter:	Martin Charvát
Art Director:	Jiří Langpaul
Client:	Bone Marrow Transplant Foundation

Free or for low price, almost new Skoda. Only 25,000 km, fully loaded, passenger side airbag, aluminium wheels. If I can't find a bone marrow donor.

Looking for anybody who would like to take care of my hamster. His name is Alfred. Terrarium, dish, plus two months' supply of sawdust. If I can't find a bone marrow donor.

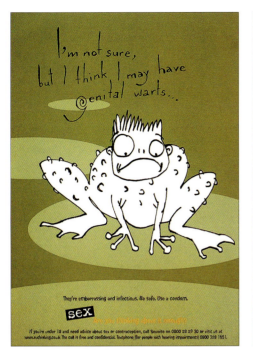

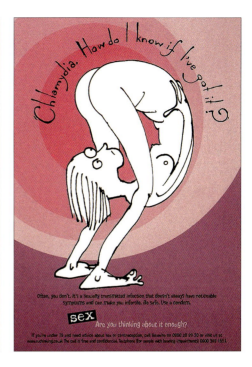

Public Interest   155

Agency:	Delaney Lund Knox Warren & Partners, London	Agency:	Reklambyrån Hjärtsjö, Stockholm
Creative Directors:	Gary Betts Malcolm Green	Copywriter:	Malin Wikerberg
Copywriter:	Jon Elsom	Art Director:	Pelle Lundh
Art Directors:	Ken Sara Tim Peckett	Client:	UNICEF
Illustrator:	Simon Spillsbury		
Client:	COI, Sex Information For Teenagers		

156 Public Interest

Agency:	Faulds Advertising, Edinburgh
Creative Director:	Billy Mawhinney
Copywriters:	Pete Bastiman Chris Muir
Art Director:	Tom Richards
Client:	Autotrader, Anti-Drink-Driving Campaign

Agency:	McCann-Erickson, Belfast	A happy young couple wait by a roadside. Their friends pull up in an old BMW and they jump in, roaring down a country lane. Rounding a bend, they collide head-on with another car. Then a third vehicle hurtles into the pile-up. The boyfriend is thrown around in a grotesque slow-motion ballet, his skull transformed into a battering ram as it connects with his girlfriend's head. Cut to a rescue worker, who is saying into his walkie-talkie: "Three dead in this vehicle, the girl is critical. They say the guy without the seatbelt did the damage." No seatbelt, no excuse.	**Agency:**	Sek & Grey, Helsinki
Creative Directors:	David Lyle		**Creative Director:**	Joanna Tavio
	Julie Anne Bailie		**Copywriter:**	Jarkko Tuuri
Copywriters:	David Lyle		**Art Director:**	Antero Jokinen
	Julie Anne Bailie		**Client:**	Central Organisation
Art Directors:	David Lyle			For Traffic Safety
	Julie Anne Bailie			In Finland
Production:	Rawi Macartney Cole, London			
Director:	Syd Macartney			
Producers:	Ruck Strauss			
	Julie Anne Bailie			
Client:	DoE, National Safety Council, "Damage"			

Public Interest

Agency:	McCann-Erickson, Zürich
Creative Director:	Claude Catsky
Copywriter:	Claude Catsky
Art Director:	Alvaro Maggini
Production:	Gap Films, Munich
Director:	Harry Patramanis
Producer:	Ossi von Richtofen
Client:	Suva Insurance Accident Prevention, "Evolution"

A chimpanzee, sitting alone in an empty room, is given a cycling helmet to play with. At first the chimp is bemused by this shiny new object, sniffing it and trying to chew it. He puts it on the ground and uses it as a pillow. Not very comfortable. Baffled, he sits and stares at it for a while. Then realisation dawns. He puts it on his head. He taps it with his knuckles, apparently quite impressed by the protective shell. If only humans could learn as quickly, there would be fewer accidents on the road.

Agency:	Propaganda, Copenhagen
Creative Director:	Frederik Preisler
Art Director:	Johnny Lund
Production:	Bullet Production
Director:	Martin Verner
Producer:	Mette Ambro
Client:	The Ministry of Environment, Recycling Center, "The Vibrator"

A woman is putting some clothes in a drawer when she notices her vibrator. With a smile, she switches it on. Her disappointed expression indicates that it no longer works. In the hall outside her apartment, she tries to drop it into a rubbish chute – but hesitates in front of a nosy neighbour. Instead, while walking her dog, she throws the thing into the river. Relieved, she sits at a waterfront café. Then her dog comes bounding up – carrying the vibrator in its mouth. Old electrical appliances should always be handed in at a recycling centre.

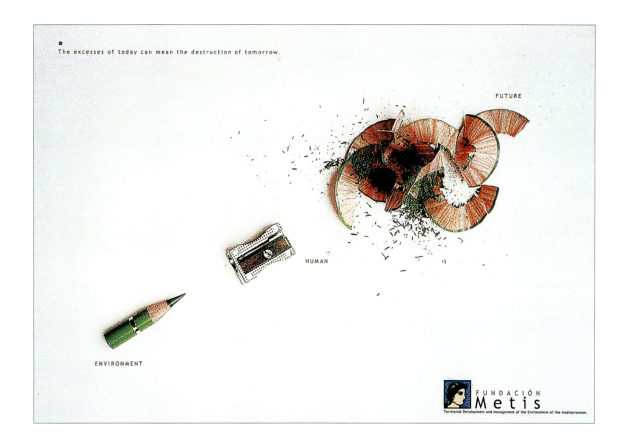

 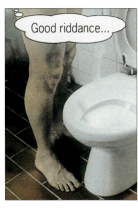   

Agency:	TBWA\España, Barcelona	Agency:	Eriksson & Gullberg, Stockholm
Creative Director:	Xavi Munill	Project Manager:	Mic Eyre
Copywriters:	Xavi Munill Miquel Sales	Copywriter:	Hanna Holmqvist
Art Directors:	Tomás Descals Alex Martín	Art Director:	Lars-Henrik Lindahl
		Photographer:	Philip Laurell
Client:	Fundacion Metis, Environmental Preservation	Client:	Stockholm Vatten, Water Utility

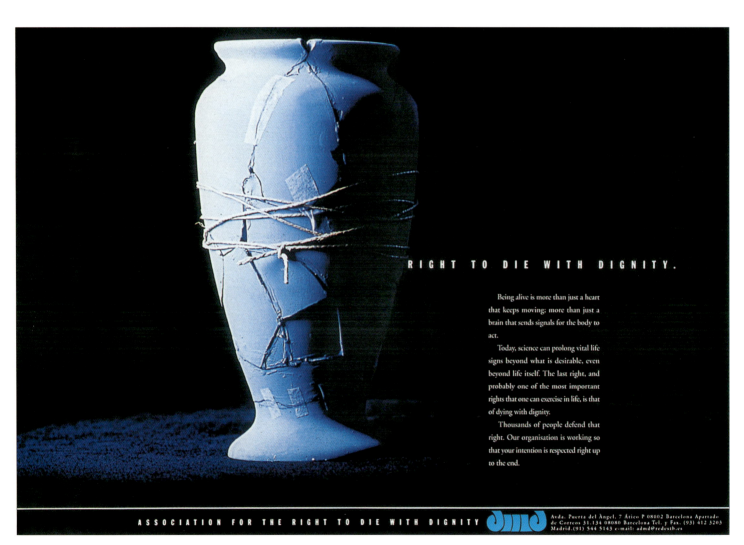

Public Interest

Agency:	Sek & Grey, Helsinki
Project Director:	Jukka Kurttila
Copywriter:	Markus Lehtonen
Art Director:	Marko Muona
Production:	Filmitalli
Director:	Mikko Lehtinen
Producer:	Hanna Salminen
Client:	Finnish Defence Forces, Recruitment, "The Operator"

"Hello. Please hold." A smartly-dressed young man is paid to answer the phone in a bland office. In a surreal touch, the 'hold' music is played by an old man with an electric piano, who sits next to him. "One more moment please." Once again he points the phone at the old man, who once again plays the same monotonous tune. The young man hangs up with a pained expression on his face. For a more exciting life, he should consider joining the Finnish Defence Forces – "a job with a cause".

Agency:	TBWA\España, Barcelona
Creative Director:	Ramón Sala
Copywriters:	Ramón Sala
	Guillermo Ramírez
	Carles Riau
Art Directors:	Jordi Sebastià
	Meritxell Horts
Photographer:	Hugo Menduiña
Client:	Euthanasia Association

Agency:	Pristop, Ljubljana	NB: The headline translates as "Only beautiful people" – a play on words which also sounds like "Only Schengen". It uses fascist imagery to criticise the EU's attitude to refugees and refers to the Schengen Convention, which is supposed to ease freedom of movement across European borders but which critics say has allowed member countries to adopt a single policy on the treatment of refugees.
Creative Director:	Radovan Arnold	
Copywriters:	Katja Kobolt	
	Aljoša Bagola	
Art Director:	Radovan Arnold	
Client:	Mladina, Refugee Awareness In the EU	

162 Communication Services

Agency:	Springer & Jacoby, Hamburg	The world is getting closer.
Creative Directors:	Thomas Walmrath Andreas Geyer Ulrich Zünkeler	
Copywriter:	Oliver Heidorn	
Art Director:	Cathrine Sundqvist	
Photographer:	Sebastian Schobbert	
Client:	Deutsche Telekom, T-DSL	

Communication Services

Agency:	BDDP & Fils, Paris
Creative Director:	Olivier Altmann
Copywriter:	Christophe Perruchas
Art Director:	Charles Guillemand
Production:	Uturn
Director:	Sébastien Chantrel
Producer:	Christine Bouffort
Client:	La Poste, "Virtual World"

A ball thrown by a child passes harmlessly through a crystal vase, as if the object were a hologram. A woman beneath an umbrella is soaked by the pouring rain. A man photocopies a book – but gets images of his hands. Coffee drains through the bottom of a cup and stains a white tablecloth. And a woman walks on the sand in boots, only to leave bare footprints. More and more objects are available online, but without somebody to deliver them, they remain virtual. What the future promises, La Poste delivers.

Agency:	Romson, Stockholm	**Agency:**	BETC Euro RSCG, Paris
Copywriter:	Martin Bartholf	**Creative Director:**	Stephane Xiberras
Art Director:	Magnus Ingerstedt	**Copywriter:**	Julie Gaillard
Production:	EPA International	**Art Director:**	Benoist Fouquet
Director:	Henrik Lagercrantz	**Photographer:**	Kevin Griffin
Producer:	Johan Persson	**Client:**	Chronopost International, Express Mail
Client:	The Swedish Post Office, "Santa's Christmas"		

Who delivers gifts to Santa's family at Christmas? This intriguing question is about to be answered as we see Santa relaxing in front of the TV after work, with his wife and two daughters. "Haven't you got an errand to run?" asks Mrs Claus pointedly. Santa agrees and disappears out of the front door. A few moments later, there is a knock – "Who can that be, children?" – and Santa enters, disguised as a postman. Sweden Post is the country's leading distributor of Christmas presents.

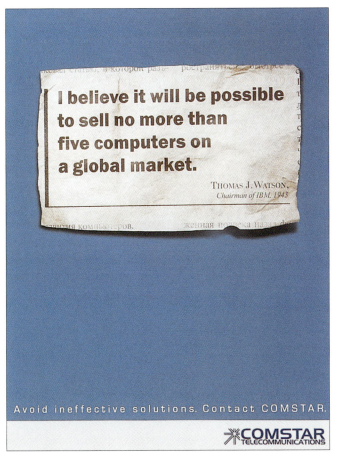
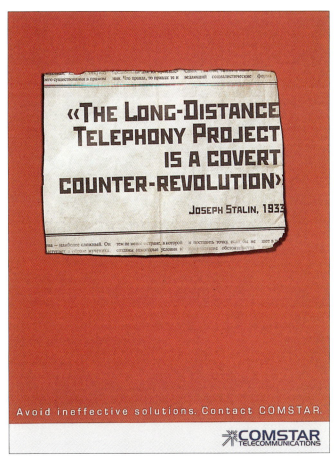

Communication Services 165

Agency:	Euro RSCG Maxima, Moscow	**Agency:**	New Deal DDB, Oslo	It looks like a typical Saturday afternoon football game, until one of the players scores. As a cheer goes up, a fat Norwegian postman charges onto the pitch and begins embracing the goal-scorer, raising a clenched fist and generally behaving as if he is a member of the team. The player looks bemused – but he shouldn't be, because the Norwegian Postal Service is always where you are…in shops, online, or at your door. Or in goal, as the postman appears to be in the last scene from the spot.
Creative Director:	Galina Dudar	**Copywriter:**	Stig Bjølbakk	
Copywriter:	Timur Lyutskov	**Art Director:**	Henrik Sander	
Art Director:	Marina Pavlenko	**Production:**	Motion Blur, Santa Monica	
Client:	Comstar	**Director:**	Harald Zwart	
		Producer:	Alison Rein	
		Client:	Norwegian Postal Service, "Football"	

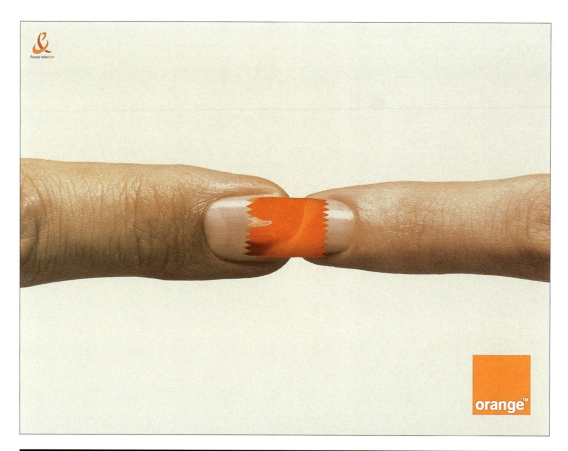
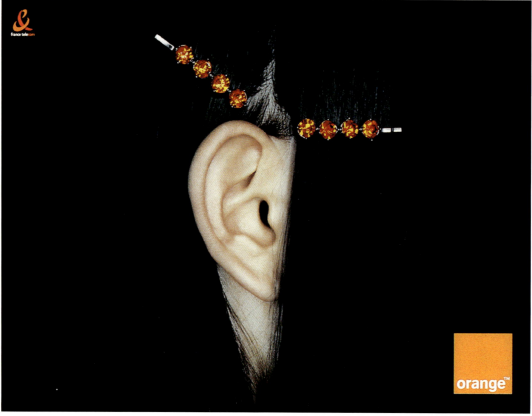

166 Communication Services

Agency:	BETC Euro RSCG, Paris
Creative Director:	Rémi Babinet
Copywriter:	Pierre Riess
Art Director:	Romain Guillon
Photographer:	John Clang
Client:	Orange

Samsung N100. Voice operated.

Agency:	BDDP & Fils, Paris	**Agency:**	TBWA\Paris	
Creative Director:	Olivier Altmann	**Creative Director:**	Eric Galmard	
Copywriter:	Olivier Couradjut	**Copywriter:**	Guilhem Arnal	
Art Director:	Rémy Tricot	**Art Director:**	Guilhem Arnal	
Photographer:	Sébastien Meunier	**Production:**	La Pac	
Client:	Samsung N100 Mobile Phone	**Director:**	Christian Lyngbye	
		Producers:	Flavie Becker, Françoise Korb	
		Client:	France Telecom, "The Dog"	

A room with a stone floor and a blazing hearth, presumably in a country mansion. A faithful hunting dog is standing tensed, muzzle raised, poised for the kill. Somewhere in the room, a duck is quacking. It happens again, and the dog growls. The camera pans across to a man sitting at his computer, trying to connect to the internet. Each time he presses the wrong button, the computer makes a quacking sound. The man needs the advice of France Telecom.

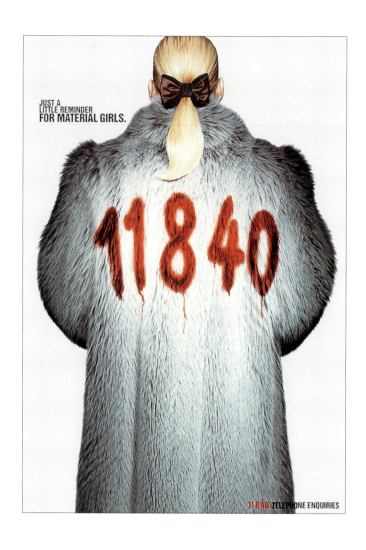
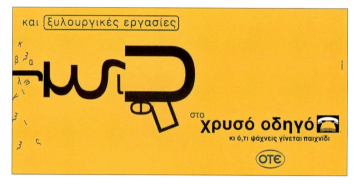

168 Communication Services

Agency:	Scholz & Friends, Berlin	Agency:	Leo Burnett, Athens
Creative Directors:	Martin Pross	Creative Director:	Vasso Skopa
	Joachim Schoepfer	Copywriter:	Vasso Skopa
Copywriter:	Beate Steiner	Art Director:	Katerina Giatra
Art Director:	Michael Winterhagen	Illustrator:	Ioanna Giotaki
Photographer:	Matthias Koslik	Client:	Greek Yellow Pages
Client:	11840 AG, Telephone Enquiry Service		

Agency:	Force, Forsman & Bodenfors, Gothenburg
Copywriters:	Mats Utberg Lisa Agnetun
Art Director:	Sara Jedenberg
Client:	The Swedish Post Office, International Mail

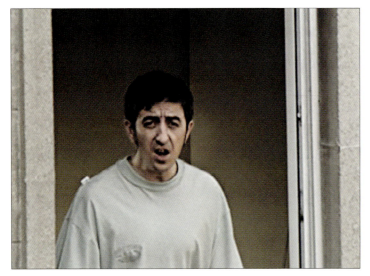

Communication Services

Agency:	Dimension, San Sebastian
Creative Director:	Guillermo Viglione
Copywriters:	Guillermo Viglione
	Mikel Aguado
Art Director:	Javier Aramburu
Production:	La Gloria, Barcelona
Director:	Miquel Alcarria
Producer:	Ricardo Bereciartua
Client:	Euskaltel Metropolitan Phone Calls, "Patxi" & "Patxi's Grandmother"

A man stands on a balcony in Barcelona, shouting the name "Patxi!" at the top of his lungs. Eventually another man appears on a balcony a couple of blocks away, and shouts back: "There must be some confusion! There's no Patxi here!" This is clearly not a good way to communicate. Doesn't Patxi's friend know that Euskaltel has just launched its cheap metropolitan phone calls service?

The man is still standing on his balcony, trying to make contact with Patxi. This time an old woman emerges from an apartment down the street. She's holding a huge cassette recorder. "Patxi isn't in. But you can leave a message after the beep." She presses the record button. Is the man still unaware that metropolitan phone calls are cheap with Euskaltel?

Communication Services	**171**
Agency:	Young & Rubicam, Prague
Creative Director:	Miroslav Pomikal
Copywriters:	František Bumbálek
	Ondrej Hubl
	Petr Stančik
Art Directors:	Lenka Sobotková
	Přemysl Ponáhlý
	Miroslav Pomikal
Client:	Český Mobil, Oskar Network

Communication Services

Agency:	Lowe Lintas, Amsterdam
Creative Directors:	Aad Kuijper Pieter van Velsen
Copywriter:	Huub Lensvelt
Art Director:	Ismaël ten Heuvel
Production:	Movie Ventures
Director:	Trevor Wrenn
Producers:	Willem van den Brandt Peter Burger
Client:	Planet Internet, "Ostrich"

A group of ostriches on a dusty African plain. One of them walks away from the others and begins to look around. In the distance, he sees mountains, and blue sky. He starts to investigate his wings, wondering if they really are useless. He flaps them tentatively. Then he flaps harder. He starts to run and flap in unison. The others watch him in alarm. Picking up speed, he leaves the ground for a few seconds. He runs faster, flapping frantically. Then he soars triumphantly into the air, free at last. With Planet Internet, there's more to explore.

Agency:	BDDP & Fils, Paris
Creative Director:	Olivier Altmann
Copywriter:	Olivier Couradjut
Art Director:	Rémy Tricot
Production:	Entropie
Director:	Pierre Salvadori
Producer:	Christine Bouffort
Client:	France Telecom – Ola Mobile Phones, "Daddy"

A father and son are sitting at home, reading. Suddenly the son says: "Dad, I want a mobile phone for Christmas." The father replies: "A mobile will make you independent, you'll leave home, your mother will start drinking and we'll divorce. Do you want to destroy this family?" He needn't have invented such an unlikely excuse – the Ola mobile phone kit is an inexpensive solution. In a second execution, the father's excuse is equally far-fetched. "Dad, can I have a mobile phone?" "No." "Why?" "Because I'm not your father."

Communication Services 173

Agencies:	E-Fact, London Springer & Jacoby, Hamburg	German literary guru Marcel Reich-Ranicki reviews the telephone book.
Creative Directors:	Ruth Holden Wolfgang Zimmerer	
Copywriters:	Marcel Reich-Ranicki Nicola Reidenbach Wolfgang Zimmerer	
Art Directors:	François Reynier Flora Maffi	
Photographer:	Matthias Heitmann	
Client:	Deutsche Telekom, Telephone Book	

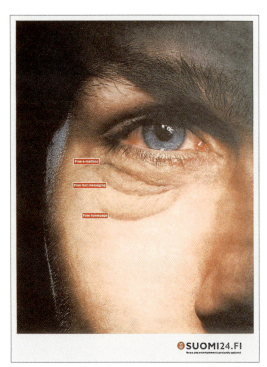

174 Communication Services

Agency:	.Start, Munich	It's easier to say it by email.
Creative Director:	Gregor Wöltje	
Copywriter:	Benedict Schreyer	
Art Director:	Kai Kier	
Photographer:	Nico Schmid-Burgk	
Client:	GMX Internet Provider	

Agency:	hasan & partners, Helsinki
Copywriters:	Jussi Turhala
	Kari Eilola
Art Director:	Magnus Ohlsson
Photographer:	Thomas Gidén
Client:	Suomi 24 Fi, Internet Portal

Agency:	Saatchi & Saatchi, Rome
Creative Directors:	Luca Albanese
	Stefano Maria Palombi
Copywriter:	Francesco Taddeucci
Art Director:	Francesca Risoolo
Photographer:	Fulvio Bonavia
Client:	Vinile.com

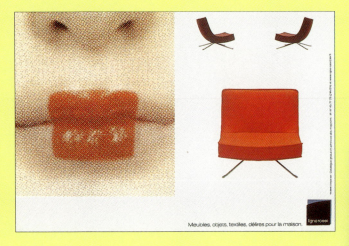
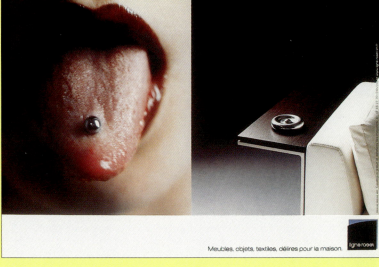

176 Homes, Furnishings & Appliances

Agency:	Callegari Berville Grey, Paris
Creative Director:	Pierre Berville
Art Director:	Patrice Jean Baptiste
Photographer:	Christian Kettiger
Client:	Ligne Roset Furnishings

Furniture, objects and textiles for the home.

Rangez.

Si vous ne le faites pas pour vous,
faites-le pour les autres.

Homes, Furnishings & Appliances

Agency:	Leagas Delaney Paris Centre	A young man shows an attractive blonde into his flat. They kiss. He manoeuvres her onto the sofa, where their embrace becomes more passionate. But suddenly she goes limp in his arms. He lifts her up – and discovers a fork stuck in her back!	In another execution, a woman is frantically searching for something in her messy flat. She peers behind shelves, wrenches open cupboards, even looks under the sofa. Whatever the missing item is, it's clearly very important. Finally, under a pile of discarded clothes beside the washing machine, she finds...her baby. The infant begins to howl in protest. Why doesn't she tidy up!	In a third film, another young man is watching his girlfriend eating spaghetti out of a bowl on the floor, in a highly erotic manner. But her mood changes when she accidentally starts chewing on one of his shoelaces. If all these people went to Ikea, they'd be able to tidy up.
Creative Director:	Pascal Gregoire			
Copywriter:	Aude Mee			
Art Director:	Sylvain Thiache			
Production:	Les Télécréateurs Satellite Films			
Director:	Brian Beletic			
Producers:	Arno Moria Marie Massis			
Client:	Ikea, "The Fork", "Under the Mess" & "Spaghetti"			

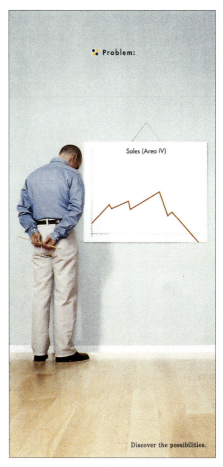

178 Homes, Furnishings & Appliances

Agency:	Grabarz & Partner, Hamburg	**Agency:**	Grabarz & Partner, Hamburg
Creative Director:	Dirk Siebenhaar	**Creative Directors:**	Dirk Siebenhaar
Copywriters:	Marek Sievers		Marek Sievers
	Stefanie Limpinsel	**Art Director:**	Gabi Schnauder
Art Director:	Gabi Schauder	**Photographers:**	Paul Bevitt
Photographer:	Manu Agah		Amselm Gaupp
Client:	Ikea	**Client:**	Ikea

Agency:	BGS D'Arcy, Milan	An Ikea worker places three of the store's armchairs in a bus shelter. Filmed by a hidden camera, citizens from all walks of life relax in the chairs while waiting for the bus, examine them, or look at the price tags. An elderly woman flops gratefully into one, laughing. A rollerblader takes a break, impressed by the chairs' stylish looks. And finally, somebody walks off with one. Ikea's democratic design appeals to everyone – and anyone can afford it.
Creative Director:	Paolo Gorini	
Copywriter:	Francesco Bozza	
Art Director:	Letizia Pettinari	
Production:	Motion Picture	
Director:	Stefano Canzio	
Producers:	Silvia Acquati Fabio Nesi	
Client:	Ikea, "Democratic Design"	

Agency:	BBDO, Moscow	A noisy child is racing around an apartment on his scooter. A voiceover asks: "What do you do with the kid when guests come? It seems you already have the solution!" Cut to a scene of the parents rolling the kid up in their Ikea carpet and standing him in the corner. When the guests arrive, he can't escape and annoy them. Obviously, Ikea has the solution to all our household problems.
Creative Director:	Igor Lutts	
Copywriter:	Andrey Amlinsky	
Art Director:	Andrey Amlinsky	
Production:	Teko Films	
Director:	Sergey Osipian	
Producers:	Marfa Pertseva Vassili Kisselev	
Client:	Ikea, "Carpet"	

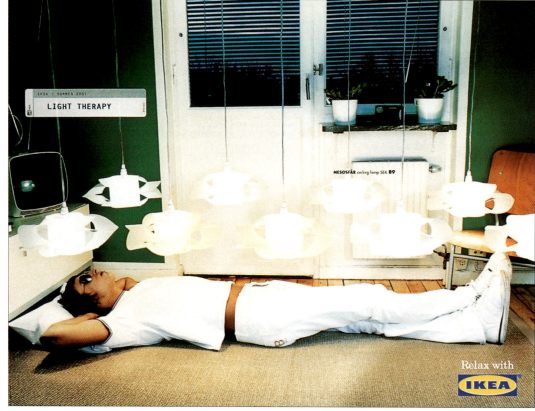

Homes, Furnishings & Appliances

Agency:	Forsman & Bodenfors, Gothenburg	**Agency:**	Forsman & Bodenfors, Gothenburg
Copywriters:	Fredrik Jansson Filip Nilsson Hjalmar Delehag	**Copywriters:**	Filip Nilsson Hjalmar Delehag
Art Directors:	Anders Eklind Karin Jacobsson	**Art Directors:**	Anders Eklind Karin Jacobsson
Photographers:	Karolina Henke	**Photographer:**	Claudia Fried-Junkins
Client:	Ikea	**Client:**	Ikea

Homes, Furnishings & Appliances 181

Agency:	St. Lukes, London
Copywriter:	Chris Wright
Art Director:	Jules Chalkley
Production:	Outsider
Directors:	dom & nic
Producers:	John Madsen
	Jo Charlesworth
Client:	Ikea, "Bathroom" & "Kitchen"

A man is taking a shower when he hears a noise in his bathroom. He wrenches the curtain aside – and is astonished to see three sinister yet well-dressed Scandinavians standing there. A fair-haired man, clearly the boss, asks: "Why have you never been to Ikea, George?" One of his henchmen shows George the Ikea brochure, suggesting some towels might brighten up his bathroom. George disagrees. In the next scene, the three men emerge from a Volvo in an underground car park, muffled banging and shouting coming from the boot... "Ikea. Come and see us – or we'll come and see you."

"Graham!" A middle-aged woman arrives home, shouting out the name of her husband. No reply. She goes into the kitchen – where the three sinister Scandinavians are waiting for her. "Ah, Dawn," says the charismatic leader. "You live near Ikea, but we know you've never been." He shows her the brochure. "How about this chair. Too wacky for you?" He turns the page – the same chair, with a man tied to it. "You see? Graham likes it!" The men begin to laugh cruelly. "Ikea. Come and see us – or we'll come and see you."

Homes, Furnishings & Appliances

Agency:	Grabarz & Partner, Hamburg	Agency:	Forsman & Bodenfors, Gothenburg
Creative Director:	Andreas Grabarz	Copywriters:	Filip Nilsson
Copywriters:	Marek Sievers		Fredrik Jansson
	Stefanie Limpinsel	Art Directors:	Anders Eklind
Art Director:	Matthias Klages		Karin Jacobsson
Photographer:	Leo Krombacher	Photographer:	Karolina Henke
Client:	Ikea	Client:	Ikea

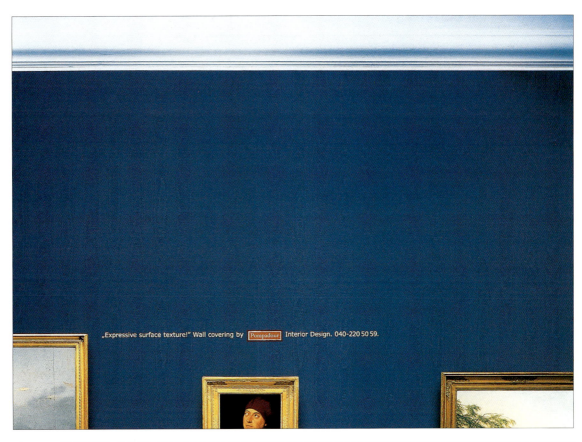

Agency:	Kolle Rebbe, Hamburg
Creative Director:	Alexander Wilhelm
Copywriter:	Melanie Schlachter
Art Director:	Melanie Schlachter
Photographer:	Giovanni Castell
Client:	Pompadour Interior Design

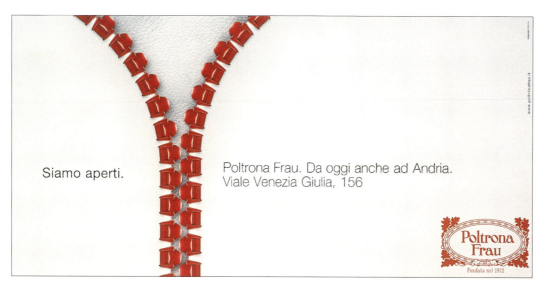

184 Homes, Furnishings & Appliances

Agency:	Armando Testa, Rome	Open from today.	**Agency:**	McCann-Erickson, Manchester
Creative Directors:	Mauro Mortaroli		**Creative Director:**	David George
	Erminio Perocco	Love of details is a gift of nature.	**Copywriter:**	Dawn Hoskinson
Copywriter:	Elio Polce		**Art Directors:**	David George
Art Director:	Marcio Cortez Melendez			Lee Manson
			Illustrator:	Rob Brown
Client:	Poltrona Frau, Furniture Retailer		**Client:**	CP Hart Bathroom Fittings

Agency:	CLM/BBDO, Paris	In a speeded-up film, we see builders constructing a house in a green valley. Then another house. A bridge appears, quickly extending into a highway. At breakneck speed, skyscrapers spring out of the ground. Traffic grows denser, overhead railways snake above the clogged streets, the sky is clouded by pollution. A sign flashes up: "You failed! Damaged environment!" Cut to a man playing a game on his laptop. He wipes the image of the city, and the green field reappears. Power is a necessity – but French utilities company EDF wants to protect the environment, too.	**Agency:**	Libens, Ghewy & Fauconnier, Brussels
Creative Directors:	Bernard Naville		**Creative Directors:**	Christophe Ghewy
	Vincent Behaeghel			Luc Libens
Copywriter:	Bernard Naville		**Copywriter:**	Paul Servaes
Art Director:	Vincent Behaeghel		**Art Director:**	Benoît Hilson
Production:	Partizan Midi-Minuit		**Photographer:**	Christophe Gilbert
Director:	Antoine Bardou-Jacquet		**Client:**	Beka Mattresses
Producers:	Georges Bergmann			
	Pierre Marcus			
Client:	EDF Electricity Supplier, "The Valley"			

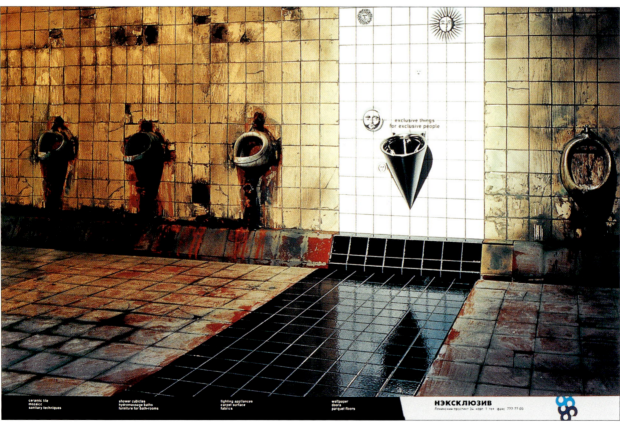

186 Homes, Furnishings & Appliances

Agency:	BBDO, Moscow
Creative Director:	Igor Lutts
Copywriter:	Andrey Amlinsky
Art Director:	Andrey Mudrov
Photographer:	Jorgen Reimer
Client:	Nexclusive Bathroom Fittings

Agency:	TBWA\Istanbul	**Agency:**	Kolle Rebbe, Hamburg	A group of drumming toy rabbits, of the kind that are often seen in battery commercials (but rarely in real life) are doing their stuff. After three hours, some of the rabbits have run out of steam. Others stay the course for six hours. But one rabbit lasts 24 hours... and then an amazing 8,763 hours. Finally we are shown his secret – not a battery at all, but a tiny solar panel on the back of his head. Conergy are specialists in harnessing energy from the sun.
Creative Director:	Derya Tambay	**Creative Directors:**	Stefan Kolle	
Copywriter:	Engin Senuysal		Thorsten Meier	
Art Director:	Mustafa Barıpoglu		Sebastian Hardieck	
Photographer:	Suleyman Kacar	**Copywriter:**	Klaus Huber	
Client:	Beko Washing Machines	**Art Director:**	Nikolaus Ronacher	
		Production:	Final Touch	
		Director:	Andreas Hoffmann	
		Producers:	Nadja Bontscheff, Axel Leyck	
		Client:	Conergy Solar Technology, "Rabbits"	

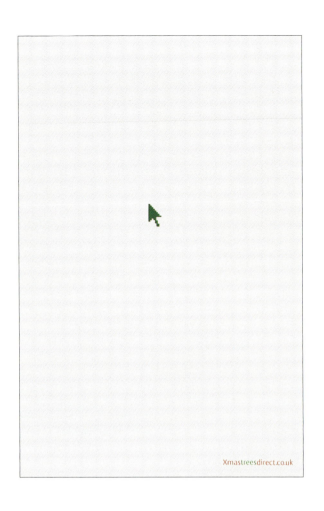

188   Homes, Furnishings & Appliances

Agency:	McCann-Erickson, Manchester	**Agency:**	Zapping, Madrid
Creative Director:	David George	**Creative Directors:**	Uschi Henkes
Copywriter:	Neil Lancaster		Urs Frick
Art Director:	Dave Price		David Palacios
Client:	xmastreesdirect.co.uk	**Copywriter:**	David Palacios
		Art Directors:	Urs Frick
			Victor Gômez
		Client:	Knight Frank Property

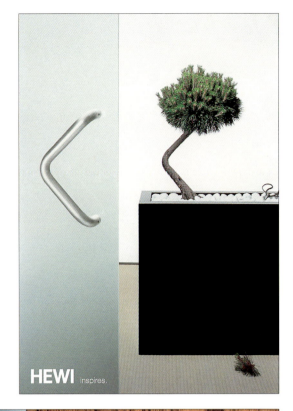

Homes, Furnishings & Appliances

Agency:	Scholz & Friends, Berlin
Creative Director:	Pius Walker
Copywriter:	Sebastian Dehrendt
Art Director:	Tim Schierwater
Photographer:	Thomas Popinger
Client:	Hewi Home Accessories

190 Household Maintenance

Agency:	Advico Young & Rubicam, Zürich
Creative Director:	Martin Spillmann
Copywriter:	Margrit Brunswick
Art Director:	Denis Schwarz
Photographer:	Kevin Summers
Client:	Tela Paper Tableware

SEEK HELP IN TIME
Spektrum advices you in big and small matters.

New special Dyrup Paint for ceilings. Paint the ceiling, not the floor.

Agency:	Thörn & Täckenström, Stockholm	**Agency:**	Young & Rubicam, Lisbon
Copywriters:	Sofie Elvestedt Johan Thörn	**Creative Director:**	Albano Homem de Melo
		Copywriter:	Albano Homem de Melo
Art Directors:	John Mara Alex Slagare	**Art Director:**	Albano Homem de Melo
Photographer:	Åsa Tällgård	**Photographer:**	João Silveira Ramos
Client:	Spektrum Paint & Wallpaper	**Client:**	Dyrup Paint

192 Household Maintenance

Agency:	Forsman & Bodenfors, Gothenburg	Agency:	Edson, FCB, Lisbon
		Creative Director:	Edson Athayde
Copywriter:	Martin Ringqvist	Copywriter:	Ricardo Miranda
Art Directors:	Kim Cramer Jonas Sjövall	Art Director:	Jorge Barrote
		Photographer:	Jarbas Teixeira Alves
Client:	Edet Wipe & Clean	Client:	Raid Insecticide

Household Maintenance   193

Agency:	Kolle Rebbe, Hamburg
Creative Directors:	Stefan Kolle
	Anke Baumeister
Copywriters:	Michael Schäfer
	Silke Maser
Art Directors:	Regina Lipowec
Photographer:	Dirk Fellenberg
Client:	Frux Fertilizer

194 Household Maintenance

Agency:	TBWA\Istanbul	**Agency:**	TBWA\España, Barcelona
Creative Director:	Derya Tambay	**Creative Director:**	Xavi Munill
Copywriter:	Ergin Koyluceli	**Copywriters:**	Xavi Munill
Art Director:	Halil Oner Sahin		Miquel Sales
Photographer:	Suleyman Kacar	**Art Directors:**	Tomás Descals
Client:	Pril Aloe Vera Dishwashing Detergent		Alex Martín
		Client:	El León Bleach

Agency:	Saatchi & Saatchi, Paris
Creative Director:	Hervé Riffault
Copywriters:	Jean-François Fournon
	Jean-François Sacco
Art Directors:	Benoît Raynert
	Gilles Fichteberg
Photographer:	David Gill
Client:	Ariel Liquitabs

Household Maintenance

196 Household Maintenance

Agency:	Vitruvio Leo Burnett, Madrid
Creative Directors:	Rafa Anton Fernando Martin
Copywriter:	Santiago Saiegh
Art Director	Sarah Okrent
Photographer:	Santiago Boil
Client:	Vileda Ultra-Mop

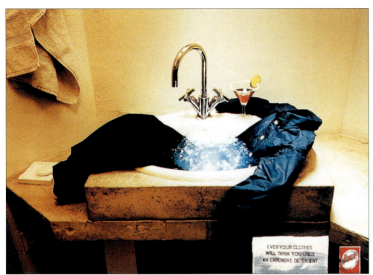

Household Maintenance

Agency:	Leo Burnett, Warsaw
Creative Director:	Darek Zatorski
Copywriter:	Arek Majewski
Art Director:	Katarzyna Macharz
Photographer:	Darek Zatorski
Client:	Bonux Detergent

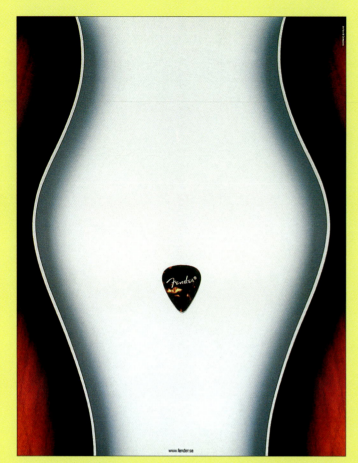

Audiovisual Equipment & Accessories

Agency:	Jerlov & Körberg, Gothenburg
Creative Director:	Fredrik Jerlov
Copywriters:	Patrik Spång
	Fredrik Jerlov
Art Director:	Magnus Tengby
Photographer:	Jesper Sundelin
Client:	Fender Guitars

Audiovisual Equipment & Accessories

Agency:	Ogilvy & Mather, Frankfurt	A chameleon is minding its own business on a branch, when a hand holding a lemon comes into frame. The chameleon obligingly turns yellow. The hand withdraws and returns, this time holding a bright red tomato. Rolling its eyes, the chameleon repeats the trick. The next time the hand returns, it is holding a Kodak film. The chameleon turns all the colours of the rainbow in succession, overloads, and drops off its perch. Nothing is able to capture colour more efficiently than Kodak film.
Creative Directors:	Christian Seifert, Patrick They	
Copywriter:	Christian Seifert	
Art Director:	Patrick They	
Production:	Neue Sentimental Film	
Directors:	Oku & Soap	
Producer:	Mirko Demschik	
Illustrator:	Christian Lau	
Client:	Kodak Germany, "Chameleon"	

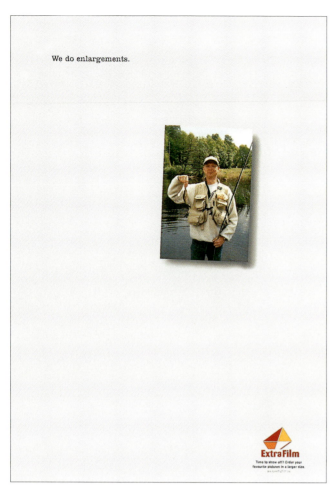

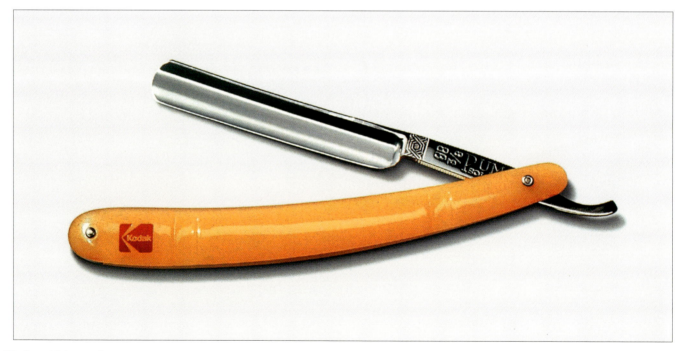

200   Audiovisual Equipment & Accessories

Agency:	Goss Reklambyrå, Gothenburg	**Agency:**	Ogilvy & Mather, Frankfurt
Copywriters:	Michael Schultz Anders Hegerfors	**Creative Directors:**	Thomas Hofbeck Dr. Stephan Vogel
Art Directors:	Gunnar Skarland Mimmi Andersson Mattias Frendberg	**Art Director:** **Photographer:** **Client:**	Marco Weber Heinz Wuchner Kodak
Client:	Extra Film Photo Developing		

Audiovisual Equipment & Accessories   201

Agency:	Hakuhodo UK, London	**Agency:**	Euro RSCG Works, Paris
Creative Director:	Tim Johnson		
Copywriter:	Peter Mabott	**Copywriter:**	Benoît Guide
Art Director:	Tim Johnson	**Art Director:**	Pauline Dubois
Photographer:	Sara Morris	**Photographer:**	Alcide Rioche
			Jean-Michel Berts
Client:	Hitachi Televisions	**Client:**	Philips Televisions

202 Audiovisual Equipment & Accessories

Agency:	Arih Advertising Agency, Ljubljana
Creative Director:	Igor Arih
Copywriter:	Slavimir Stojanović
Art Director:	Slavimir Stojanović
Photographer:	Aljoša Rebolj
Client:	Duracell Batteries

Agency:	Saatchi & Saatchi, Madrid
Executive Director:	César Garcia
Creative Directors:	Miguel Roig
	Osky
Copywriter:	Jose Luis Alberola
Art Director:	Amabel Minchan
Photographer:	Luis Enrique González Tortosa
Client:	Sony Handicam

Handycam Digital 8. Compatible with your 8mm recording. Don't throw away your memories.

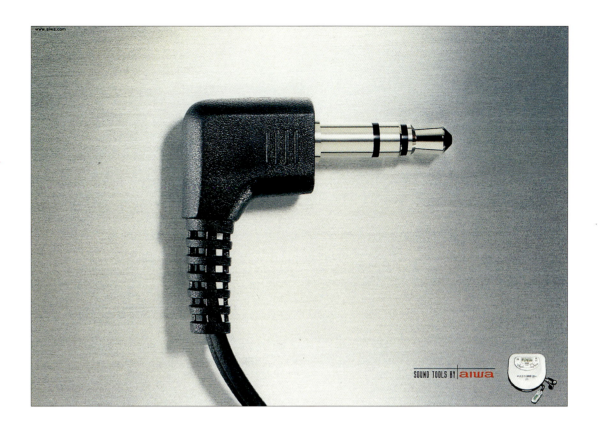

Audiovisual Equipment & Accessories 203

Agency:	SKA, Porto	Agency:	Jung von Matt, Zürich
Creative Director:	Celso Muniz	Creative Directors:	Daniel Meier
Copywriter:	Pedro Lima		Alexander Jaggy
Art Director:	Giselle Kyrillos	Copywriter:	Christoph Hess
Photographer:	Francisco Prata	Art Director:	Daniel Meier
Client:	Aiwa	Photographers:	Staudinger & Franke
	Portable CD Players	Client:	Panasonic Batteries

204   Toiletries & Health Care

Agency: Michael Conrad & Leo Burnett, Frankfurt
Creative Director: Christoph Barth
Copywriter: Guido Masson
Art Director: Guido Masson
Client: Tip Lady Shaver

Agency:	McCann-Erickson, Manchester	A young man walks down a cobbled street. He is followed by an enormous army of men dressed as sperm. When he looks at his watch, they mimic his movements. He enters the city's main square, the sperm in hot pursuit. At the other side of the wide expanse, he spots his date. The sperm charge forward, trampling the man in their haste to get to the pretty girl. But they are stopped by the latex barrier of an enormous condom. The man brushes himself down and leads his date away. Durex – vital for a hundred million reasons.
Creative Director:	David George	
Copywriter:	Neil Lancaster	
Art Director:	Dave Price	
Production:	Spectre	
Director:	Daniel Kleinman	
Producers:	Bertie Miller Sara Clementson	
Client:	Durex Condoms, "Square"	

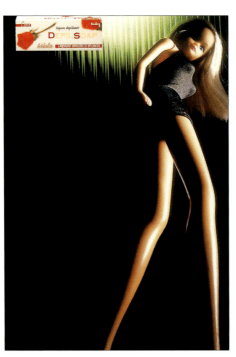

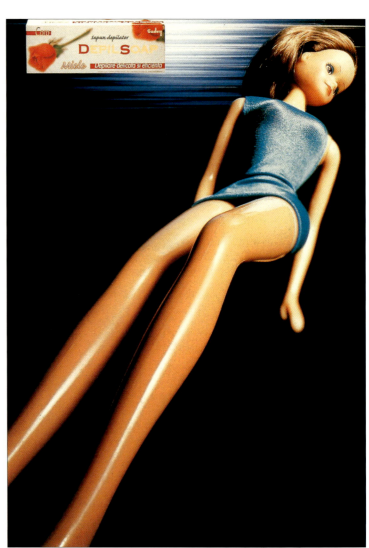

206 Toiletries & Health Care

Agency:	TBWA\España, Madrid	**Agency:**	ADDV Euro RSCG, Bucharest
Creative Director:	Quico Vidal	**Creative Director:**	Dorian Pascuci
Copywriter:	Lay Aguayo	**Copywriters:**	Ioana Slaniceanu
Art Director:	Marco Pitzolu		Vlad Dâmboviceanu
Client:	Onda Salud Healthcare Website	**Art Director:**	Dorian Pascuci
		Photographer:	Ionut Macri
		Client:	DepilSoap

Toiletries & Health Care 207

Agency:	Callegari Berville Grey, Paris	With brusque, vigorous movements, a chamber maid is cleaning a luxurious room. She polishes handles until they shine, puts plenty of elbow grease into wiping surfaces, and plumps pillows like a boxer hitting a punch-bag. Until it's time to dust a painting – Courbet's L'Origine du Monde, an intimate depiction of the female body. The maid plucks a single feather from her duster, and runs it very gently over the canvas. Intimate areas require gentle cleansing.	**Agency:**	Sudler & Hennessey, Milan	When you travel you always pick something up. Enterogermina – for exotic bellies.
Creative Director:	Pierre Berville		**Creative Directors:**	Angelo Ghidotti Bruno Stucchi	
Copywriter:	Corinne Assuerus Trugeon				
Art Director:	Hélène Bremond Le Guay		**Copywriter:**	Angelo Ghidotti	
Production:	Cake Films		**Art Director:**	Bruno Stucchi	
Director:	Jean Baptiste Leonetti		**Illustrator:**	Luigi Russo	
Producer:	Marie-Thérèse Diot		**Client:**	Enterogermina	
Client:	Rogé Cavaillès Intimate Soap, "The Painting"				

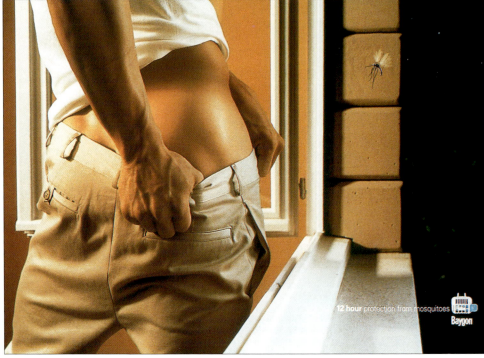

208 Toiletries & Health Care

Agency:	BDDP & Fils, Paris	**Agency:**	CLM/BBDO, Paris
Creative Director:	Olivier Altmann	**Creative Directors:**	fred&farid
Copywriter:	Bruno Delhomme	**Copywriters:**	Mathieu Degryse
Art Director:	Damien Bellon		Yves-Eric Deboey
Photographer:	Vincent Dixon	**Art Directors:**	Mathieu Degryse
Client:	Manix Gel		Yves-Eric Deboey
		Photographer:	Marc Hom
		Client:	Baygon Insect Repellent

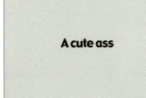 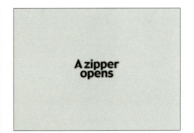

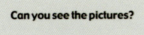  

Agency:	Ogilvy & Mather, Frankfurt
Creative Directors:	Thomas Hofbeck, Dr. Stephan Vogel
Copywriters:	Jörg Schrod, Jens Frank
Art Director:	Jens Frank, Jörg Schrod
Production:	La Fourmi, Paris
Director:	Pierre Coffin
Producer:	Andreas Botschka
Client:	Kondomshop.org, "Penguins"

A trio of baby cartoon penguins are jumping up and down beside their father on an iceberg, making plaintive bleating noises. The father looks long-suffering. Finally, he flexes his webbed foot – and kicks one of the babies into the sea. The remaining pair are shocked into silence, especially when a killer whale's fin briefly surfaces. Then they start bleating even louder than before. 73% of parents are stressed. Don't forget Kondomshop.org.

Agency:	McCann-Erickson, Hamburg
Executive Director:	Christian Daul
Production:	The Shack
Producers:	Markus Skroblies, Guntram Krasting
Client:	Durex Condoms, "Reminder"

The story is told entirely in subtitles, to a soundtrack of heavy, rhythmic, breathing. "A sexy blonde. Luscious lips. Perfect breasts. A cute ass. A zipper opens. Can you see the pictures? What you cannot see... AIDS."

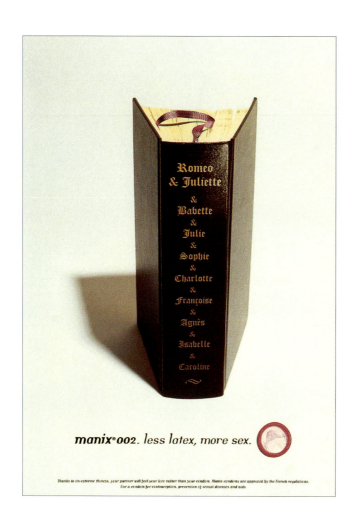

Toiletries & Health Care

Agency: BDDP & Fils, Paris	**Agency:** McCann-Erickson, Milan
Creative Director: Olivier Altmann	**Creative Director:** Stefano Campora
Copywriter: Bruno Delhomme	**Copywriter:** Guglielmo Pezzino
Art Director: Damien Bellon	**Art Director:** Federico Pepe
Photographer: Damien Bellon	**Photographer:** Rankin
Client: Manix Condoms	**Client:** Durex Hatu, Condoms

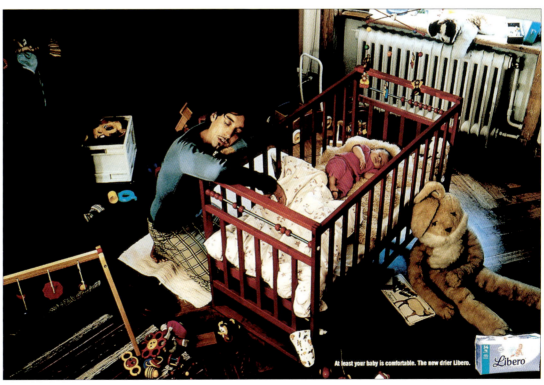

Toiletries & Health Care 211

Agency:	Advico Young & Rubicam, Zürich	Agency:	Forsman & Bodenfors, Gothenburg
Creative Directors:	Martin Spillmann Urs Schrepfer	Copywriter: Art Director:	Jonas Enghage Kim Cramer
Copywriter:	Stefan Ehrler	Photographer:	Jesper Brandt
Art Director:	Roland Scotoni	Client:	Libero Diapers
Photographer:	Julien Vonier		
Client:	Hakle Sensitive Toilet Paper		

212 **Beauty Products**

Agency:	Mother, London
Creative Directors:	Robert Saville
	Mark Waites
Copywriter:	Caroline Pay
Art Director:	Kim Gehrig
Client:	Organics Shampoo, "Do Me, Do Me", "You, You, You" & "Competition"

The campaign features two young women competing over the condition of their hair. In the first, the pair debate whose hair looks the best, until they end up arguing. One even pulls the other's hair. They seem to have made up by the second film, in which the dark-haired girl tells the blonde: "Love your hair!" The blonde thanks her and wanders off, annoying her friend by not returning the compliment. And finally, a hair-flicking contest turns into a full-scale dance routine, when the girls shake their stuff to the tune Duelling Banjos from the film Deliverance.

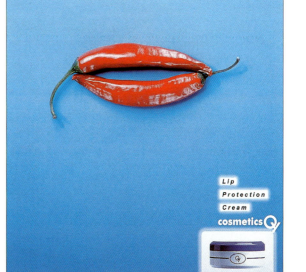

Agency:	TBWA\España, Barcelona	Agency:	Jean & Montmarin, Paris	Kids never worry about too much sun. Coppertone – sun protection for kids.
Creative Director:	Kike Fernández	Creative Director:	Gérard Jean	
Copywriter:	Kike Fernández	Copywriter:	Pierre-Marie Faussurier	
Art Director:	Marielo Gil	Art Director:	Sébastien Zanini	
Photographer:	Vicens San Nicolás	Photographer:	Martin Timmermann	
Client:	Cosmetics Oy Skin Creams	Client:	Coppertone	

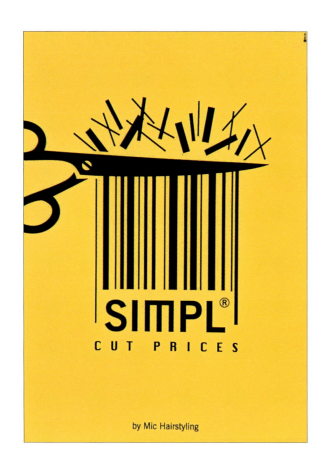

Beauty Products

Agency:	Arih Advertising Agency, Ljubljana	
Creative Director:	Igor Arih	
Copywriter:	Gal Erbežnik	
Art Director:	Slavimir Stojanović	
Client:	Simpl Hairstyling Salons	

Agency:	Lowe Lintas, Amsterdam
Creative Directors:	Aad Kuijper
	Pieter van Velsen
Copywriter:	Stan Lommers
Art Director:	Patrick de Zeeuw
Photographer:	Carli Hermès
Client:	Rexona Deodorants & Bodysprays

Rexona for men: surprisingly dry and fresh.

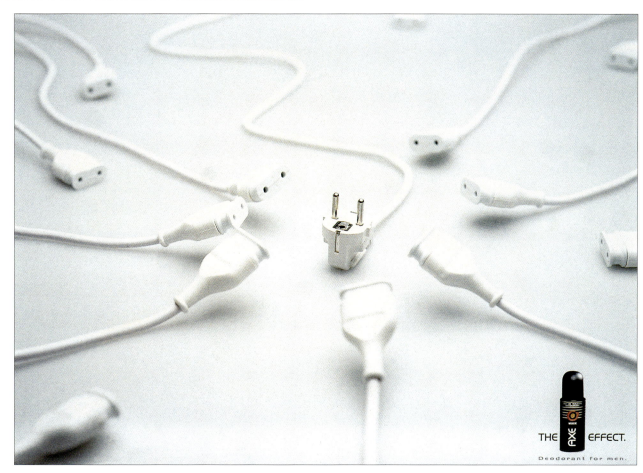

Beauty Products

Agency:	Lintas Middle East North Africa, Dubai
Creative Director:	Nirmal Diwadkar
Copywriter:	Manoj Ammanath
Art Director:	Adham Obeid
Photographer:	Tejal Patni
Client:	Axe Deodorants

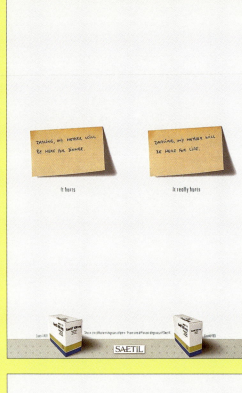

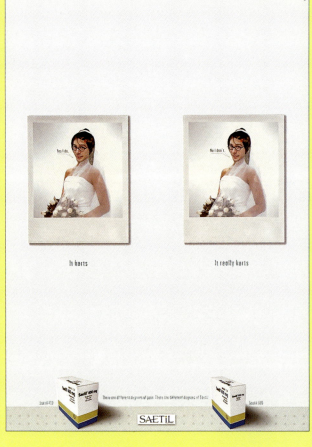

Prescription Products

Agency:	Springer & Jacoby, Barcelona	It hurts. It really hurts. There are different degrees of pain, so there are different degrees of Saetil. For example, an empty condom box is distressing – but not as much as a full one that has passed its expiry date.
Creative Director:	Rafa Blasco	
Copywriter:	Albert Saurina	
Art Director:	Marc Cardona	
Client:	Saetil Pain Reliever	

Prescription Products   217

Agency:	Junction 11 Advertising, Weybridge	Agency:	JBR McCann, Oslo
Creative Directors:	Richard Rayment, John Timney	Creative Director:	Paal Tarjei Aasheim
Copywriter:	Richard Rayment	Copywriter:	Petter Gulli
Art Director:	John Timney	Art Director:	Joachim A. Haug
Photographer:	Bob Wing	Photographer:	Albert Boullet
Client:	Trizivir HIV Therapy	Client:	Imigran Pain Reliever

218 Prescription Products

Agency:	Sudler & Hennessey, Milan	When pain attacks.	Agency:	Paradiset DDB, Stockholm
Creative Directors:	Bruno Stucchi		Copywriter:	Jens Englund
	Angelo Ghidotti		Art Director:	Andreas Lönn
Copywriter:	Angelo Ghidotti		Photographer:	André Wolf
Art Directors:	Massimiliano Luzzani		Illustrator:	Patrik Andersson
	Bruno Stucchi		Client	Pfizer Image Campaign
Photographer:	Occhiomagico			
Client:	Oramorph Pain Reliever			

Prescription Products   219

Agency:	Torre Lazur McCann, London
Creative Director:	Don Nicolson
Copywriters:	Matt Reid
	Len Faith
Art Director:	David Dalley
Client:	Cipramil Antidepressant

220 Automobiles

Agency: DDB, Brussels
Creative Director: Michel De Lauw
Copywriter: Georges Amerlynck
Art Director: Georges Amerlynck
Client: Volkswagen TDI

Automobiles

Agency:	Saatchi & Saatchi, Frankfurt
Creative Directors:	Benjamin Lommel
	Harald Wittig
	Carsten Heintzsch
Copywriter:	Harald Wittig
Art Director:	Benjamin Lommel
Production:	Jo! Schmid, Berlin
Director:	Martin Schmid
Producers:	Michael Schmid
	Jutta Schroll
Client:	Audi Multitronic Transmission, "The Fan"

An Elvis fan is driving along in his old sports car, the little Elvis figurine on his dashboard twirling and gyrating each time he crashes through the gears. Then his old banger breaks down, and he is given a lift by a glamorous young woman. She lets him play his tape of The King, and even stick his toy on the dashboard. But her Multitronic transmission is so smooth that the figure doesn't move – until she gives it a nudge.

Automobiles

Agency:	Strat, Lisbon
Creative Director:	Joaquim Pena
Copywriter:	Evandro Lima
Art Director:	Evandro Lima
Production:	Elástica
	Mixturas
Director:	Alexandre Sorriso
Producers:	Isabel Sá Coutinho
	Pedro Gaspar
Client:	Audi, "Puddle"

A large puddle. A crash of thunder. The subtitles read: "Enjoy the winter." The first four drops of rain hit the water, and the four spreading rings form the familiar shape of the Audi logo. With an Audi, even bad weather conditions are something to look forward to.

Agency:	Red Cell, Milan
Executive Director:	Pietro Maestri
Creative Director:	Paul Meijer
Production:	Serious Pictures, London
Director:	Michael Haussman
Executive Producer:	Donnie Masters
Producer:	Carla Beltrami
Client:	Alfa Romeo 147, "Quads"

Are identical siblings telepathic? They are in this film about female 'quads', who we first see in a series of childhood photographs. Cut to the present day, and one of them is driving her new Alfa 147. As she revels in the orgasmic delight of putting her foot down and blasting the car down an ocean-side highway, her three sisters experience the same emotion – even though they are respectively in an art gallery, a posh restaurant, and a business meeting.

Agency:	BGS D'Arcy, Turin
Creative Directors:	Luciano Nardi
	Roberto Molino
Copywriter:	Michela Grasso
Art Director:	Daniele Ricci
Production:	Academy, London
Director:	David Kellogg
Producers:	Laura Kaufman
	Sarah Patterson
Client:	Fiat Doblò, "Jamaica"

A beach in Jamaica. Four men are doing a variety of weird exercises – leaning from side-to-side in a beached canoe, sitting on a vibrating washing machine, or holding giant blocks of ice. When they get into their spacious car, we see the most bizarre sight of all – a bobsleigh strapped to its roof. The Fiat Doblò, with its unique character, is the official car of the Jamaican bobsleigh team.

You should always control your path.

ESP, electronic stability program as standard.

Automobiles

Agency:	Louis XIV DDB, Paris
Creative Directors:	Sylvain Guyomard
	Jocelyn Devaux
Copywriter:	Olivier Apers
Art Director:	Hugues Pinguet
Production:	Why Us?
Director:	Sadry Adhami
Producer:	Jean-Luc Bagur
Client:	Volkswagen ESP, "Tea", "Bar" & "Soap"

A man is pouring tea Chinese-style, from high up – but a violent sneeze does not affect the flow of liquid into the cup. A barman slides a glass down a bar – and it swerves to avoid a basket of bread rolls before reaching its target. And a bar of soap slips out of a pair of hands, only to arrive unerringly in the soap dish. People who have this amount of directional control must be Volkswagen ESP drivers.

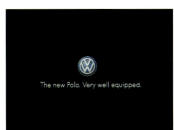

Agency:	Louis XIV DDB, Paris	**Agency:**	King, Stockholm
Copywriter:	Alexandre Hervé	**Copywriters:**	Peter Fjäll
Art Director:	Samuel Kadz		Ola Gatby
Production:	Ninety Nine	**Art Directors:**	Johan Boije
Directors:	Yanis Mangematin		Frank Hollingworth
	Samuel Kadz	**Production:**	Kingfilm
Producer:	Jean-Luc Bagur	**Client:**	Volkswagen Golf GTI,
Client:	Volkswagen Polo		"Bye Bye"
	Match, "The Tree"		

Firemen arrive to rescue a woman who has somehow got herself stuck up a tall tree. The voiceover explains: "Helen, 32, relatively sane according to friends and family, recently heard that there's a new Polo with air conditioning, sound system, CD player, electric sunroof, ABS, GPS and four airbags – all standard. She then swore that nothing was impossible, and that she would jump from her roof in order to fly."

A man watches tearfully as his old Golf GTI is loaded onto a tow truck. The car has clearly come to the end of its life. The soundtrack plays "Seasons In the Sun", a nostalgic lament for times past, as the truck drives away. The tagline reads: "Thanks for the first 25 fun years". It's the 25th anniversary of the GTI.

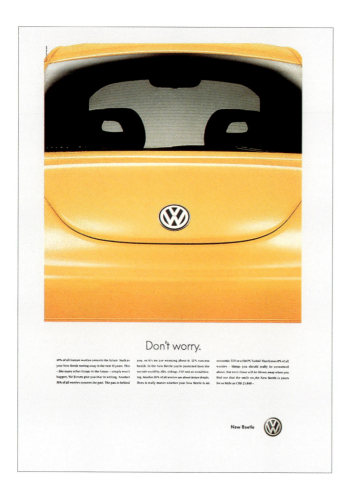
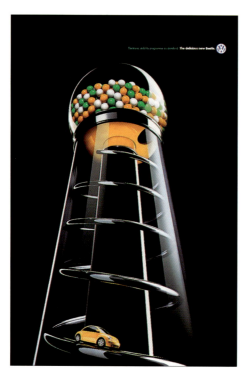

226 Automobiles

Agency:	Lowe Lintas, Zürich	**Agency:**	Team/Young & Rubicam, Dubai	Electronic stability programme as standard.
Creative Director:	Mark Stahel	**Creative Director:**	Sam Ahmed	More miles per gallon.
Copywriters:	Ueli Haller	**Copywriter:**	Shahir Ahmed	The delicious new Beetle.
	Lukas Schmid	**Art Directors:**	Sam Ahmed	
Art Directors:	Alfred Burkard		Shahir Ahmed	
	Philipp Sträuli	**Photographers:**	Paul Cox	
Client:	Volkswagen Beetle		Richard Butterfield	
			Suresh Subramanian	
		Illustrators:	Anil Palyekar	
			Rajeev Sangdhore	
		Client:	Volkswagen Beetle	

Golf TDI 150 hp.

Agency:	Louis XIV DDB, Paris	**Agency:**	Louis XIV DDB, Paris	
Creative Directors:	Sylvain Guyomard	**Copywriter:**	Alexandre Hervé	
	Jocelyn Devaux	**Art Director:**	Samuel Kadz	
Copywriter:	Olivier Apers	**Production:**	HLA, London	
Art Director:	Hugues Pinguet	**Director:**	Rob Sanders	
Client:	Volkswagen	**Producer:**	Jean-Luc Bagur	
	Golf TDI 130	**Client:**	Volkswagen	
			Golf 4 Motion,	
			"The Trick"	

A magician appears to cut a woman in half, but she's a contortionist curled up inside the cabinet. Wrestlers fake vicious-looking blows. A woman hangs from a vertiginous building – which is in fact a horizontal stage set. And a VW Golf glides through snowbound streets, unaffected by the thick drifts that have buried other cars. The VW Golf with permanent four wheel drive. There's a trick to everything.

The S 400 CDI.
The most powerful diesel car in the world.

Mercedes-Benz
The Future of the Automobile.

Mercedes-Benz

Automobiles

Agency:	Springer & Jacoby, Hamburg
Creative Directors:	Stefan Meske, Arno Lindemann
Copywriter:	Michael Meyer
Production:	Tempomedia
Director:	Pucho Mentasti
Producers:	Vera Portz, Natascha Teidler
Client:	Mercedes-Benz S 400 CDI, "Jazz"

A man is driving through the city streets, his son by his side. Dad is listening to a lush, smooth, jazz track – until his son reaches forward and changes the dial to a rap station. Using a button on the steering wheel, dad changes it back. This happens a few times, until the car hits the open road. As the boy reaches forward, dad puts his foot down – and the kid is flung back into his seat by the acceleration. The S 400 CDI is one of the most powerful diesel cars on the market.

Agency:	Springer & Jacoby, Paris
Creative Director:	Franck Rey
Copywriter:	Aude Commissaire
Art Director:	Franck Rey
Production:	The Gang Films
Directors:	Fabrice Carazo, Rachel Carazo
Producers:	Jean Villiers, Laurent Burdin
Client:	Mercedes-Benz, "The Road"

A woman walks her newborn baby down a hospital corridor, which is decorated with a mural of a country road. She suddenly notices that the infant's fingertips are stained black, and wipes them clean. A few seconds later, when she looks away, it happens again. What can be causing this phenomenon? Then we see things from the baby's perspective – as her mother walks along, the child is trailing her fingers lovingly over the picture of the road. On her wrist, a name tag: Mercedes.

Automobiles

Agency:	Springer & Jacoby, Hamburg
Creative Directors:	Alexander Schill Axel Thomsen Hans-Jürgen Lewandowski
Copywriter:	Alexander Schill
Art Director:	Axel Thomsen
Production:	Cobblestone Pictures
Director:	Sébastien Grousset
Producers:	Axel Heldens Natascha Teidler
Client:	Mercedes-Benz C-Class Sportcoupé, "Eighteen"

A teacher is asking her pupils what jobs they eventually want to do. "Astronaut," says one, "waitress" another, while a third wants to be a "soccer player". One of the pupils is distracted, staring out the window at a gleaming Mercedes C-Class. The teacher says: "And Sebastian, what do you want to be?" He looks at her, and responds firmly: "Eighteen."

Agencies:	Colnaghi & Manciani–Springer & Jacoby, Milan
Creative Directors:	Mauro Biagini Michael Engelbrecht
Copywriter:	Mauro Biagini
Art Director:	Michael Engelbrecht
Production:	Film Master
Director:	Dario Piana
Producer:	Michela Gabelli
Client:	Mercedes-Benz A-Class, "Parking Lot"

A perfectionist car park attendant sees two Mercedes A-Class cars parked next to one another, but they aren't lined up. He pushes one of them so the front bumpers are in line, but then notices that the rears are out of alignment. He gets a colleague to help, and after a lot of pushing and shoving they realise that although the cars are identical in every other way, one of them is bigger. The A-Class now comes in a longer wheelbase version.

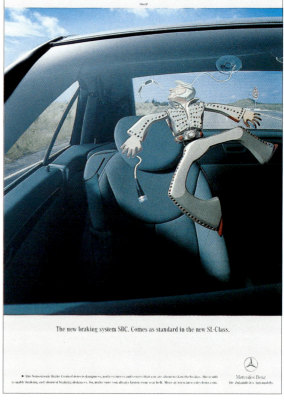

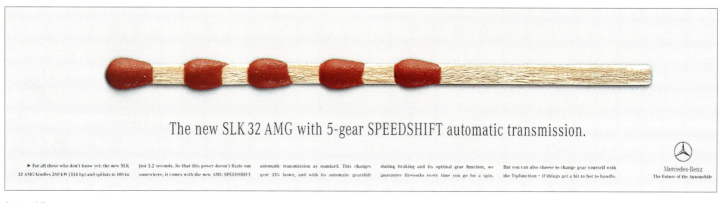

Automobiles

Agency:	Springer & Jacoby, Hamburg	NB: The Elvis ad is Mercedes' response to Audi's Multitronic commercial (see p. 221).	Agency:	Springer & Jacoby, Hamburg
Creative Directors:	Dirk Häusermann, Torsten Rieken, Jan Ritter		Creative Directors:	Kurt Georg Dieckert, Stefan Schmidt
Copywriter:	Tobias Ahrens		Copywriter:	Stefan Schmidt
Art Director:	Frank Bannöhr		Art Director:	Johannes Hofmann
Photographer:	Thomas Strogalski		Photographer:	Adam Mitchinson
Client:	Mercedes-Benz SL-Class		Client:	Mercedes-Benz, Innovations

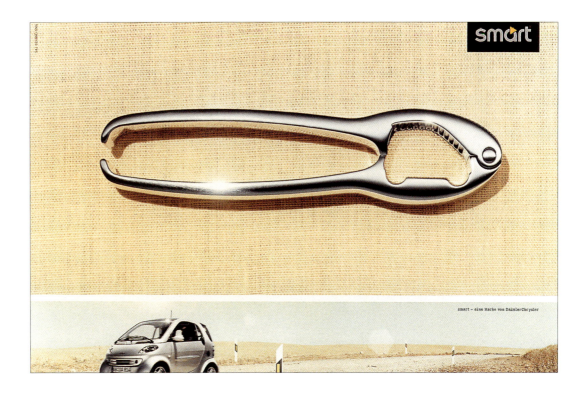

Your whole life using quattro.

Automobiles 231

Agency:	Springer & Jacoby, Hamburg	Agency:	Tandem Campmany Guasch DDB, Barcelona
Creative Directors:	Florian Grimm Antje Hedde Amir Kassaei	Creative Directors:	Danny Ilario Alberto Astorga
Copywriters:	Daniel Grether Michael Meyer	Copywriter:	Nuria Argelich
Art Directors:	Frank Aldorf Jeannette Bergen	Art Director:	Fernando Codina
Photographers:	Uwe Düttmann Martin Wellermann	Client:	Audi Quattro
Client:	Smart Micro-Cars		

232　Automobiles

Agency:	BBH, London
Creative Director:	Will Awdry
Copywriter:	Nick O'Bryan Tear
Art Director:	Al Welsh
Production:	Spectre
Director:	Daniel Kleinman
Producers:	David Botterell
	Andy Gulliman
Client:	Audi A6 Quattro, "Wakeboarder"

A beach at low tide. A man gets onto his wakeboard – a cross between a water ski and a surfboard – and is towed into a series of stunning manoeuvres, curving, gliding and skimming across the shallow waves. We see that he is being towed not by a motorboat, but by an Audi quattro. He completes his routine by jumping a beached boat. The car rolls to a halt. The man puts his board in the boot, and gets in. The Audi drives off, unaffected by the ankle-deep seawater.

Agency:	BBH, London
Creative Director:	Tom Hudson
Copywriter:	Nick Gill
Art Director:	Nick Gill
Production:	Therapy Films
Director:	Malcolm Venville
Producers:	Daniel Todd
	Helen Powlette
Client:	Audi A4, "Symphony"

Animation techniques are used to show us the different parts of a car working separately, accompanied by various musical instruments – the gear stick, the seat, the headlights and the engine all have their own distinctive sounds. These various parts are then assembled, much like instruments are introduced into a symphony, until they make up a harmonious whole. The Audi A4 Cabriolet is "the complete car".

Automobiles

Agency:	Tandem Campmany Guasch DDB, Barcelona
Creative Directors:	Danny Ilario Alberto Astorga
Copywriter:	Nuria Argelich
Art Director:	Fernando Codina
Client:	Audi Range

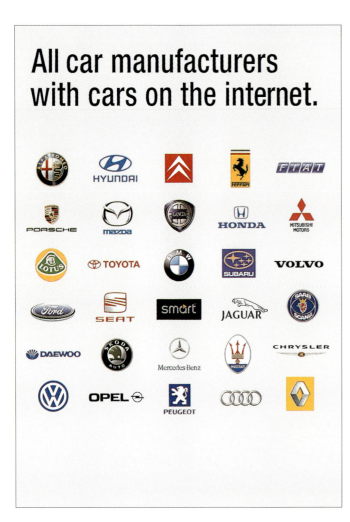

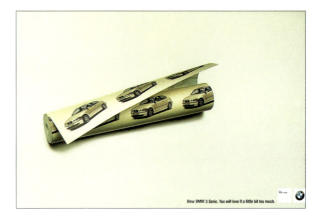

234 Automobiles

Agency:	Jung von Matt, Munich	Agency:	TBWA\Paris
Creative Directors:	Till Hohmann	Creative Director:	Eric Galmard
	Bernhard Lukas	Copywriter:	Vincent Lobelle
Copywriters:	Eva Goede	Art Directors:	Stephen Cafiero
	Sven Nagel		Cédric Moutaud
Art Directors:	Alice Hoffmann	Photographer:	Kevin Summers
	Tomas Tulinius	Client:	BMW 3 Series
Client:	BMW ConnectedDrive		

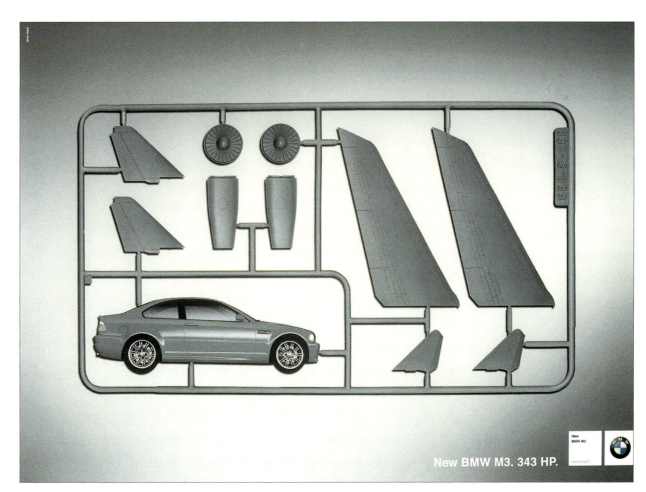

Automobiles

Agency:	D'Adda, Lorenzini, Vigorelli, BBDO, Milan
Creative Directors:	Maurizio D'Adda, Gian Pietro Vigorelli
Copywriter:	Vicky Gitto
Art Director:	Gian Pietro Vigorelli
Photographer:	Pier Paolo Ferrari
Client:	BMW Financial Services

Agency:	TBWA\Paris
Copywriter:	Vincent Lobelle
Art Director:	Stephen Cafiero
Photographer:	Thomas François
Client:	BMW M3

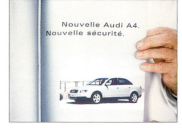

Automobiles

Agency:	Louis XIV DDB, Paris
Creative Director:	Hervé Plumet
Copywriter:	Jean Williaume
Art Director:	Hervé Plumet
Production:	Stink, London
Director:	Jen Jonsson
Client:	Audi A4, "Paradise"

After a road accident involving a collapsing crane, a man finds himself quite literally on the stairway to heaven. In paradise, he explains to various bureaucrats that there must have been a mistake. He finally reaches the highest authority of all, who checks his files and discovers that our hero is indeed scheduled to live until 2051. In a flash, the man finds himself back at the wheel – where his Audi's reliable brakes save his life.

Agency:	Tandem Campmany Guasch DDB, Barcelona
Creative Directors:	Danny Ilario, Alberto Astorga
Copywriters:	Nuria Argelich
Art Directors:	Fernando Codina
Production:	Lee Films Int'l, Madrid Microscope
Director:	Pep Bosch
Producers:	Angel Recio, Julia Carrasco, Vicky Moñino
Client:	Audi A3 Quattro, "Wheels"

Sitting in his garden, a man explains that he has always lacked control over his life. Flashbacks demonstrate how objects with wheels – a pram, a shopping trolley, an office chair, and even a hospital stretcher – seem to go out of control as soon as he gets into them. "Not being able to control what happens to you… I wouldn't wish it on anyone. I couldn't go through that again." And so he drives an Audi A3 quattro.

Agency:	Jung von Matt, Hamburg	**Agency:**	Jung von Matt, Hamburg
Creative Directors:	Oliver Voss Deneke von Weltzien Goetz Ulmer Thomas Wildberger	**Creative Directors:**	Deneke von Weltzien Oliver Voss
Copywriter:	Alexandra Weczerek	**Production:**	Propaganda Film, London
Art Director:	Julia Meyran	**Director:**	Dante Ariola
Photographer:	Daniel M. Hartz	**Producers:**	Natalie Hill Mark Rota
Client:	BMW Mini	**Client:**	BMW Mini, "Sunset"

A young couple are on a cliff top watching a romantic sunset, their Mini parked just behind them. But the woman looks a bit impatient. As soon as the sun has vanished below the horizon, she says briskly: "Right – shall we go then?" and strides off towards the Mini. She seems much happier at the wheel, speeding through the country lanes. Is it love?

238 Automobiles

Agency:	TBWA\Paris	Agency:	TBWA\España, Barcelona
Creative Directors:	Medhi El Alj	Creative Director:	Xavi Munill
	Ivan Pierens	Copywriters:	Xavi Munill
Copywriter:	Vincent Lobelle		Miquel Sales
Art Director:	Stephen Cafiero	Art Directors:	Tomás Descals
Photographer:	Jacques de Marcillac		Alex Martín
Client:	Nissan X-Trail	Photographers:	Tomás Descals
			Alex Martín
		Client:	Nissan

...AND OVER

Automobiles 239

Agency:	D'Adda, Lorenzini, Vigorelli, BBDO, Milan	Agency:	FCB, Frankfurt
Creative Directors:	Rozzi Pino	Creative Director:	Robert Mitchell
	Roberto Battaglia	Copywriters:	Dodo Appel
Copywriter:	Vicky Gitto		Frank Dovidat
Art Director:	Roberto Battaglia	Art Directors:	Klaus Engelhardt
Photographer:	Pier Paolo Ferrari		Holger Bultmann
Client:	Land Rover	Photographer:	Allan McPhail
		Client:	Jeep Grand Cherokee

240 Automobiles

Agency:	BETC Euro RSCG, Paris
Creative Directors:	Daniel Fohr
	Antoine Barthuel
Copywriter:	Marc Rozier
Art Director:	Jean-Marc Tramoni
Production:	Première Heure
Director:	Frédéric Planchon
Producers:	Fabrice Brovelli
	Simon Chatter Robinson
Client:	Peugeot 406, "Upside Down"

Due to some unexplained cataclysm, the world has literally been turned upside down. Trucks and cars plunge from streets, kids play football on the underside of a flyover, water gushes into the sky from fire hydrants, and office workers are forced to walk on ceilings. But everyone in this topsy-turvy world looks around as a Peugeot 406 glides by, still gripping the upturned tarmac. The car was designed to hold the road.

Agency:	BBDO Portugal, Lisbon
Creative Director:	Pedro Bidarra
Copywriter:	Diogo Anahory
Art Director:	José Bomtempo
Production:	Tangerina Azul
Director:	Sérgio Henriques
Producers:	Miguel Varela
	Manuel Teixeira
	Ricardo Cansado
Client:	Nissan Micra Elegance, "Crowd"

A man is in a bar, showing off about his new car for the umpteenth time. "Did I tell you about the door handles?" he asks. His bored friends begin listing some of the car's features. So do the people at the neighbouring table. Finally, the whole bar has joined in, so familiar are they with the man's rapturous descriptions. The man looks sheepish. Nobody loves their car like a Micra driver.

Automobiles   241

Agency:	Saatchi & Saatchi, Paris
Creative Director:	Hervé Riffault
Copywriter:	Jean-François Sacco
Art Director:	Gilles Fichteberg
Photographer:	Carli Hermès
Client:	Toyota
	Rav4 Turbo Diesel

242 Automobiles

Agency:	Ubachs Wisbrun, Amsterdam	Agency:	Agence .V., Paris
Creative Directors:	Wim Ubachs, Kees Sterrenburg	Creative Director:	Christian Vince
Copywriter:	Maarten Klep	Copywriter:	Christian Vince
Art Director:	Roland Tielman	Art Director:	Christian Vince
Photographer:	Jaap Vliegenthart	Photographer:	Yann Robert
Client:	MGF	Client:	Skoda Octavia

Agency:	Forsman & Bodenfors, Gothenburg	Agency:	hasan & partners, Helsinki
Copywriters:	Filip Nilsson Johan Olivero	Copywriter: Art Director:	Antti Einiö Nono Alakari
Art Directors:	Anders Eklind Andreas Malm Mikko Timonen	Production: Director: Producers:	Harry Douglas, Stockholm Musse Hasselvall Anna Persson Mary Lee Copeland
Photographer:	Jesper Brandt		
Client:	Volvo C70 Convertible	Client:	Honda Civic 5D, "Wish"

It's Jake's birthday party, and all his neighbours are there. His wife brings in the cake, and before he blows out the candles, urges him to make a wish. "I hope you all get new Volvos," he says. The following morning, as he steps out onto the drive, a family waves to him from a passing Volvo: "Thanks Jake!" His neighbours have a shiny new Volvo too. In fact, all his friends have them. Jake looks worried, and opens his garage door. He sighs with relief – his Honda Civic is still there. It's nice to be different.

Automotive & Accessories

Agency:	Scholz & Friends, Berlin
Creative Directors:	Martin Pross
	Joachim Schoepfer
Copywriter:	Matthias Schmidt
Photographer:	Calvin Dolley
Client:	Mercedes-Benz Commercial Vehicles

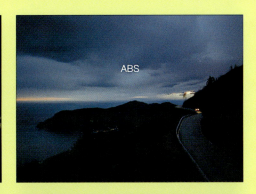

Automotive & Accessories 245

Agency:	Jung von Matt, Munich
Creative Directors:	Till Hohmann
	Bernhard Lukas
Copywriters:	Till Hohmann
	Bernhard Lukas
Art Director:	Gudrun Muschalla
Production:	Arden Sutherland-Dodd, London
Director:	Paul Arden
Producers:	Nick Sutherland-Dodd
	Moritz Merkel
Client:	BMW C1 Motorbike, "Magic Car"

Two headlights approach from the end of a long tunnel, and we follow them on their way down a hillside. The subtitles read: "Safety passenger cell. Seatbelt system, ABS. Is that anything special? On two wheels it is." At a fork in the road, the headlights divide and we see that we are looking at two BMW C1 motorbikes.

246 Automotive & Accessories

Agency:	D'Adda, Lorenzini, Vigorelli, BBDO, Milan	Agency:	Jung von Matt, Munich
Creative Directors:	Pino Rozzi Roberto Battaglia	Creative Directors:	Till Hohmann Bernhard Lukas
Copywriter:	Vicky Gitto	Copywriters:	Heinz Helle Sven Nagel
Art Director:	Stefano Rosselli	Art Directors:	Gudrun Muschalla Martin Besl
Photographer:	Marco Biondi	Photographer:	Thomas Strogalski
Client:	BMW C1 Motorbike	Client:	BMW C1 Motorbike

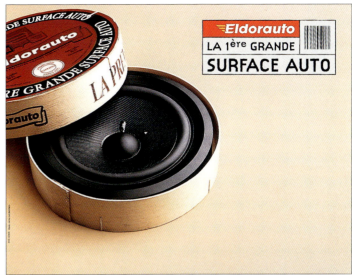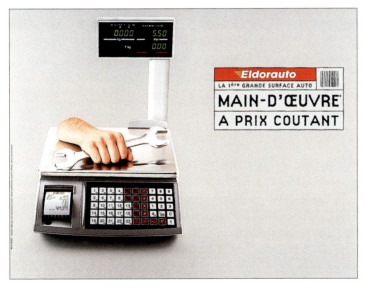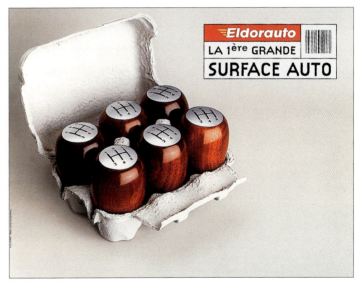

Automotive & Accessories

Agency:	Euro RSCG Works, Paris	The first car supermarket.
Creative Director:	Frédéric Temin	
Copywriter:	Jacques Marsily	
Art Director:	Jean-Luc Collard	
Photographer:	Jenny van Sommers	
Client:	Eldorauto Automotive Retailer	

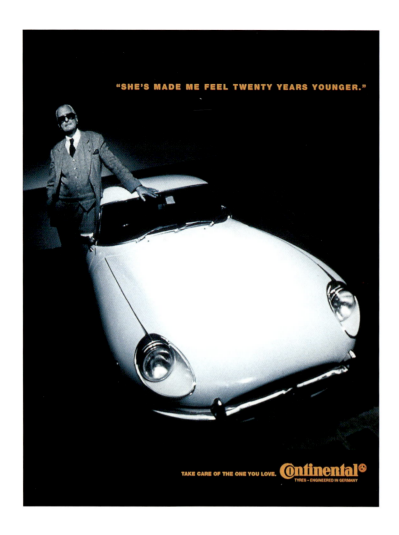

248 Automotive & Accessories

Agency:	Palmer Hargreaves Mint, Leamington Spa
Creative Director:	Randy Weeks
Copywriter:	Jody Williams
Art Director:	And O'Donnell
Client:	Continental Tyres

Agency:	TBWA\Berlin
Creative Director:	Christoph Klingler
Copywriters:	Christoph Klingler
	Athanassios Stellatos
Art Directors:	Boris Schwiedrzik
	Philip Borchardt
Production:	Caspari Film, Düsseldorf
Director:	Oliver Julius
Producers:	Thomas Caspari
	Gerald Heinemann
	Nina Steiger
Client:	Kawasaki Ninja ZX 6R, "Experience"

A motorcycle is moving at incredible speed down a mountain road – blasting through tunnels, screeching around hairpin bends and ripping through narrow passes. After a breathtaking journey, the rider parks and dismounts. Then he is violently sick. The Ninja ZX 6R offers an experience your senses will never forget. Can you handle it?

Agency:	Publicis España, Madrid	Agency:	Paltemaa Huttunen Santala TBWA, Helsinki
Creative Directors:	Tony Fernández-Mañés Antonio Milanés David R. Vega	Creative Directors:	Mira Leppänen Unto Paltemaa
Copywriter:	Nines Montero	Copywriter:	Mira Leppänen
Art Director:	Alejandro de Antonio	Art Director:	Unto Paltemaa
Client:	Autodisco, Firestone/Bridgestone Tyres	Photographer:	Markku Lähdesmäki
		Client:	Nokian Tyres

Automotive & Accessories

Automotive & Accessories

Agency:	CLM/BBDO, Paris
Creative Director:	Anne de Maupeou
Copywriters:	Valérie Larrondo
	Matthew Branning
Production:	Stink, London
Director:	Lawrence Hamburger
Producers:	Robert Herman
	Pierre Marcus
Client:	Midas, "Baby"

On a crowded bus, a woman's baby is crying at the top of its lungs. The other passengers look annoyed. A kind-looking man leans forward, offering to hold the baby and see if there's anything he can do. She agrees. But when he takes the child, the man "tunes it up" by pulling gently on its foot, so that when he gives it back it's whining like a high performance sports car. A Midas car mechanic's job is never done.

Agency:	Scholz & Friends, Berlin
Creative Director:	Martin Pross
Copywriters:	Matthias Schmidt
	Peter Quester
Art Director:	Sandra Schilling
Photographer:	Nina Mallmann
Client:	Mercedes-Benz Sprinter

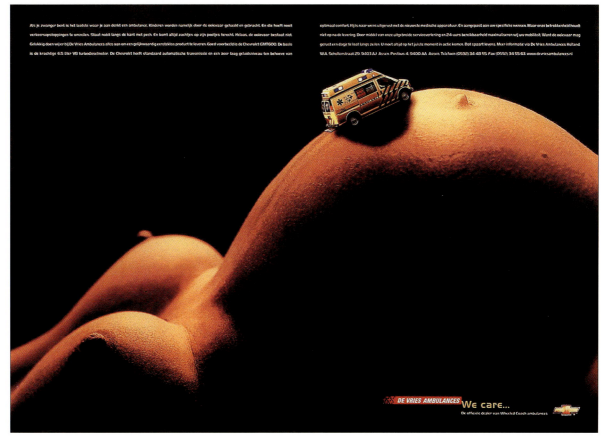

Automotive & Accessories	**251**
Agency:	AGH & Friends, 'S-Hertogenbosch
Creative Director:	Wieke van der Aa
Art Director:	Patrick van der Heijden
Photographer:	Frank Tielemans
Client:	De Vries Ambulances

252 Office Equipment

Agency: BDDP & Fils, Paris
Creative Director: Olivier Altmann
Copywriter: Jean-Gabriel Causse
Art Director: Xavier Beauregard
Photographer: Marc Abel
Client: Microsoft Office

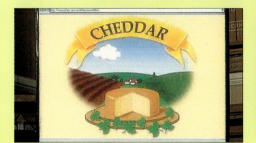

Agency:	Ogilvy & Mather, Paris
Creative Director:	Susan Westre
Copywriter:	Fergus O'Hare
Art Director:	Tim Knox
Production:	Pytka Productions, Venice, California
Director:	Joe Pytka
Producers:	Kathy Rhodes
	Leslie Vaughn
	Lee Weiss
Client:	IBM Europe, "Cheese Wars"

We're in Cheddar – "This historic city of cheese" – and in the town hall, a dignitary is about to unveil a new website. "When I push this button, the Cheddar website will open the markets of the world to us!" But only seconds after the screen has been unveiled, crude animations appear on the site – a lump of blue cheese and the words: "Vive le Roquefort! Cheddar stinks!" The town official is scandalised. "What's happened?" he demands. His colleague provides the answer: "We've been hacked." IBM can help solve your security problems.

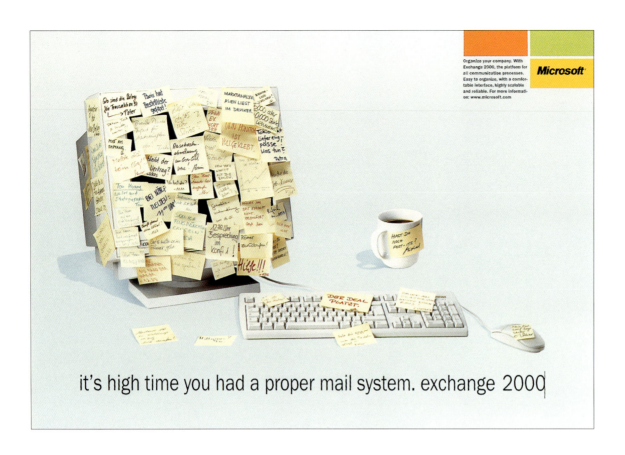

254 **Office Equipment**

Agency:	Jung von Matt, Hamburg
Creative Directors:	Bernhard Lukas, Burkhart von Scheven
Copywriter:	Bjoern Lockstein
Art Director:	Mirjam Heinemann
Client:	Microsoft Exchange 2000

Agency:	Jung von Matt, Hamburg
Creative Directors:	Bernhard Lukas, Burkhart von Scheven
Copywriter:	Bjoern Lockstein
Art Director:	Mirjam Heinemann
Client:	Microsoft Windows 2000

Agency:	Michael Conrad & Leo Burnett, Frankfurt
Creative Director:	Christoph Barth
Copywriter:	Nicola Wassner
Art Director:	Guido Masson
Photographer:	Uwe Düttmann
Client:	Trend Micro Anti-Virus Software

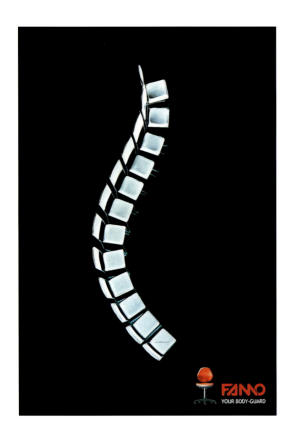

256 Office Equipment

Agency:	Opal, Porto	**Agency:**	Scholz & Friends, Berlin
Creative Director:	Vasco Cordovil	**Creative Directors:**	Martin Krapp
Copywriter:	Zeza Leites		Lutz Pluemecke
Art Director:	France Grosjean	**Copywriter:**	Jan Froescher
Client:	Famo Office Chairs	**Art Director:**	Oliver Seltmann
		Client:	ON-Computing, Apple Service

Agency:	Sandberg Trygg, Malmö
Creative Director:	Peer Eriksson
Copywriter:	Gary Gunning
Art Director:	Peer Eriksson
Photographer:	Dawid
Client:	Ericsson Bluetooth Technology

258 Business Services

Agency:	Lamtar, Paris	Lyon: not far. Marseille: further.
Creative Director:	Philippe Boutié	Imagine a world beyond measure.
Copywriter:	Philippe Boutié	
Art Directors:	Patrick Modé	
	Philippe Boutié	
Photographer:	Patrick Modé	
Client:	Mediametrie	
	Audience Measurement	

Better temporary jobs you'll find at our employment agency.	**randstad** working your way — Employment Agency	

Business Services 259

Agency:	McCann-Erickson, Zürich
Creative Director:	Claude Catsky
Copywriter:	Claude Catsky
Production:	Wirz & Fraefel Productions
Director:	Claude Catsky
Producer:	Stefan Fraefel
Client:	Randstad Employment Agency, "Hitchhiker"

A man stands by a roadside, holding a piece of cardboard with the word 'Zürich' scrawled on it. He stands there for hours, even days, in wind and rain – but nobody stops to give him a lift. Finally a van pulls up, and two workmen get out. They are carrying a smart new road sign: 'Zürich', it says. The man wasn't a hitchhiker – he was standing in for the sign. One of the workmen pays him and gives him a new piece of cardboard. It reads: 'Vladivostok'. Looking for a better temporary job? Better go to Randstad.

Business Services

Agency:	Try Advertising, Oslo
Creative Director:	Kjetil Try
Copywriter:	Petter Bryde
Art Director:	Thorbjørn Ruud
Production:	Paradox
Director:	Kasper Wedendahl
Client:	Adecco Employment Agency, "Midwife"

A fat, jolly woman is in the kitchen with her daughter. She encourages the daughter to throw her an apple, but fails to catch it. The same thing happens outside, when the newspaper boy throws the daily paper at her. She doesn't have much luck with a child's football, either. Even a friend's little dog slips through her arms. Then we see her at work, in a hospital, where she's helping to deliver a baby. As the mother strains, she gets ready to catch... Not everyone is suited to the same job. Adecco makes the right match.

Agency:	hasan & partners, Helsinki
Copywriter:	Antti Einiö
Art Director:	Magnus Ohlsson
Production:	Atmosfär, Stockholm
Director:	Johan Tappert
Producers:	Berit Tilly, Mary Lee Copeland
Client:	TieToenator, "Basketball"

Tough-looking youths are playing basketball. A meek, chubby bloke is watching them. When the ball accidentally lands at his feet, instead of giving it back, he executes a perfect shot. The youths look surprised. One of them rolls the ball back to him – a challenge. He picks it up and does the same thing again. Then he walks off. Cut to his job in a kitchen, where he is breaking eggs and tossing the shells accurately into a bin on the other side of the room. The more you focus on something, the better you become. TieToenator focuses on its customers.

TRY TURNING OFF A BILLBOARD.

GIRAUDY
BILLBOARD NETWORK

YOU CAN FALL ASLEEP IN FRONT OF YOUR TV. NOT IN FRONT OF A BILLBOARD.

GIRAUDY
BILLBOARD NETWORK

WITH BILLBOARDS, YOU CAN'T GO TO THE BATHROOM LIKE YOU CAN DURING OTHER COMMERCIALS.

GIRAUDY
BILLBOARD NETWORK

Business Services

Agency:	BDDP & Fils, Paris
Creative Director:	Olivier Altmann
Copywriter:	Eric Elias
Art Director:	Jorge Carreno
Photographer:	Sébastien Meunier
Client:	Giraudy Outdoor Advertising

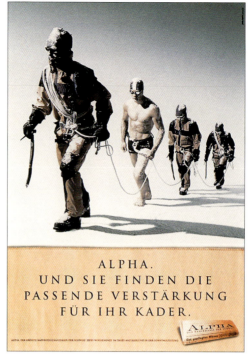
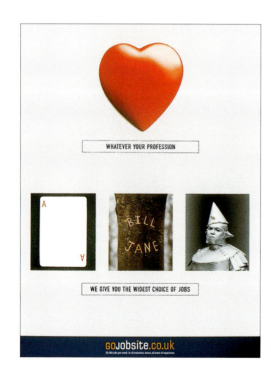
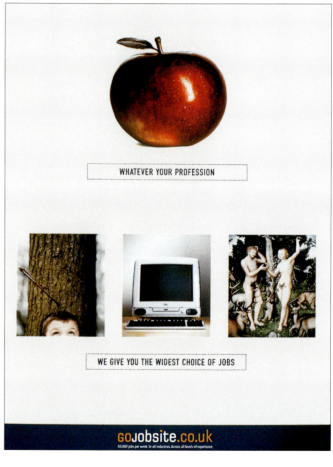

262 Business Services

Agency:	Jung von Matt, Zürich	Where you'll find the better match for your management team.
Creative Directors:	Daniel Meier	
	Alexander Jaggy	
Copywriter:	Christoph Hess	
Art Director:	Simon Staub	
Photographer:	Nicolas Monkewitz	
Client:	Alpha Recruitment	

Agency:	Springer & Jacoby, London
Creative Directors:	Kurt Georg Dieckert
	Stefan Schmidt
Copywriter:	Thomas Chudalla
Art Director:	Tony Hector
Photographer:	Chris Frazer Smith
Client:	GoJobsite, Recruitment Site

Agency:	Vitruvio Leo Burnett, Madrid	**Agency:**	Ogilvy & Mather, Frankfurt
Creative Director:	Rafa Anton	**Creative Director:**	Pat They
Copywriter:	Rafa Anton	**Copywriter:**	Annette Jans
Art Directors:	Eivind Homboe Javier Alvarez	**Art Director:**	Stefanie Bodenstedt
Photographers:	Rodrigo Zabala Aurelio Rodriguez	**Photographer:**	Vincent Dixon
Client:	Starcom Media Planning	**Client:**	Jobpilot Recruitment Site

Business Services

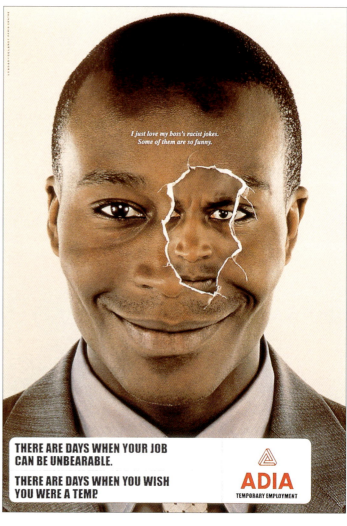

Business Services

Agency:	Ogilvy & Mather, Paris	**Agency:**	Leagas Delaney Paris Centre, Paris
Creative Director:	Susan Westre		
Copywriter:	Fergus O'Hare	**Creative Director:**	Pascal Grégoire
Art Director:	Tim Knox	**Copywriter:**	Patrice Chatelain
Illustrator:	Gilbert Noury	**Art Director:**	Olivier Goguet
Client:	IBM Europe	**Photographer:**	Rose Neige
		Client:	Adia Employment Agency

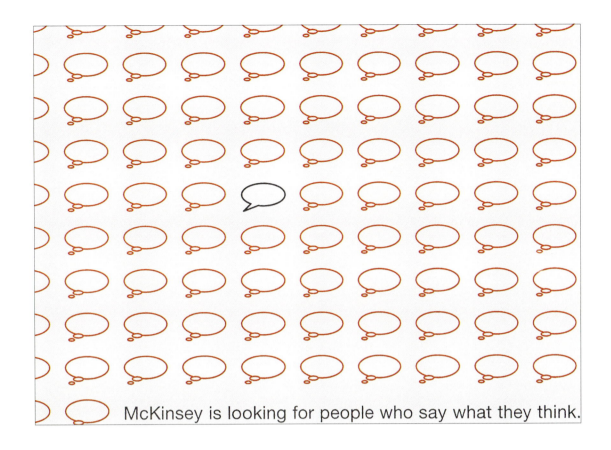

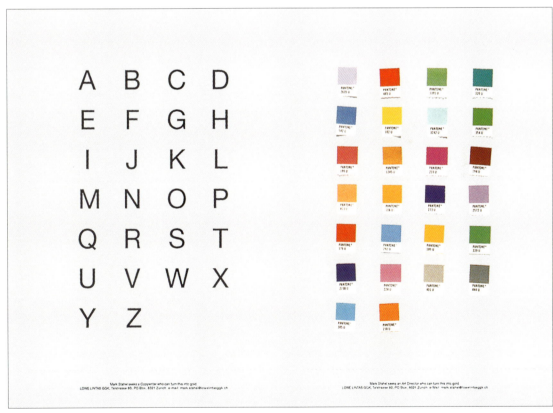

Agency:	Springer & Jacoby, Hamburg	Agency:	Lowe Lintas GGK, Zürich	Mark Stahel seeks a copywriter/art director who can turn this into gold.
Creative Directors:	Timm Weber, Bettina Olf	Creative Director:	Mark Stahel	
Copywriter:	Sascha Hanke	Copywriter:	Lukas Schmid	
Art Director:	Regina Wysny	Art Director:	Philipp Sträuli	
Client:	McKinsey & Company	Photographer:	Bruno Oberhänsli	
		Client:	Lowe Lintas GGK, Recruitment Ad	

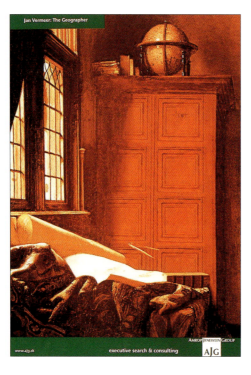

Business Services

Agency:	1576 Advertising, Edinburgh	Interests: wine tasting.	**Agency:**	Wiktor/Leo Burnett, Bratislava
Creative Directors:	David Reid		**Creative Director:**	Raffo Tatarko
	Adrian Jeffery	Hobbies: art.	**Copywriter:**	Vlado Slivka
Copywriter:	James Betts	We see through the CV.	**Art Director:**	Rast'o Záležák
Art Director:	Rufus Wedderburn		**Client:**	Amrop Jenewein Group, Executive Search
Photographer:	Victor Albrow			
Client:	ID Recruitment Consultants			

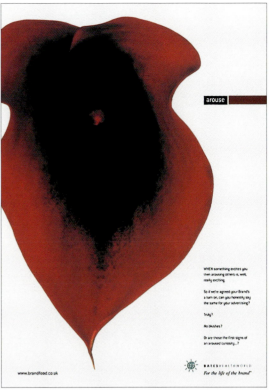
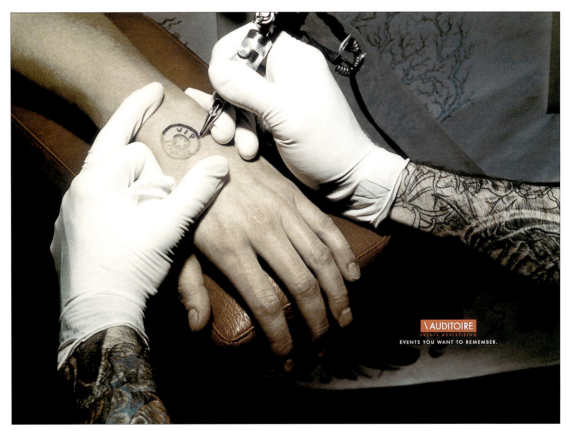

Business Services

Agency:	Bates Healthworld, London	Agency:	BDDP & Fils, Paris
Creative Director:	Adrian Parr	Creative Director:	Olivier Altmann
Copywriter:	Paul McCarthy	Copywriter:	Thierry Albert
Art Director:	John Green	Art Director:	Charles Guillemand
Photographer:	Matthew Shave	Photographer:	Sébastien Meunier
Client:	Bates Healthworld, Self-Promotion	Client:	Auditoire Events Agency

Agency: Creative Center Cardea, Sarajevo
Copywriter: Anur Haoziomerspahić
Art Director: Anur Haoziomerspahić
Photographer: Max Zambelli
Graphic Designer: Ajna Zlatar
Client: Iskraemeco Electric Meters

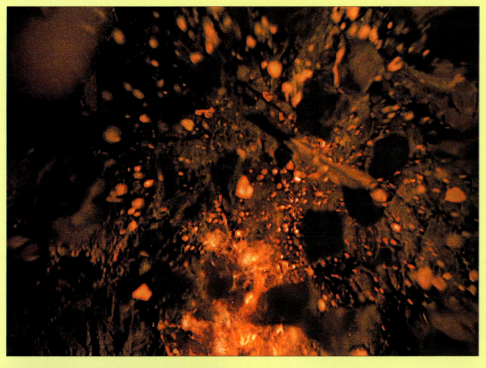

 Industrial & Agricultural Equipment

Agency:	Euro RSCG Corporate, Paris	A camera tunnels through the earth, from the core to the surface. And then it continues upwards, offering us cross-section views of an underground railway, workmen in a manhole, a shopping mall, a stock exchange, a gymnasium and busy offices. Throughout the entire journey, there is nothing but cacophony and stress. Finally we burst through the top of the building, soar over the city, and break through the cloud cover – into tranquil, silent blue skies. Airbus: travel in peace.
Creative Director:	Olivier Moulierac	
Copywriter:	Chermine Assadian	
Art Director:	Bruno Banaszuk	
Production:	Entropie	
Directors:	Les Frères Poireaud	
Producers:	Stephane Kooshmanian Christine Murzeau	
Client:	Airbus, "The Magma"	

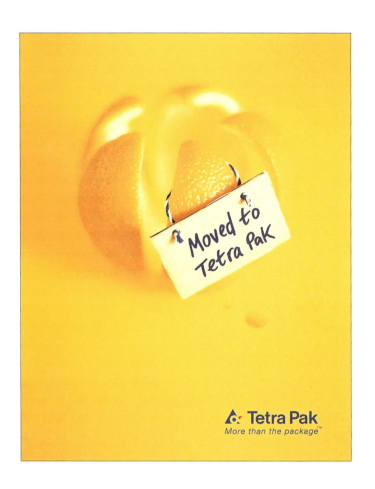

270 **Industrial & Agricultural Equipment**

Agency:	Lowe Lintas Digitel, Zagreb	Agency:	Happy F&B, Gothenburg
Creative Director:	Dario Vince	Creative Director:	Anders Kornestedt
Copywriter:	Nini Cinotti	Art Director:	Andreas Kittel
Art Director:	Goran Štimac	Photographer:	Branko
Photographer:	Ivana Vucic	Client:	Munkedals Papermill
Client:	Tetra Pak, Packaging		

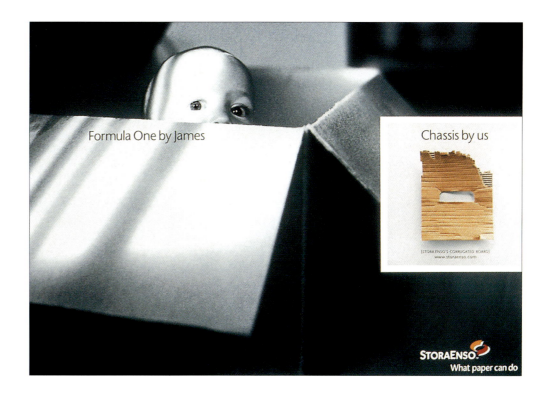

Industrial & Agricultural Equipment   271

Agency:	Lowe Brindfors, Stockholm	Agency:	Springer & Jacoby, Hamburg
Creative Director:	Jari Ullakko	Creative Directors:	Timm Weber
Copywriter:	Sean Duffy		Uli Gürtler
Art Director:	Alan Moore		Bettina Olf
Photographer:	Jens Mortensen	Copywriter:	Sven Keitel
Client:	Stora Enso, Paper Products	Art Director:	Claudia Tödt
		Photographers:	Uwe Düttmann
			Heribert Schindler
		Client:	European Steel Alliance

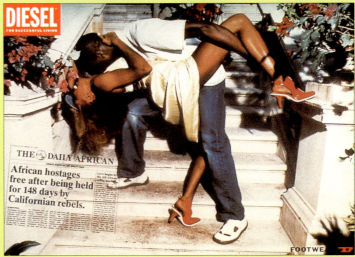

Agency:	Paradiset DDB, Stockholm
Creative Director:	Joakim Jonason
Copywriter:	Björn Rietz
Art Director:	Tove Langseth
Photographers:	Ellen von Unwerth
	Peter Alendahl
Illustrator:	Patrik Andersson
Client:	Diesel
	Jeans & Workwear

 Clothing & Fabrics

Agency:	Lowe Lintas, London
Creative Director:	Charles Inge
Copywriter:	Tony Barry
Art Director:	Vince Squibb
Production:	Gorgeous Enterprises
Director:	Frank Budgen
Producers:	Paul Rothwell
	Charles Crisp
Client:	Reebok, "Sofa"

A bored-looking guy is slumped on his old sofa, watching telly. Finally he clicks off the TV and stands up. But what's this? The sofa jolts forward so that he falls back onto its cushions. He tries again. The same thing happens, only now the sofa has turned into a living thing, and it's trying to suffocate him. He wrenches himself free and is pursued around the room. Snatching up his Reebok sports bag, he makes a dive for the door. He escapes with seconds to spare, the psychotic sofa wedged in the narrow doorframe. Reebok sportswear helps you escape the sofa.

274 Clothing & Fabrics

Agency:	Paradiset DDB, Stockholm	Agency:	CLM/BBDO, Paris
Copywriters:	Ola Lax	Creative Director:	Anne de Maupeou
	Camilla Hilarius	Copywriter:	Olivier Dermaux
Art Director:	Kjell Doktorow	Art Director:	Mathieu Vinciguerra
Photographer:	Calle Stoltz	Photographer:	Rankin
Illustrator:	Patrik Andersson	Client:	Kookaï
Client:	Björn Borg		

Clothing & Fabrics 275

Agency:	Armando Testa, Milan	Agency:	RG Wiesmeier, Munich
Creative Directors:	Maurizio Sala	Creative Directors:	Claudia Hammerschmidt
	Michele Mariani		Susanne Ahlers
Copywriter:	Sonia Cosentino	Copywriter:	Carlos Obers
Art Director:	Paola Balestreri	Art Director:	Susanne Ahlers
Photographer:	Brigitte Niedermair	Photographer:	Anatol Kotte
Client:	Allegri	Client:	Oui Fashions

Clothing & Fabrics

Agency:	Miles Calcraft Briginshaw Duffy, London
Creative Directors:	Paul Briginshaw, Malcolm Duffy
Copywriter:	Malcolm Duffy
Art Director:	Paul Briginshaw
Production:	Gorgeous Enterprises
Director:	Peter Thwaites
Producers:	Paul Rothwell, Fiona Marks
Client:	Aristoc Slimline System Tights, "Subtitles"

We appear to be watching an arty Italian movie from the 1960s, complete with subtitles. A young couple are talking in a minimalist room, but the subtitles obscure the leggy young woman's face. "Something's wrong Paolo," she says. "It's these stupid subtitles. Why aren't they at the bottom of the screen? No-one can see my face." Paulo tells her that it's because she's wearing Aristoc Slimline System Tights, which make her legs look fabulous. He adds: "It would be a crime to cover them up."

Agency:	Republica, Albertslund
Creative Director:	Joachim Rosenstand
Copywriter:	Torben Andersen
Art Director:	Anne Skarbye
Production:	Nordisk Film Commercial, Copenhagen
Director:	Kasper Barfoed
Producers:	Stig Lauritsen, François Grandjean
Client:	Kvickly, "Friends"

Two mothers with young daughters greet each other in a suburban street. As they chat, the toddlers size each other up, as if deciding whether or not to be friends. They smile at each other. And then, as their mothers hug one another goodbye, the kids launch into a complicated greeting ritual, which involves slapping hands, touching fists and doing "high fives" – as if they were rappers meeting on an LA street. There's nothing like making friends.

Agency:	Louis XIV DDB, Paris	Agency:	Springer & Jacoby, Hamburg
Copywriter:	Olivier Moine	Creative Directors:	Stefan Meske
Art Director:	Nicolas Chauvin		Arno Lindemann
Photographer:	Geoffroy de Boismenu	Copywriter:	Stefan Meske
Client:	La City	Art Directors:	Arno Lindemann
			Uli Gürtler
		Photographer:	Peter Gehrke
		Client:	Mustang Jeans

Clothing & Fabrics

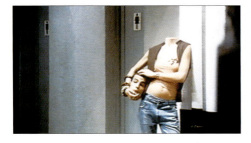

Clothing & Fabrics

Agency:	BBH, London
Creative Director:	Russell Ramsay
Copywriter:	Mark Hunter
Art Director:	Tony McTear
Production:	Gorgeous Enterprises
Director:	Frank Budgen
Producers:	Paul Rothwell
	Andy Gulliman
Client:	Levi's Engineered Jeans, "Twist"

A bunch of trendy kids in a retro car pull up outside a diner. Right away we can tell they're different – as they stretch their legs, they are able to twist into all sorts of contorted positions. Even the kids themselves seem impressed by their powers. Is it magic? Are they aliens? They put on a full display of their prowess for the astonished customers, bending this way and that, and even exchanging limbs. As the car pulls away, one of them leaves a hand behind – but a little dog runs after them with it in his mouth.

Agency:	ANR BBDO, Gothenburg
Creative Director:	Christer Allansson
Copywriter:	Håkan Larsson
Art Director:	Hans-Erik Andreasson
Production:	Efti, Stockholm
Director:	Felix Herngren
Producers:	Carl Molinder
	Cornelia Opitz
	Joakim Brinkenberg
Client:	Fristads Workwear, "The Door"

"This can't be right," says a young man to a workman, who has done a bad job of replacing his front door. The workman asks indignantly: "What do you mean 'can't be right'?" The young man demonstrates – when the door is shut, there's a 5cm wide gap all the way round. Daylight floods through. "Oh, you mean the gap!" says the workman. "That'll be okay. The wood will expand. In the autumn." Not only professionals, it seems, wear Fristads workwear.

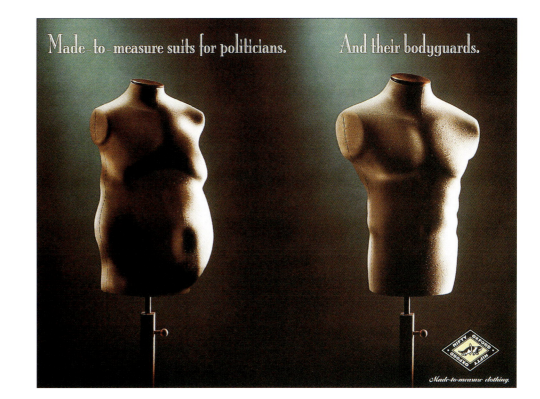

Agency:	Publicis, Zürich	**Agency:**	Springer & Jacoby, Hamburg
Creative Directors:	Markus Gut Markus Ruf	**Creative Directors:**	Stefan Meske Arno Lindemann
Copywriter:	Markus Ruf	**Copywriter:**	Tobias Stutznäcker
Art Director:	Markus Gut	**Art Directors:**	Thomas Knobloch Ulrike Letulé
Photographers:	Stefan Minder Felix Schregenberger	**Photographer:**	Tom van Heel
Client:	Nifty Oxford, Made-to-Measure Clothing	**Client:**	Bogner Jeans

Clothing & Fabrics

DesCriBE YoUR PerFecT ParTNer iN a woRd.

FiT.

The perfect partner is just like Mey's webbed waistband. It gives you the support you need, but you won't feel restricted. It's got a flexible attitude. It always stays in shape. And it will stick with you through thick and thin. How can you resist? Find out more at www.mey.de

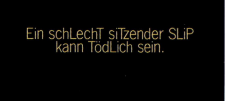

Ein schLechT siTzender SLiP kann TödLich sein.

Clothing & Fabrics

Agency:	Jung von Matt, Hamburg	**Agency:**	Jung von Matt, Hamburg	We're in the middle of a Sergio Leone-style Western. Two gunslingers face each other on a dusty street. Sweat pours down their faces. Their fingers twitch nervously over their holsters. Then one of the men unexpectedly reaches down to adjust his undergarments. The other takes advantage of this distraction to shoot him dead. Ill-fitting underwear can cost you your life.
Creative Directors:	Kathrin Berger, Michael Ohanian	**Creative Directors:**	Kathrin Berger, Doerte Spengler-Ahrens	
Copywriters:	Christina Coates, Andy Dankelmann	**Production:**	Markenfilm, Wedel	
Art Director:	Vera Hoescheler	**Director:**	Marc Schoelermann	
Photographer:	Uwe Duettmann	**Producers:**	Jörg Fudickar, Moritz Merkel	
Client:	Mey Fine Bodywear	**Client:**	Mey Fine Bodywear, "Duel"	

Clothing & Fabrics   281

Agency:	Air Paris
Creative Director:	Tho Van Tran
Art Director:	David Loretti
Photographers:	Warren du Preez
	Nick Thornton Jones
Client:	Marithé & François Girbaud

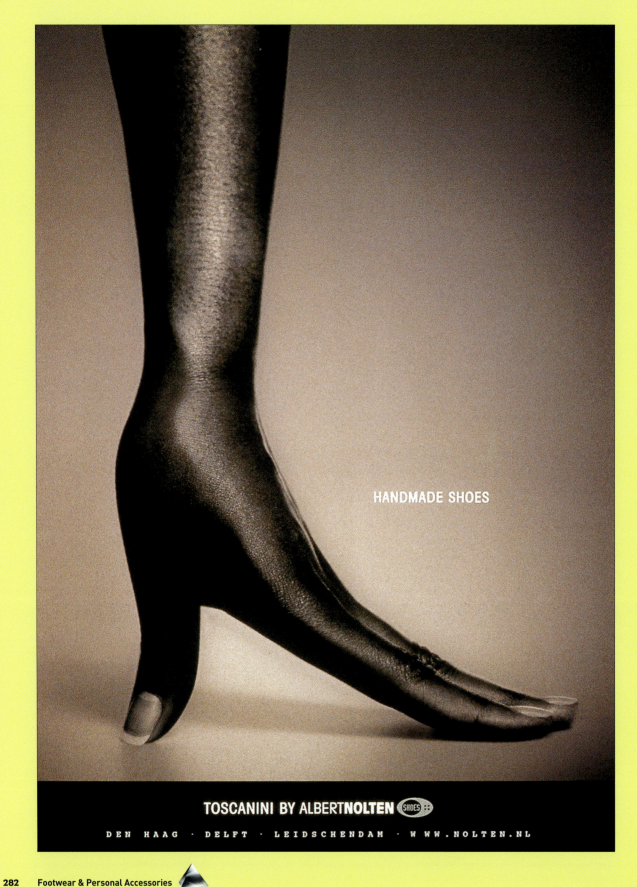

282 Footwear & Personal Accessories
Agency: YokYor, Amsterdam
Creative Directors: Mart Groen
Ralph Wilmes
Photographer: Edo Kars
Client: Albert Nolten Shoes

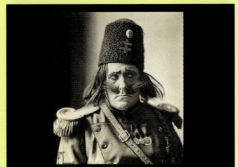

Footwear & Personal Accessories 283

Agency:	Kolle Rebbe, Hamburg	Using an ingenious script and a series of amusing, comically appropriate photographs, this three-minute cinema ad tells the story of an ill-fated rendezvous between Jean and the love of his life, Mirabelle, in Paris. The result can only be described as "surrealism meets Monty Python". The narrator describes how Jean's adventures began when he spotted Mirabelle in a café, and asked for a light for his cigarette. What he really wanted, of course, was her telephone number. Or did he? Viewers are invited to decide.
Creative Directors:	Erik Hart	
	Bernd Huesmann	
Copywriter:	Alexander Baron	
Art Director:	Florian Scherzer	
Production:	Das Werk	
	Hastings	
Producers:	Bianca Mack	
	Sandra Monse	
	Axel Leyck	
Client:	Gauloises Cigarettes, "Rendezvous"	

Footwear & Personal Accessories

Agency:	Springer & Jacoby, Hamburg	Agency:	Sixpack, Düsseldorf
Creative Directors:	Thomas Walmrath Olaf Oldigs	Creative Directors:	Frank Berger Robert Röhrbein
Copywriter:	Thomas Walmrath	Copywriter:	Malin Bögel
Art Director:	Holger Schäfers	Art Director:	Andrée Dietsch
Client:	P&S Cigarettes	Photographer:	Thomas Herbrich
		Client:	Asics Sport Shoes

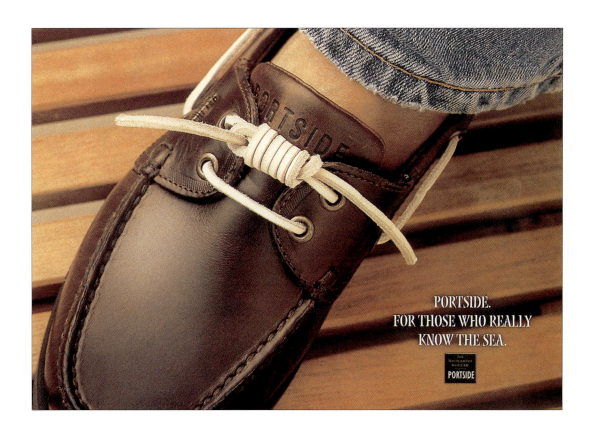

PORTSIDE.
FOR THOSE WHO REALLY
KNOW THE SEA.

Footwear & Personal Accessories

Agency:	Young & Rubicam, Lisbon	**Agency:**	Aimaq Rapp Stolle, Berlin
Creative Director:	Albano Homem de Melo	**Creative Directors:**	André Aimaq
Copywriter:	João Ribeiro		Lars Oehlschlaeger
Art Director:	Lourenço Thomaz	**Copywriter:**	Oliver Frank
Photographer:	João Silveira Ramos	**Art Director:**	Alexander Reiss
Client:	Portside Shoes	**Production:**	Markenfilm
		Director:	Jan Wentz
		Producer:	Jörg Fudickar
		Client:	Nike, "Night's Rest"

Two young guys are practising basketball on the front drive of a suburban home – at the dead of night. The shooter scores every time, the ball arcing through the air and dropping silently through the net without grazing the backboard. He achieves this feat maybe half a dozen times. Suddenly, the ball bounces off the hoop with a clanging noise. Bedroom lights go on as the unusual sound echoes down the street. "Sorry!" says the boy. The lights go off, and they keep playing.

286 Footwear & Personal Accessories

Agency:	180 Communications, Amsterdam
Creative Director:	Lorenzo De Rita
Copywriter:	Lorenzo De Rita
Art Director:	Dean Maryon
Production:	RSA, London
Director:	Lawrence Dunmore
Producers:	Amanda Tassre, Esther Hielckert
Client:	Adidas Footwear & Sportswear, "Adidas Makes You Cool"

In Rome, a barman is explaining how the city's traffic used to make its citizens boil with rage – "People screaming like baboons" – until tennis ace Martina Hingis showed up. We see her playing in a city square, tennis balls glancing off a rotating sign which smoothly directs the traffic. "She was wearing this," says another witness, holding up an Adidas shirt. "And now everyone wears them." A traffic cop adds: "Everyone is cool now." A young mother can barely express her gratitude. "I wanted to call him Martina," she says, displaying her new baby. "But he's a boy."

Agency:	180 Communications, Amsterdam
Creative Director:	Lorenzo De Rita
Copywriter:	Lorenzo De Rita
Art Director:	Dean Maryon
Production:	RSA, London
Director:	Lawrence Dunmore
Producers:	Helen Williams, Esther Hielckert
Client:	Adidas Footwear & Sportswear, "Adidas Makes You Light"

A metro security guard recalls that watching the escalators on closed circuit TV used to be dull – until athlete Ato Boldon decided to practice on them. "When Ato came, he brought light," recounts a metro passenger, as we see Boldon sprinting up the 'down' escalators. Commuters join in, and soon the metro has become a makeshift gym. "Now it's like watching a sports channel," says the security guard, who adds that he has started wearing Adidas shoes in homage to Ato. "Very funky, huh?"

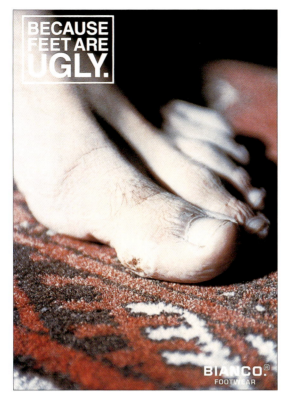
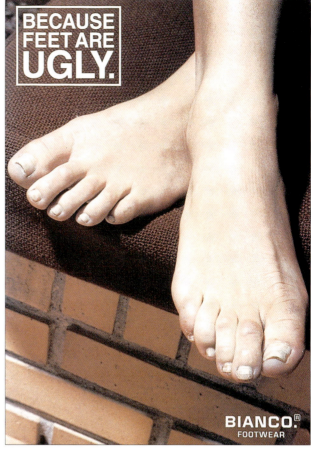
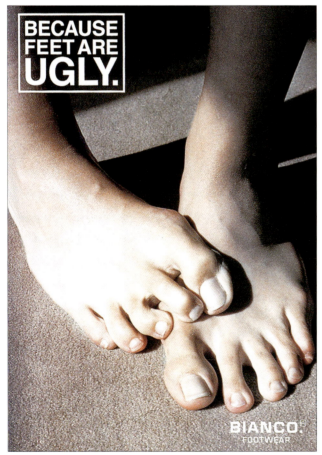

Agency:	&Co., Copenhagen
Art Directors:	Thomas Hoffmann
	Robert Cerkez
Production:	Locomotion
Director:	Jens Mikkelsen
Producer:	Mariusz Skronski
Client:	Bianco Footwear

Footwear & Personal Accessories

Agency:	D'Adda, Lorenzini, Vigorelli, BBDO, Milan
Creative Directors:	Gian Pietro Vigorelli, Pino Rozzi
Copywriter:	Pino Rozzi
Art Director:	Gian Pietro Vigorelli
Photographer:	Ilan Rubin
Client:	Biasia Handbags

Agency:	devarrieuxvillaret, Paris	No woman's body has been exploited for this ad.
Copywriter:	Pierre-Dominique Burgaud	
Art Director:	Stéphane Richard	
Photographer:	John Akehurst	
Client:	Eram Shoes	

Footwear & Personal Accessories

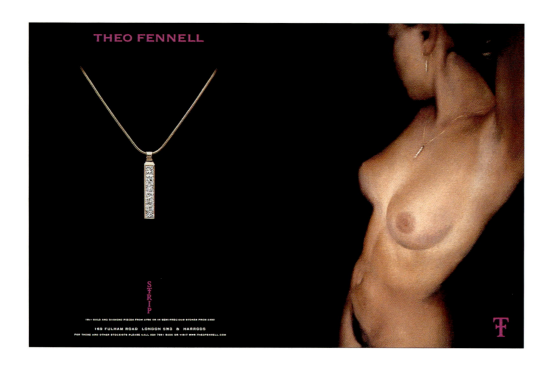

290 Footwear & Personal Accessories

Agency:	G3, London	**Agency:**	FCB, Brussels
Creative Director:	Richard Melik	**Creative Directors:**	François Milliex
Art Director:	Richard Melik		Yves Dupuis
Photographer:	Paul Biddle	**Copywriter:**	Fréderic Petitjean
Illustrator:	Jonathan Yeo	**Art Director:**	Domenico de Mico
Client:	Theo Fennell Jewellery	**Photographer:**	Christophe Gilbert
		Client:	Eastpak Backpacks

Agency:	Vinizius Young & Rubicam, Barcelona	Agency:	TBWA\Brussels
Creative Director:	Muntsa Dachs	Creative Director:	André Rysman
Copywriter:	Mauricio Alarcon	Copywriter:	Frank Marinus
Art Director:	David Garriga	Art Director:	Jan Macken
Client:	Swatch Scuba Collection	Photographer:	Hans Kroeskamp
		Client:	Samsonite Luggage

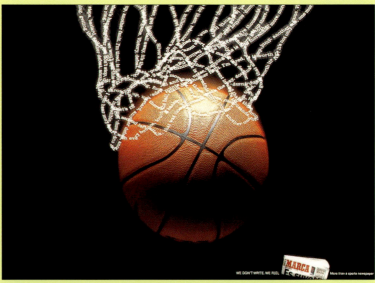

Agency:	Publicis España, Madrid
Creative Directors:	Tony Fernández-Mañéz
	Antonio Milanés
	María Jesús Herrera
	Juanma Pérez-Paredes
Copywriter:	María Jesús Herrera
Art Director:	Juanma Pérez-Paredes
Photographer:	Antonio Díaz
Client:	Marca Sports Newspaper

Agency:	Mother, London
Creative Directors:	Robert Saville
	Mark Waites
Copywriters:	Jim Thornton
	Ben Mooge
	Graham Linehan
Client:	QTV Music Channel, "The Danster"

"Feedback is my evil mistress." Meet 'The Danster', a failed musician dreaming of stardom. At his local music store, we see him returning a piece of equipment. "I bought this last week. But I don't know what it is." In another spot, a waitress hands him a piece of paper. He signs his autograph with a flourish – but in fact she's giving him the bill. And he even bores a taxi driver with a droning monologue about his musical influences when all the driver wanted to know was where he wanted to go. QTV – thousands who've made it, for the millions who haven't.

Agency:	JBR McCann, Oslo		**Agency:**	Edson, FCB, Lisbon
Creative Director:	Paal Tarjei Aasheim		**Creative Director:**	Edson Athayde
Copywriter:	Bjørnar Buxrud		**Copywriter:**	Edson Athayde
Art Directors:	Jannicke Østlie		**Art Director:**	Paulo Pereira
	Joachim A. Haug		**Production:**	Show Off
Production:	EPA International, Stockholm		**Director:**	Aleandre Montenegro
Directors:	Calle Aastrand		**Producers:**	Raul Nunes
	Christoffer von Reis			César Monteiro
Producers:	Johan Persson		**Client:**	Editorial Notícias, Publisher, "Bathroom"
	Tonje Østbye			
Client:	Dagbladet Newspaper, "Strong Pensioners"			

A politician is visiting an old peoples' home. He shakes their hands, hugs them, and generally grabs every available photo opportunity. But the way he furtively wipes his hand after one handshake reveals his true feelings. Then he meets a frail woman, who appears to be blind. She traces the contours of his face with her hands, knocking his glasses askew. Then she slaps him. The politician retreats, scandalised. The woman smiles and picks up her copy of Dagbladet newspaper. She's not blind at all – but like the paper, she has strong opinions.

We see a man on the toilet, inexplicably trying to balance a bulky PC screen and a keyboard on his lap. The subtitles explain: "They say computers will replace books." The man presses a button on his keyboard, and the whole top-heavy ensemble falls off his lap and smashes on the floor. Subtitles: "Yeah, sure." The message is clear: the printed word is still the most practical communication tool.

Media 295

Agency:	Edson, FCB, Lisbon	Agency:	Van Walbeek Etcetera, Amsterdam
Creative Director:	Edson Athayde	Creative Director:	Willem van Harrewijen
Copywriter:	Frederico Saldanha	Copywriter:	Antoine Houtsma
Art Director:	Fabiano Bonfim	Art Director:	Raymond van Schaik
Photographer:	Francisco Prata	Photographer:	Jan Holtslag
Client:	Jornal de Notícias Newspaper	Client:	Veronica Magazine

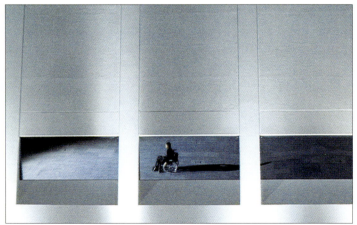

Agency:	Malcolm Moore Deakin Blazye, London	**Agency:**	Springer & Jacoby, Hamburg
Creative Directors:	Guy Moore Tony Malcolm	**Creative Directors:**	Alexander Schill Axel Thomsen
Copywriter:	Gary Ruby	**Copywriters:**	Alexander Weber Annette Steffens
Art Director:	Nick Williamson	**Art Director:**	Bastian Kuhn
Production:	Gorgeous Enterprises	**Production:**	Cobblestone Pictures
Director:	Tom Carty	**Director:**	Sébastien Grousset
Producers:	Ciska Faulkner Helen Routledge	**Producers:**	Angelika Esslinger Jenny Krug
Client:	MTV, "Eggcentric"	**Client:**	Die Welt Newspaper, "Wheelchair"

An improbably trendy young man gets into an apartment block lift with his shopping, which consists entirely of eggs. As he cooks scrambled eggs for supper, we notice that there are eggshells everywhere – made into hanging decorations, dropped into the fish tank, stuck on the wall. The man serves eggs to his dog, and a heart-shaped fried egg to his girlfriend. Finally, he has what he needs – one last egg box to complete his soundproofed room, enabling him to blast out MTV Hits without disturbing his neighbours.

We see a man in a wheelchair, wheeling himself around a hi-tech glass and steel office building. He takes a lift, crosses crowded walkways and negotiates open plan offices. Suddenly, in another corridor, one of the chair's wheels gets stuck in a grid concealing under-floor wiring. He tugs violently at the chair, trying to free it. Then, miraculously, he stands up – and takes out a notebook to jot the incident down. He is Uwe Grahl, architect. The world belongs to those who think in new ways.

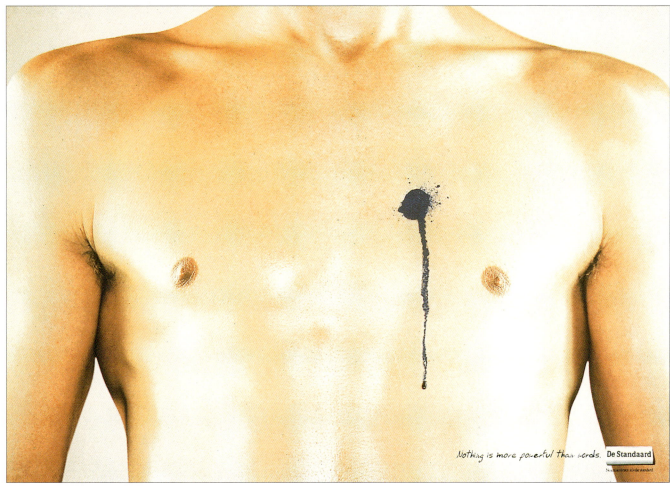

Agency:	Lowe Lintas & Partners, Brussels
Creative Director:	Georges Lafleur
Copywriters:	Dominique van Gilbergen
	Joeri van den Broeck
Art Director:	Joost Berends
Photographer:	Frank Uyttenhove
Client:	De Standaard Newspaper

Media

Agency:	Lowe Brindfors, Stockholm
Creative Director:	Johan Nilsson
Copywriter:	Björn Hjalmar
Art Director:	Mitte Blomqvist
Photographer:	Henrik Halvarsson
Client:	UPC Cable TV

Agency:	Lowe Brindfors, Stockholm
Creative Director:	Johan Nilsson
Copywriter:	Björn Hjalmar
Art Director:	Mitte Blomqvist
Photographer:	Henrik Halvarsson
Client:	UPC Cable TV

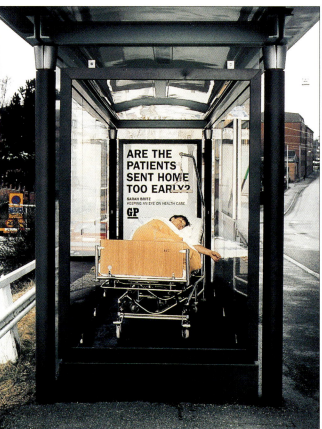

Agency:	Forsman & Bodenfors, Gothenburg	**Agency:**	Forsman & Bodenfors, Gothenburg
Copywriter:	Björn Engström	**Copywriters:**	Björn Engström
Art Directors:	Staffan Forsman		Martin Ringqvist
	Staffan Håkanson	**Art Directors:**	Staffan Forsman
Photographer:	Peter Boström		Staffan Håkanson
Client:	Göteborgs-Posten Newspaper	**Photographer:**	Jens Assur
		Client:	Göteborgs-Posten Newspaper

Agency:	Forsman & Bodenfors, Gothenburg
Copywriter:	Björn Engström
Art Directors:	Staffan Forsman
	Staffan Håkanson
Client:	Göteborgs-Posten Newspaper

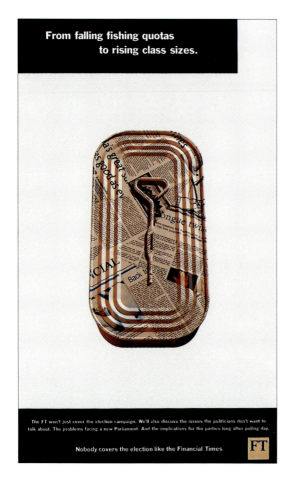

Agency:	Delaney Lund Knox Warren & Partners, London	Agency:	Dinamo Reklamebyrå, Lysaker
Creative Directors:	Gary Betts Malcolm Green	Copywriters:	Bjarte A. Storbråten Espen D. Hagen
Copywriter:	Richard Warren	Art Director:	Mats Nyquist
Art Director:	John Sutcliffe	Photographer:	Glen Røkeberg
Illustrator:	Meiklejohn	Client:	Aftenposten Newspaper
Client:	Financial Times		

Agency:	Jung von Matt, Berlin	**Agency:**	Young & Rubicam, Frankfurt
Creative Director:	Roland Schwarz	**Creative Directors:**	Matthias Berg
Copywriters:	Alex Römer		Helmut Schulte
	Steffen Pejas	**Copywriter:**	Helmut Schulte
Art Directors:	Craig Lovelidge	**Art Director:**	Norbert Huebner
	Birgit Schuster	**Photographer:**	Christian Stoll
Client:	Max Magazine	**Client:**	HR Skyline, Financial Radio Station

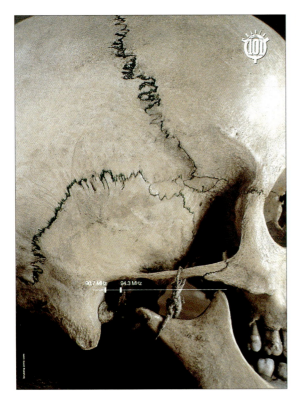
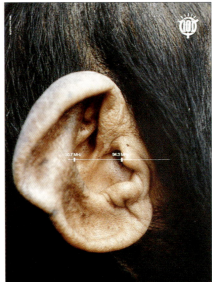
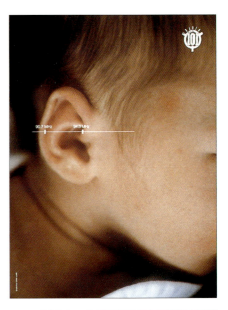
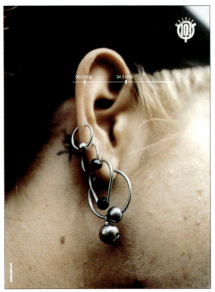
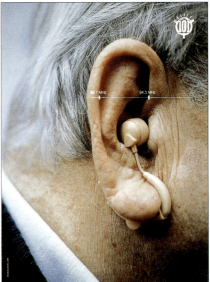

304 Media

Agency:	Bruketa & Zinic, Zagreb	Agency:	Faulds Advertising, Edinburgh
Creative Directors:	Bruketa Davor / Zinic Nikola	Creative Director:	Billy Mawhinney
Copywriters:	Bruketa Davor / Zinic Nikola	Copywriter:	Pete Bastiman
Art Directors:	Bruketa Davor / Zinic Nikola	Art Director:	Steve Mawhinney
Photographer:	Vanja Solin	Photographer:	Giblin & James
Client:	Radio 101	Client:	Key 103 FM

Agency:	Jung von Matt, Berlin	Agency:	Umwelt, Copenhagen
Creative Director:	Jürgen Vossen	Photographer:	Martin Moos
Copywriter:	Alex Römer	Client:	Børsen Daily
Art Director:	Craig Lovelidge		Business Newspaper
Photographer:	Reinhard Hunger		
Client:	WirtschaftsWoche Magazine		

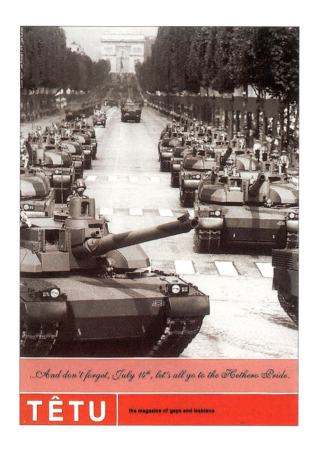

Agency: Leo Burnett, Paris	Agency: Kolle Rebbe, Hamburg
Creative Directors: Christophe Coffre, Nicolas Taubes	Creative Directors: Sebastian Hardieck, Holger Bultmann
Copywriter: Christophe Coffre	Art Director: Nikolaus Ronacher
Art Director: Nicolas Taubes	Photographer: Robert Grischek
Client: Têtu Magazine	Client: TwenFM

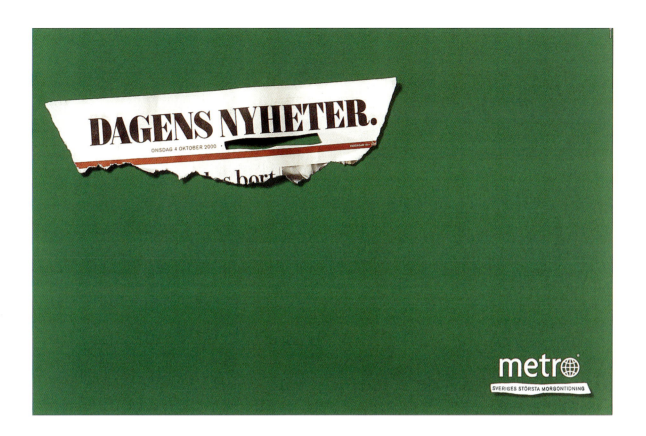

Media   307

Agency:	Abby Norm, Stockholm	NB: The idea of the ad was to dramatise the fact that the underdog free daily newspaper Metro has become bigger than the traditional household newspaper Dagens Nyheter. So Metro steals DN's tagline, "Sweden's leading morning paper", and makes it its own.	**Agency:**	Citigate Albert Frank, London
Copywriter:	Ulrika Granlund Kukulska		**Creative Director:**	Paul Anderson
Art Director:	Emil Frid		**Copywriters:**	Paul Anderson
Photographer:	Pelle Berglund			Linda Spencer
Client:	Metro Newspaper		**Art Director:**	Paul Anderson
			Photographer:	Martin Barraud
			Illustrator:	Carlo De-Martini
			Client:	Investment Week Trade Publication

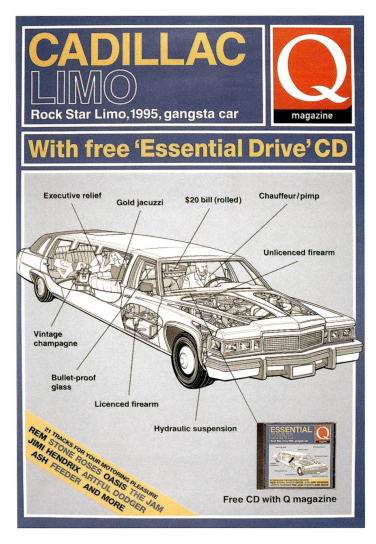
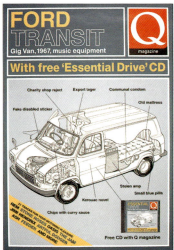
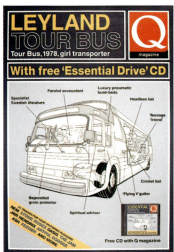
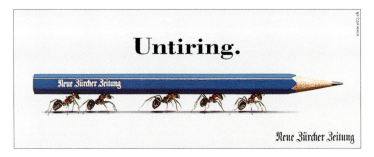

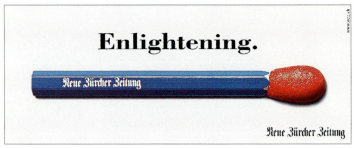

Agency:	Mother, London	Agency:	Publicis, Zürich
Creative Directors:	Robert Saville	Creative Director:	Markus Gut
	Mark Waites	Copywriter:	Johnny Jost
Copywriter:	Joe de Souza	Art Director:	Ralph Halder
Art Director:	Sam Walker	Client:	Neue Zürcher Zeitung
Client:	Q Music Magazine		Newspaper

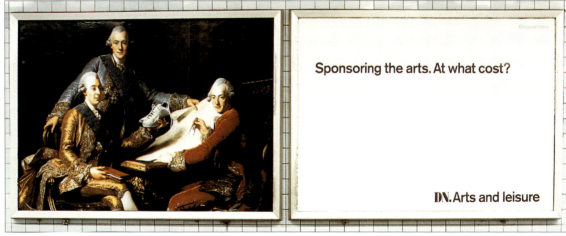

Agency:	Lowe Brindfors, Stockholm
Creative Director:	Johan Nilsson
Copywriters:	Johan Nilsson
	Björn Persson
	Amalia Pitsiava
Art Directors:	Patrick Waters
	Kristofer Mårtensson
	Lisa Engart
Photographers:	Jens Gustafsson
	Tobias Regell
Client:	Dagens Nyheter Newspaper

310 Recreation & Leisure

Agency:	hasan & partners, Helsinki
Account Manager:	Petteri Anttila
Copywriters:	Timo Everi
	Sari Mikkonen-Mannila
Art Director:	Kimmo Kivilahti
Client:	Kansallis National Museum

TÆNK HVIS DU VANDT...

Agency:	Lowe Lintas, Copenhagen
Creative Director:	Hans-Henrik Langevad
Copywriter:	Kim Juul-Andersen
Art Director:	Mads Kold
Production:	EPA International, Stockholm
Director:	Axel Lindström
Producer:	Annelie Lindström
Photographer:	Carl Sundberg
Client:	Danish Lottery, "Keep on Dreaming"

Cruising a California highway in his red convertible, a young man is living the American dream. Things couldn't get any better – until he picks up a pretty hitchhiker. He puts his hand on her knee. She smiles. Then he hears: "I don't know where you're going, young man – but I get off at the next stop." Cut to the interior of a train carriage, where he has put his hand on the knee of a thickset elderly woman. He snaps out of his daydream, noticing that the 'hitchhiker' is sitting opposite. He looks down at his lottery ticket. Imagine winning...

Recreation & Leisure

Agency:	TBWA\Paris
Creative Directors:	Eric Holden
	Remi Noel
Copywriter:	Remi Noel
Art Director:	Eric Holden
Production:	1/33
Director:	David Charhon
Producer:	Nathalie Gueirard
Client:	Sony Playstation, Formula One 2001, "The Pit"

A young guy is playing Formula One 2001 on his Sony Playstation. When the commentary says: "And the German driver has just entered the pits," his family get in on the act, playing the part of mechanics as they dust him down, top up his orange juice and vacuum under his seat. The flag drops, and he's off.

Agency:	TBWA\Paris
Creative Directors:	Eric Holden
	Remi Noel
Copywriter:	Remi Noel
Art Director:	Eric Holden
Photographer:	Nick Meek
Client:	Sony Playstation, Gran Turismo 3

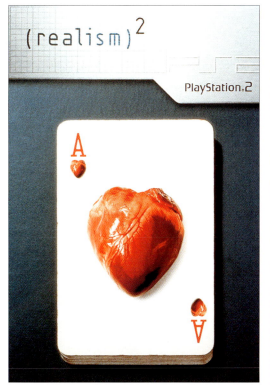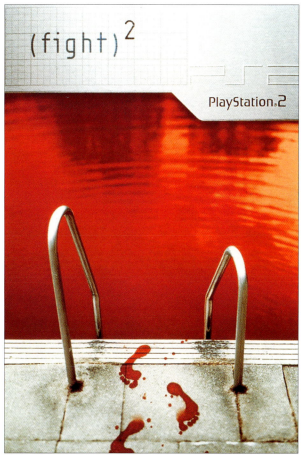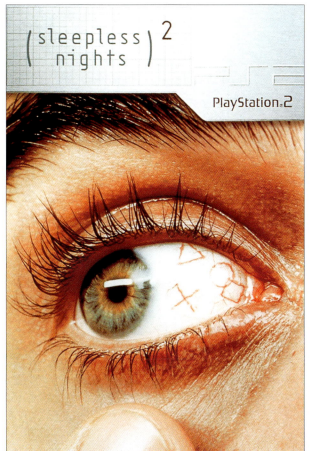

Recreation & Leisure   313

Agency:	TBWA\Paris
Creative Directors:	Jorge Carreno
	Eric Helias
Copywriter:	Eric Helias
Art Director:	Jorge Carreno
Photographers:	Joe Magrean
	Oliver Rheindorf
Client:	Sony Playstation 2

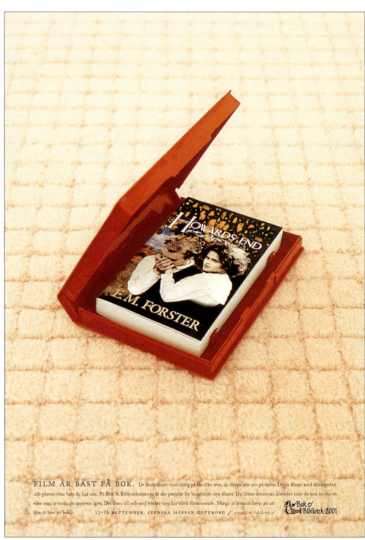

314 Recreation & Leisure

Agency: Young & Rubicam, Lisbon	**Agency:** Jerlov & Körberg, Gothenburg	Films are best as books.
Creative Director: Albano Homem de Melo	**Creative Director:** Pelle Körberg	
Copywriter: Gabriela Hunnicutt	**Copywriters:** Johan Brink, Patrik Vult von Steyern	
Art Director: Claudio Quartilho	**Art Director:** Ola Lundin	
Client: Porto 2001, Horror Film Festival	**Photographers:** Magnus Cimmerbeck, Magnus Johansson	
	Client: Gothenburg International Book Fair	

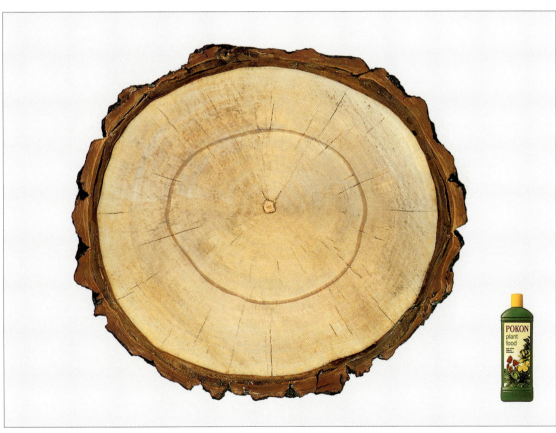

Agency:	Xynias, Wetzel, von Büren, Munich	Agencies:	PMSvW/Y&R, Amsterdam
Creative Directors:	Thilo von Büren Marc Strotmann	Creative Directors:	Marcel Hartog Jeroen van Zwam
Copywriter:	Marc Strotmann	Copywriter:	Jaap Langenberg
Art Director:	Chris Mayrhofer	Art Director:	Michiel Keser
Photographer:	Alex Herzog	Photographer:	David Kater
Client:	Leo's Sports Club	Client:	Pokon Plant Food

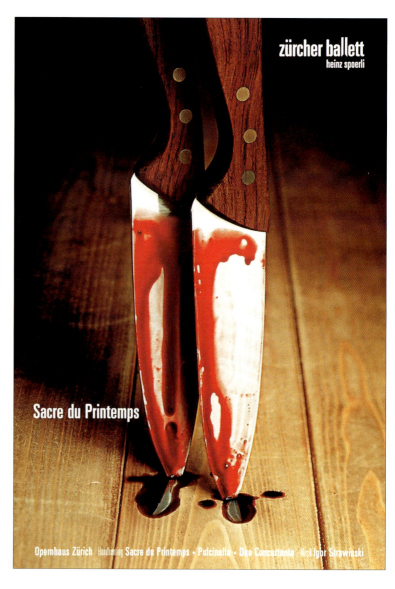

316 Recreation & Leisure

Agency:	Young & Rubicam, Lisbon	Agency:	McCann-Erickson, Geneva
Creative Supervisors:	Susana Sequeira Lourenço Thomaz	Creative Director:	Frank Bodin
Creative Director:	Albano Homem de Melo	Art Directors:	Lisa Leuch Sarah Mundhenke
Copywriter:	Pedro Lima	Photographer:	Volker Möhrke
Art Director:	Andre Navarro	Client:	Zürich Ballet
Client:	Leaf, Lisbon Erotic Advertising Festival		

The Nutcracker

The Rites of Spring

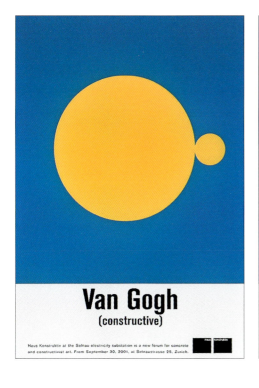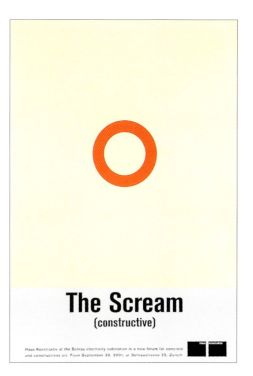

Agency:	Wirz Werbung, Zürich	**Agency:**	TBWA\London
Creative Director:	Matthias Freuler	**Creative Director:**	Trevor Beattie
Copywriter:	Roy Spring	**Copywriter:**	Sam Taylor
Art Director:	Marietta Albinus	**Art Director:**	Tony St. Leger
Client:	Haus Konstruktiv, Art Museum	**Production:**	Mustard
		Producers:	John Doris Catharine Chesterman
		Client:	Sony Playstation 2, "Jimmy Dynamite"

We're at an audition, and a man holds up a card reading: "Jimmy Dynamite." He looks trendy, in an off-beat kind of way, and wears impenetrable dark glasses. Off-camera, a woman says: "Would you mind taking your glasses off for just a minute?" Jimmy refuses – he never takes off his shades. He makes a strange grimace, and looks pleased with himself. "They're part of my face," he adds. In fact, Jimmy is perfect casting for a Playstation 2 ad – he plays by his own rules.

Recreation & Leisure

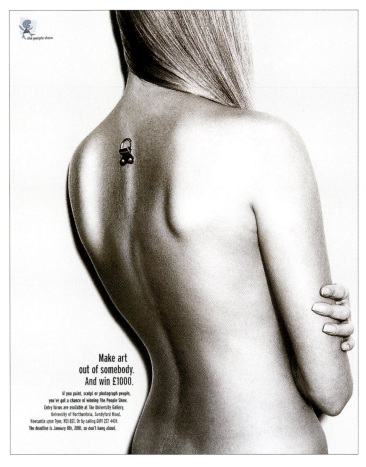
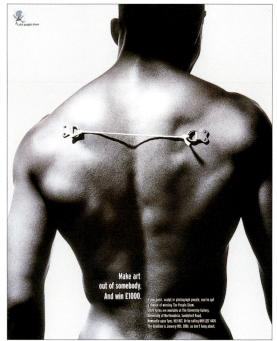

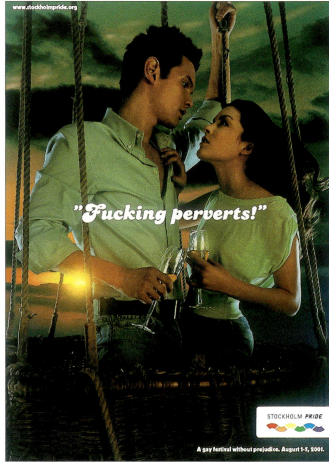

Recreation & Leisure

Agency:	Cravens Advertising, Newcastle Upon Tyne	**Agency:**	Ogilvy Advertising, Stockholm
Creative Director:	Peter Straughan	**Creative Director:**	Mats Fridehall
Copywriter:	Stephen Carrol	**Copywriter:**	Johannes Ivarsson
Art Director:	Phil Barnes	**Art Director:**	Richard Mellberg
Photographer:	Michael Baister	**Photographer:**	Calle Stoltz
Client:	University of Northumbria Art Competition	**Client:**	Stockholm Pride Festival

Agency:	Jung von Matt, Hamburg
Creative Directors:	Niels Alzen
	Thim Wagner
Copywriters:	Willy Kaussen
	Jens Daum
Art Directors:	Christian Reimer
	Hans Weishaeupl
	Raphael Milczarek
Illustrator:	Felix Reidenbach
Client:	CinemaxX Cinemas

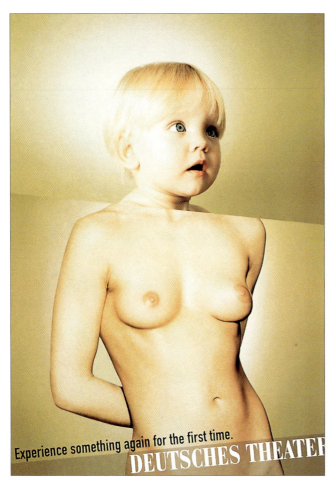
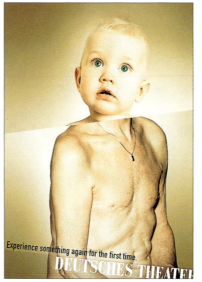
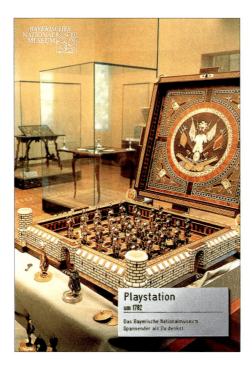
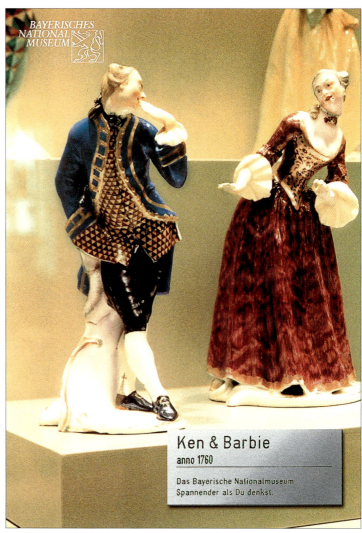

Agency: Scholz & Friends, Berlin	**Agency:** Serviceplan, Munich
Creative Directors: Pius Walker, Johannes Krempl	**Creative Director:** Sabine Brugge
	Copywriter: Stefan Kroiss
	Art Director: Therese Stuessel
Photographer: Uwe Düttmann	**Photographer:** Thomas Spiessl
Client: Deutsches Theater	**Client:** Bayerisches National Museum

Agency: Renommé, Oslo **Creative Director:** Jarle Ryne **Copywriter:** Øyvind Try-Leiner **Art Director:** Jarle Ryne **Photographer:** Roger Nabben **Client:** Jarlsberg Race Track	**Agency:** Klaar Kiming, Hamburg **Creative Directors:** Peer Hartog Oliver Jochens **Copywriter:** Peer Hartog **Art Director:** Oliver Jochens **Production:** Petersen Naumann **Director:** Steven Wilhelm **Client:** Nawrot Reduta Acting School, "Dives"	A Strauss waltz complements scenes of soccer players 'diving' – in other words, faking fouls or injuries in order to gain time or penalties. In what appears to be a well-choreographed ballet, the players crash to the ground, clutch their limbs, writhe in agony, or simply fall over on the spot, as if knocked over by a giant, invisible hand. With acting skills as poor as these, the ad suggests, they should enrol at the Nawrot Reduta Acting School.

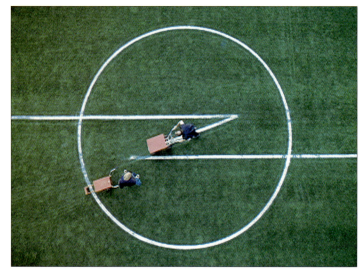

322 Recreation & Leisure

Agency:	Lowe Lintas, Copenhagen
Creative Director:	Hans-Henrik Langevad
Copywriter:	Kim Juul-Andersen
Art Director:	Mads Kold
Production:	Parafilm
Director:	Søren Fauli
Producer:	Christina Bostofte
Client:	Danish Lottery, "Arab"

A Dane is cycling down a quiet street, when a limousine glides out of a driveway and knocks him off his bike. A well-dressed Arab emerges and begins apologising profusely in Arabic. He offers the Dane a Ferrari in recompense, dangling the keys. Misunder—standing, the furious Dane accuses the Arab of showing off. Mortified, the Arab offers the Dane his house. But the cyclist still doesn't get it. "Yes, you came from there, I came from here – it's still your fault." He cycles off. Some people never give their luck a chance – but you can, by playing the lottery.

Agency:	McCann-Erickson, Frankfurt
Creative Director:	Dietmar Reinhard
Copywriter:	Peter Römmelt
Art Director:	Simon Oppmann
Production:	Petersen Naumann Film, Hamburg
Director:	Christoph Klenzendorf
Producer:	Justine Coggins
Client:	Opel Football Tournament, "Jubiläums Trailer"

Two men are painting a white line on a playing field, approaching each other from either side of the pitch. But when they get to the middle – surprise, surprise – they've missed each other completely. They scratch their heads. Then one of the men just shrugs and joins the lines together, creating a 'Z'. But it's okay – seen from above, the design looks just like the Opel logo, and the marque is sponsoring the event.

Agency:	Ogilvy & Mather, Frankfurt	Agency:	Duval Guillaume, Brussels
Copywriter:	Cora Walker	Creative Director:	Jens Mortier
Art Director:	Alexander Heil	Copywriter:	Jens Mortier
Client:	Museums of Frankfurt	Art Director:	Philippe de Ceuster
		Photographer:	Frank Uyttenhove
		Illustrator:	Mark Borgions
		Client:	Belgian Olympic Committee

Agency:	The Leith Agency, Edinburgh
Creative Director:	Gerry Farrell
Copywriter:	Dougal Wilson
Art Director:	Dougal Wilson
Director:	Dougal Wilson
Producer:	Dougal Wilson
Client:	The Leith Agency, "Xmas Card"

This Christmas greeting, sent via email to clients and contacts, features a kitsch 'snow dome' containing a small building with the words 'The Leith Agency' on it. A hand comes into frame and shakes the dome. Then we see the effect inside the agency, where staffers tumble from side-to-side in corridors, collapse under piles of falling video cassettes, and are thrown from their seats around the boardroom table. The hand replaces the dome. Merry Christmas, from The Leith Agency.

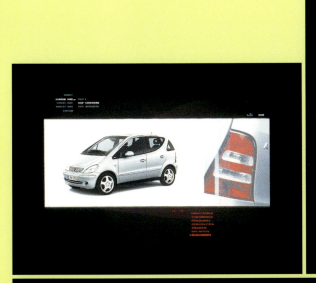
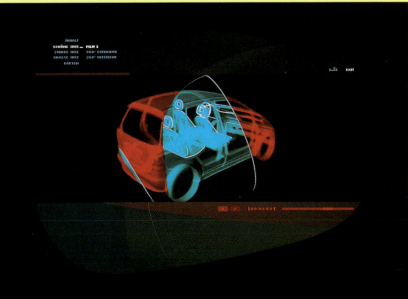
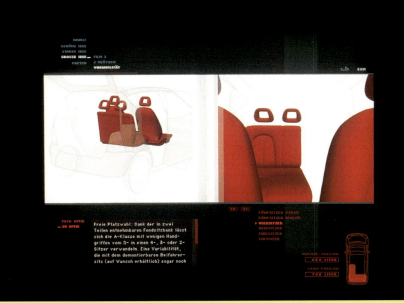
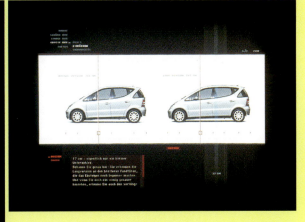

 Interactive: CD Roms 325

Agency:	Scholz & Volkmer, Wiesbaden	This interactive CD-Rom was designed to communicate the style and sleekness of the A-Class, as well as its technical features, and the introduction of the longer wheelbase model for those who need more space. Different levels include interactive test drives, crash-test videos, three-dimensional animations, and finally all the facts that help buyers determine exactly what they want from their car.
Creative Director:	Michael Volkmer	
Copywriter:	Katharina Schlungs	
Art Director:	Heike Brockmann	
Client:	Mercedes-Benz A-Class CD Rom	

326   Interactive: Banners

Agency:	Forsman & Bodenfors, Gothenburg	An animated toddler gets up to all sorts of mischief in a living room, while a link to the Libero website provides access to information about child safety in the home.
Copywriters:	Jesper Lövkvist	
	Jonas Enghage	
Art Directors:	Tobias Ottahall	
	Kim Cramer	
	Mattias Stridbeck	
	Marcus Edin	
Client:	Libero Up & Go Diapers	

Agency:	Framfab Denmark, Copenhagen
Creative Director:	Lars Bastholm
Copywriter:	Jamie McPhee
Art Director:	Rasmus Frandsen
Client:	Nike Freestyle Website

Working in tandem with a Nike advertising campaign, which showed basketball, football and skateboard pros improvising tricks and techniques to music, the interactive site enabled visitors to watch individual stars strutting their stuff. Bios, personalised screen savers, wallpaper and the soundtrack to the ad could also be downloaded, and there was also an opportunity to design and sign your own sports shoe.

328 Interactive

Agency:	The Leith Agency, Edinburgh
Creative Director:	Gerry Farrell
Copywriters:	Chris & Lee
Production:	Iodine Media
Director:	Michael Keillor
Producers:	Michael Keillor, Pete Thornton
Client:	Balderdash Game, "Taxi", "Office" & "Bed"

Three email films illustrating the art of bluffing to promote the Balderdash game. In the first, a man demonstrates how to get a free taxi ride by chewing a piece of soap that makes him foam at the mouth. In the second, a young man pretends to have been violently sick at work – by pouring two tins of vegetable soup onto his desk and lying face-down in the mess. And in the final spot, a man has wet the bed, and bluffs his way out of it by blaming the dog. Balderdash – you have to bluff, to win.

Agency:	The Leith Agency, Edinburgh
Creative Director:	Gerry Farrell
Copywriters:	Chris & Lee
Production:	MTP
Director:	Dougal Wilson
Producers:	James Jeffries, Dougal Wilson
Client:	Articulate Game, "Seat", "Chicken" & "Coffee"

Three compromising situations. In the first, a man sits in a waiting room. When the receptionist leaves for a few moments, he crosses to her seat and begins sniffing it. But she catches him in the perverse act. In the second, things get worse – a man's wife discovers him naked, in front of the fridge, using an uncooked chicken as a masturbation aid. And in the third spot, a young office worker wreaks revenge on his colleagues by urinating into the coffee pot – but he hasn't spotted one of them trying to repair the photocopier. Articulate – get ready to do some talking.

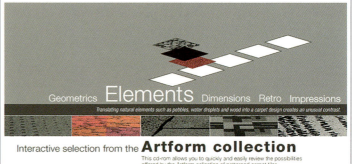

Interactive

Agency:	Libens, Ghewy & Fauconnier, Brussels		**Agency:**	AGH & Friends, 'S'Hertogenbosch
Creative Directors:	Christophe Ghewy, Luc Libens		**Creative Director:**	Kees de Vos
Copywriter:	Antoine Wellens		**Copywriters:**	Martijn van der Ven, Paula Terreehorst
Art Director:	Laurent Duffaut		**Art Director:**	Jurgen van Zachten
Director:	Laurent Duffaut		**Photographer:**	Josée Riele
Producer:	Hans Roels		**Client:**	Desso, Carpet Tiles CD Rom
Client:	De Streekkrant Free Newspaper, "Post Box", "Chair" & "Pellet"			

Three email films. In the first, a newspaper boy cycles up to a mailbox and drops the free newspaper inside. The box crashes to the ground. In the second, a man sits at his desk, and picks up the paper. His chair buckles under the weight. And finally, two men are larking around in their office, throwing balls of paper at each other. But a page torn from De Streekkrant sends one of the men flying off his seat. The newspaper adds weight to your ads.

The CD-Rom enabled users to create their own flooring using Desso carpet tiles. A toolbox contained 60 different colours, six possible structures and 35 possible designs.

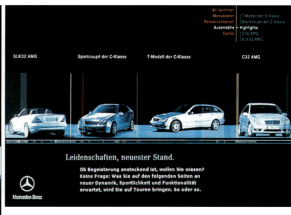

Agency:	Scholz & Volkmer, Wiesbaden	The website was developed specifically for the North American International Motor Show 2001 in Detroit. It included the latest news from the event, as well as a history of Mercedes, which was celebrating its 100th anniversary. At the heart of the site was a 'personalities' section, containing details of all those who had made a difference to the Mercedes brand, from founders to racing drivers. Elsewhere, users could view the latest Mercedes models.	Agency: Scholz & Volkmer, Wiesbaden
Creative Director:	Anette Scholz		Creative Director: Michael Volkmer
Copywriter:	Chris Kohl		Art Director: Heike Brockmann
Art Director:	Oliver Aumann		Client: Ralf Wengenmayr, Composer
Client:	Mercedes-Benz		

The site was designed to promote Ralf Wengenmayr, the German composer of film and advertising theme music. Its aim was to demonstrate the broad range of his work, with details of some of his projects. Users could click on his biography and references, send a contact message – and most importantly of all, listen to the music.

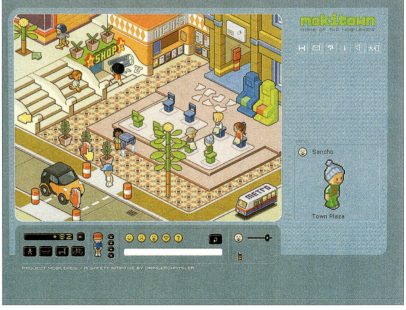

332 Interactive

Agency:	BBDO InterOne, Munich
Creative Director:	Stefan Kurzweg
Copywriter:	Julia Grunenberg
Art Directors:	Wolfgang Hofmann
	Rüdiger Woerner
Client:	Mi Adidas Workout Camp

Running in tandem with an offline campaign, the Mi Adidas website was adapted to include a fitness programme for women, with links to products.

Agency:	Neue Digitale, Frankfurt
Creative Director:	Olaf Czeschner
Copywriter:	Sascha Bosio
Art Director:	Rolf Borcherding
Client:	Mokitown

Supported by the car manufacturer DaimlerChrysler, the site was designed to educate children about road safety. Moki (Mo-bile Ki-ds) Town was a virtual landscape where kids between eight and twelve could come and play, learning in the process how to pay attention to the hazards presented by traffic.

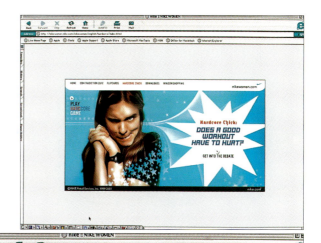

Agency:	AGI, Stuttgart	**Agency:**	Framfab, Copenhagen
Creative Director:	Christian Schwarm	**Creative Director:**	Lars Bastholm
Copywriter:	Stefanie Katzschke	**Copywriter:**	Jamie McPhee
Photographer:	Brigitte Richter	**Art Director:**	Lars Cortsen
Client:	Ca'n Roses Hotel	**Client:**	Nike Women Site

Some places don't lend themselves to description – they must be experienced. This was the thinking behind a highly visual site designed to introduce visitors to one of Mallorca's most charming hotels.

The humorous site enables women to view the latest Nike gear, send messages to friends, air problems, and download wallpaper and screensavers that reflect their daily lives and concerns.

Interactive

Agencies:	Moonwalk, Stockholm St. Lukes, Stockholm	Speedy Tomato is a portal enabling access to the web through mobile phones and other hand-held devices. For the company's website, the agency invented the Monster Without A Mouth – a rather sad character who can't communicate, thus representing the direct opposite of the Speedy Tomato communication experience.	**Agency:**	Moonwalk, Stockholm	Get Some Real is an anti-internet porn campaign run by women's magazine Darling. The website gives female users the option of designing fake internet porn pages – with a selection of phrases such as Horny In Hungary or Naked Russian Girls. When men click to access the sites, they receive a message: "Get Some Real – porn is fake, girls are real."
Creative Director:	C. Sjönell & T. Hearn		**Creative Director:**	Calle Sjönell	
Copywriters:	F. Lundgren & N. Cooper		**Copywriter:**	Anna Ander	
Art Directors:	J. Mogren, J. Westmen & Y. Zu Innhausen und Knyphausen		**Art Director:**	Jesper Löfroth	
			Production:	Jessica Olander	
			Peter Janson	Didde Brockman	
Production:	Fido Film		**Producers:**	Sofia Nilsson Johanna Järnfeldt	
Producers:	Linus Nicklasson Felix af Ekenstam Didde Brockman		**Client:**	Darling Magazine, Get Some Real Campaign	
Client:	Speedy Tomato				

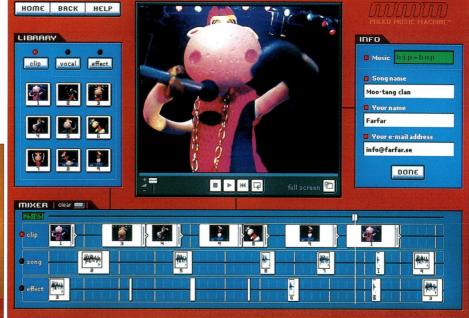

Agency:	TBWA\E-Company, Amsterdam	
Creative Director:	Jurrienne Ossewold	
Art Director:	Margo Rouwhorst	
Client:	Van Gogh Museum, Light Exhibition	

The Light! Exhibition opened at the Van Gogh museum in Amsterdam on 20 October 2000, and detailed the evolving relationship between light and society from 1750 to 1900. The site contained images of the works shown in the exhibition, online experiments with light, and a timeline detailing the advances man has made in lighting his environment.

Agency:	Romson, Stockholm
Copywriter:	Jacob Nelson
Art Director:	Magnus Ingerstedt
Production:	Farfar, Stockholm
Producer:	Matias Palm-Jensen
Client:	Milko Fruit Yoghurt

With the Milko Music Machine website, you could create your own rock video – featuring wannabe star The Mountain Cow – and mail it to friends.

Interactive 335

336 New Media

Agency:	Publicis, Amstelveen
Copywriter:	Pim Gerrits
Art Director:	Ben Lammers
Photographer:	Sylvester van der Vlugt
Client:	Bonzo Dogfood

These posters were placed in parks in several Dutch cities. They emitted an ultrasonic noise which humans could not hear, but dogs could. The curious hounds were drawn towards the posters, and began to bark. The posters were programmed to emit the sound at intervals, otherwise the owners would have had a hard time pulling their dogs away!

Agency:	Publicis, Zürich	Agency:	Edson, FCB, Lisbon
Creative Director:	Markus Gut	Creative Director:	Edson Athayde
Copywriter:	Markus Tränkle	Copywriter:	Ricardo Miranda
Art Director:	Ralph Halder	Art Director:	Liliana Dantas
Photographer:	Felix Streuli	Client:	Raid Insecticide
Client:	APG Billboards		

Passers-by could see the owl clearly during the day, but only its glowing eyes were visible at night – promoting the benefits of APG luminous billboards.

These 'magic glasses' enabled users to see what Raid did to insects in their home – in fact, they disappeared – thanks to an optical effect.

Agency:	Maestro Design & Advertising, Amsterdam
Client:	Amsterdam City Council

"Cut it out!" Public service advertising became temporary art when these cut-out dogs were placed in the heart of Amsterdam early one morning. Information brochures were handed out, urging dog owners to clean up after their pets, using newly-installed 'dog dirt' bins.

Agency:	Michael Conrad & Leo Burnett, Frankfurt
Creative Director:	Andreas Pauli
Copywriter:	Mathias Henkel
Art Director:	Thomas Ruffert
Client:	Focus Book of Doctors

"Doctor?" Focus magazine's annual list of doctors is Germany's most comprehensive guide. The 'guerrilla advertising' campaign used strategically placed 'plasters' to point out that a specialist is always close by.

Agency:	Jung von Matt, Hamburg	In 1999 two newborn babies were found dead on a rubbish heap in Hamburg. The horrific discovery led to the creation of the Project Foundling Baby Hatch. This is literally a series of booths, or 'hatches', in which mothers leave their unwanted babies - to be received and cared for on the other side - thus guaranteeing the mothers complete anonymity. The poster reads: "Do you think this picture is too much? Your donation deletes a square."	
Creative Director:	Deneke von Weltzien		
Copywriter:	Diana Pauser		
Art Director:	Gertrud Eisele		
Photographer:	Michaela Rehn		
Client:	Project Foundling		

Agency: Springer & Jacoby, Hamburg
Creative Directors: Thomas Walmrath, Andreas Geyer, Ulrich Zünkeler
Copywriter: Jan Krause
Art Directors: Cathrine Sundqvist, Tanja Ritter
Photographer: Sebastian Schobbert
Client: Deutsche Telekom

"Make love" suggests this giant installation at the Brandenburg Gate in Berlin, on the occasion of the Love Parade.

Agency:	Juraj Vaculík – Creative Studio, Bratislava	As the climax of a campaign utilising the comic potential of pop groups' names, the agency created a "musical" installation, enabling passers-by to press a button and hear songs by the likes of The Police, or Earth, Wind & Fire.	Agency:	Michael Conrad & Leo Burnett, Frankfurt	Trendy night-clubbers also tend to take pride in their appearance. Where could they get shoulders so broad that their clothes would need a giant hanger? At the Fitness Company gym, whose ingenious marketing tool was placed in the cloakrooms of hip bars and nightclubs in Frankfurt.
Creative Director:	Juraj Vaculík		Creative Directors:	Uwe Marquardt Kerrin Nausch	
Copywriter:	Juraj Vaculík		Copywriter:	Jörg Hoffmann	
Art Director:	Adrian Leško		Art Director:	Mariko Neumeister	
Client:	Radio B1		Client:	Fitness Company	

Agency:	Publicis, Zürich	Mirrors installed in buses suggested that those looking in them might be in need of certain services – such as a solarium, a hairdresser, or even a plastic surgeon!	**Agency:**	D'Arcy, Amsterdam	The Hague's accordion bus suggested that it was the most efficient mode of transport for getting to the North Sea Jazz Festival.
Creative Director:	Jean Etienne Aebi		**Copywriter:**	Piebe Piebenga	
Copywriters:	Michael Kathe		**Art Director:**	Darre van Dijk	
	Michael Manzardo		**Photographer:**	Reinoud Klazes	
Art Director:	Ralf Kostgeld		**Client:**	The Hague	
Client:	Yellow Pages			Public Transport Service	

Agency:	BDH\TBWA, Manchester	Installed at bus shelters, the slightly convex mirror made those looking into it appear slimmer – demonstrating the benefits of drinking Diet Tizer.
Creative Director:	Danny Brooke-Taylor	
Copywriter:	Michael Murray	
Art Director:	Chris Lear	
Client:	Diet Tizer	

Agency:	Maher Bird Associates, London	Dwarfs were hired to distribute 2,700 miniature popcorn boxes around London, to promote the Soho Short Film Festival.
Creative Director:	Graham Kerr	
Copywriter:	Patrick Robertson	
Art Director:	Darren McKay	
Photographer:	Darren McKay	
Client:	Soho Short Film Festival	

Agency:	Mediamix, Maribor	"It's taxi time!" Slovenia has a high number of alcohol-related car accidents. This responsible advertising message was placed on the bottoms of glasses in bars, becoming visible when a person had finished their drink – and would be ill-advised to drive home.	Agency:	Advico Young & Rubicam, Zürich	"Forgotten" luggage placed on airport carousels reminded travellers of Kuoni's advertising promise: vacations that make you forget everything.
Creative Director:	Toni Tomašek		Creative Director:	Martin Spillmann	
Art Director:	Iztok Virant		Copywriter:	Peter Rettinghausen	
Photographer:	Andrej Cvetnič		Art Director:	Hélène Forster	
Client:	Taxi Plus		Client:	Kuoni Reisen Travel	

New Media

Agency:	Force, Forsman & Bodenfors, Gothenburg	During the summer of 2001, people dressed as walking post offices – complete with boxes strapped to their backs – allowed people to buy postcards and stamps, write a message to a friend, and post it there and then.
Copywriters:	Mats Utberg	
	Lisa Agnetun	
Art Director:	Sara Jedenberg	
Client:	The Swedish Post Office	

Agency:	Springer & Jacoby, Hamburg	This giant newspaper, placed inside a regular daily newspaper, contained colourful stories illustrating people's passion for the Mercedes brand. It was the largest ad ever placed in a daily paper.
Creative Directors:	Alexander Schill	
	Axel Thomsen	
Copywriter:	Christoph Hildebrand	
Art Directors:	Sven Klohk	
	Kirsa Plewnia	
Client:	Mercedes-Benz	

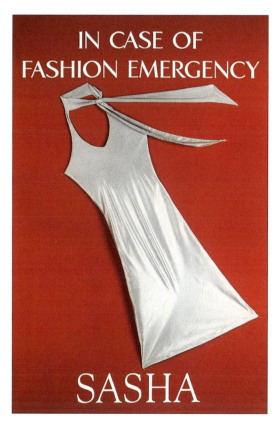
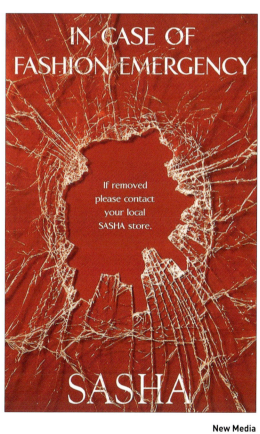

Agency:	FCB, Berlin	The couple shown on this double page spread were separated by a third page representing the Berlin Wall to promote SAT 1's TV film, "The Tunnel".
Creative Directors:	Patrick Thiede, Waldemar Konopka	
Copywriter:	Torben Wrobel	
Art Director:	Kati Paech	
Client:	SAT 1	

Agency:	AFA Advertising, Dublin	The campaign used real garments – items from Sasha's winter range – placed behind the glass sides of bus shelters. Other shelters nearby were mocked up to look as if the glass had been smashed and the covetable item stolen. "If removed, contact your local Sasha store." Newspaper ads in the style of articles detailing the 'crimes' supported the campaign.
Creative Director:	Joe Collins	
Art Director:	Greg Murray	
Photographer:	Eugene Langan	
Client:	Sasha Winter Collection	

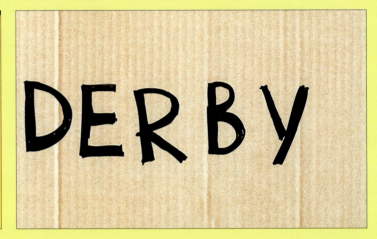

Direct Marketing

Agency:	Harrison Troughton Wunderman, London
Creative Directors:	Graham Mills Jack Nolan
Copywriter:	Stephen Timms
Art Director:	Anthony Cliff
Client:	AA Roadside Assistance

AA Roadside Assistance is the UK's biggest breakdown recovery service. This mailing was sent to those whose membership had lapsed, suggesting that hitchhiking would be the only way to get home if they did not re-join the service. The cards were digitally personalised to show the recipients' home town.

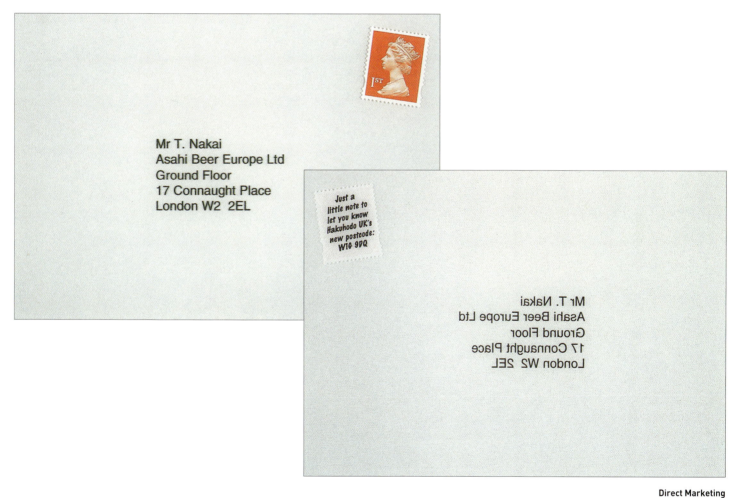

Direct Marketing 347

Agency:	JBR McCann Direkte, Oslo
Creative Director:	Jan Petter Ågren
Copywriter:	Erik Ingvoldstad
Art Director:	Charlotte Havstad
Client:	DMA Chicago 2001

To promote the Direct Marketing Association conference in Chicago, each potential delegate received a goldfish in a bag, a fish bowl and sand, a plastic skyline of the city and a brochure. The fish were all named after famous Chicago personalities, such as sportsmen Shoeless Joe Jackson and Fred "The Refrigerator" Perry, and were personally delivered with care instructions to make sure they came to no harm. They could also be returned if recipients did not want them.

Agency:	Hakuhodo UK, London
Creative Director:	Tim Johnson
Copywriter:	Tim Johnson
Art Director:	Tim Johnson
Client:	Hakuhodo UK, Change of Postcode

This note reminding clients about a change of postcode was written on the back of a stamp, stuck to a transparent postcard!

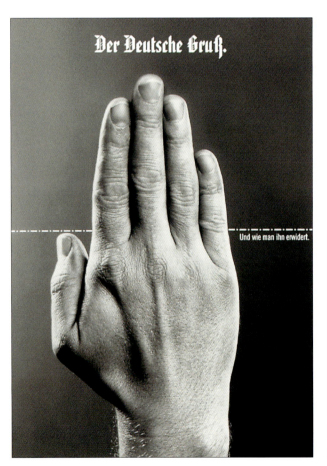
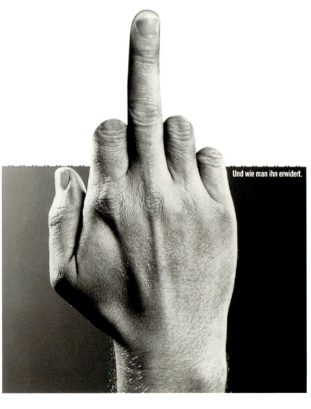

Direct Marketing

Agency:	Jerlov & Körberg, Gothenburg
Creative Director:	Pelle Körberg
Copywriters:	Patrik Vult von Steyern, Johan Brink
Art Director:	Ola Lundin
Client:	Classic Garden Outdoor Furniture

Two imaginative invitations. The Champagne bottle top was a teaser for the launch of a new range of metal garden chairs. Promoting a separate event for the same client, the note on the grass-stained chinos says: "Classic Garden invites you to a summer lunch in the garden."

Agency:	Scholz & Friends, Berlin
Creative Directors:	Stephan Ganser, Eric Urmetzer
Copywriter:	Axel Lawaczeck
Art Director:	Sven Drobnitza
Client:	Anti-Nazi Initiative

"The German salute...and how to reply." Half of the perforated postcard folds back, leaving enough of the hand visible to show the right response to a Nazi salute.

Agency:	Forsman & Bodenfors, Gothenburg	This letter was sent to law firms just before Christmas, asking them to do some of the work that the Salvation Army does...Or if they couldn't handle it, to donate money.
Copywriter:	Martin Ringqvist	
Art Directors:	Staffan Forsman, Staffan Håkanson	
Client:	Salvation Army	

Agency:	Jerlov & Körberg, Gothenburg	Ever seen a movie that was better than the book? "Films are best when they're in books," is the message behind this campaign promoting one of the world's biggest book fairs. It utilised books inserted into the video boxes of the films they inspired.
Creative Director:	Pelle Körberg	
Copywriters:	Johan Brink, Patrick Vult von Steyern	
Art Director:	Ola Lundin	
Client:	Gothenburg International Book Fair	

Direct Marketing

Direct Marketing

Agency:	DEC, Barcelona
Creative Director:	Berta Loran
Copywriter:	Gabriel Catalá
Art Director:	Valentín Soto
Client:	Fundació Èxit

Fundació Èxit aims to offer a better future to underprivileged adolescents, by retraining them and helping them find jobs. The mailing, aimed at businesses in Catalonia, featured a cardboard box with a litter bin inside. At the bottom of the bin was a crumpled piece of paper, which unfolded into a poster of a teenager. "This is Luis. You can help him or throw him back into the bin." The poster went on to describe the work of the foundation, and give details of what the reader could do to help. Follow-up mailings tracked Luis's success and introduced other teenagers in need of help.

Agency:	OgilvyOne Worldwide, Frankfurt
Creative Director:	Christine Blum-Heuser
Copywriter:	Susanne Lippert
Art Director:	Christine Schmidt
Client:	Dresdner Bank

The objective was to convince chief executives that Dresdner Bank could care for their company through all the stages of its development – symbolised by the growth rings of a tree. The living Bonsai tree, which was mailed out with a brochure, also reminded recipients that their investments needed careful tending every day.

Agency:	Jerlov & Körberg, Gothenburg	**Agency:**	Arih Advertising Agency, Ljubljana	The greeting card in this envelope is made of paper that contains pine seed. Don't keep it and don't throw it in the garbage! Throw it away in the forest by the end of January. Even better, dig a shallow hole in the ground and bury it there. Maybe you will plant a natural air freshener.
Creative Director:	Fredrik Jerlov	**Creative Director:**	Igor Arih	
Copywriter:	Elisabeth Berlander	**Copywriter:**	Gal Erbežnik	
Art Director:	Mia Stangertz	**Art Director:**	Slavimir Stojanovič	
Client:	IHM Business School	**Client:**	Arih Advertising, New Year's Greeting Card	

352 **Direct Marketing**

Agency:	Euro RSCG Catapult, Zürich	This headed paper has 18 holes, of course.
Creative Directors:	Frank Bodin Hanspeter Wüthrich	
Art Director:	Miro Beck	
Client:	IAA & Basler Mediengruppe Golf Cup	

Agency:	Scholz & Friends, Berlin	To encourage businesses to invest in Baden-Württemberg, they were sent a box containing one of the location's most famous products: a teddy bear, to remind them of their childhood affection for products from the region.
Creative Directors:	Martin Pross Sebastian Turner Joachim Schoepfer	
Copywriter:	Benedikt Goettert	
Art Directors:	Angela Franchini Marco Fusz	
Client:	Baden-Württemberg	

Agency:	JBR McCann Direkte, Oslo	Feeling hungry for some digital freshware? As an invitation to an e-business seminar, the bank's customers and prospects were sent a variety of confectionary technology products – including a chocolate CD-Rom showing the seminar's date, and a chocolate box laptop with a keyboard displaying the names of the speakers.	**Agency:** claydonheeleyjonesmason, London
Creative Director:	Jan Petter Ågren		**Creative Directors:** Pete Harle, Dave Woods
Copywriter:	Børge Skråmestø		**Copywriter:** Christina Mitsis
Art Director:	Anette Waage Mohn		**Art Director:** Cathryn Jayne
Client:	Gjensidige NOR Savings Bank		**Client:** British Airways, Turks & Caicos Route

Mailer to promote a new BA flight to the Caribbean islands of Turks and Caicos, "taking you straight to paradise". On the shell was written: "Listen."

Direct Marketing

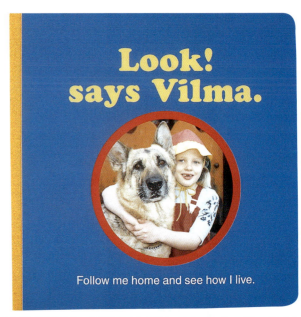
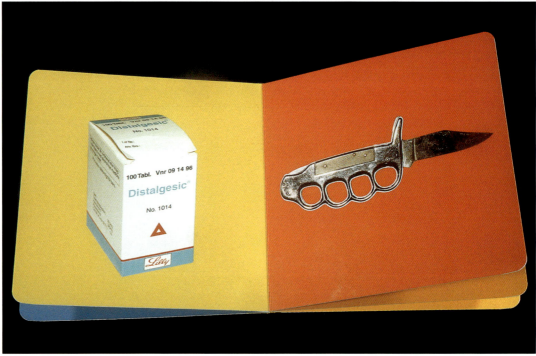

Direct Marketing

Agency:	Ehrenstråhle & Co., Stockholm
Copywriter:	Mats Brun
Art Director:	Bertil Timan
Client:	Infonet

"All you need to know to create a global internet solution." The title of a book that contained only one word – Infonet. All other pages were blank.

Agency:	ANR BBDO, Gothenburg
Creative Director:	Christer Allansson
Copywriter:	Håkan Larsson
Art Director:	Hans-Erik Andreasson
Photographer:	Mikael Olsson
Client:	Gothenburg Homeless Shelter

What looked like a classic children's book was actually designed to raise awareness of the way homeless kids are under threat from drugs and violence.

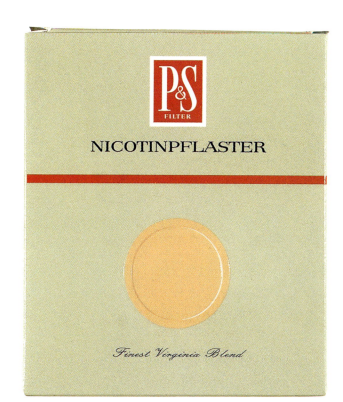

Agency:	Springer & Jacoby, Hamburg	The first nicotine patch with the "finest Virginia blend" from P&S cigarettes. Handed out in cinemas and airports to keep smokers comfortable during non-smoking films or flights.	Agency:	WWAV Rapp Collins, Edinburgh	The mailer was aimed at existing whisky drinkers who had not adopted Macallan as their favourite brand. The aim was to get them to try the whisky, but in a way that reflected the brand's quirky positioning. And so the miniature bottle was "hidden" from prying eyes inside an eye-glazing tome about Albanian shopping malls.
Creative Directors:	Peter Jooss Paul Holcmann Thomas Walmrath		Creative Director:	Paul Readman	
Copywriters:	Gordon Hollenga Richard Brim		Copywriter:	Dawn Kermani	
Art Directors:	Holger Schäfers Greg Mitchell		Art Director:	Mark Flett	
Client:	P&S Cigarettes		Client:	The Macallan Single Malt Scotch Whisky	

Because you can only learn so much from a CV.

356 Direct Marketing

Agency:	1576 Advertising, Edinburgh	**Agency:**	Fredag Reklamebyrå, Oslo
Creative Directors:	David Reid, Adrian Jeffery	**Creative Director:**	Sigurd Gaston Larsen
Copywriter:	James Betts	**Copywriter:**	Sigurd Gaston Larsen
Art Director:	Rufus Wedderburn	**Art Director:**	Anneli Hole
Client:	ID Recruitment	**Photographer:**	Katja Krogh
		Client:	Konika Film

This direct marketing initiative aimed at photography stores ran alongside a consumer campaign using the idea of double exposures. The tagline was: "Treat yourself to an extra film this summer." Meanwhile, retailers were sent a disposable camera containing undeveloped shots of in-store display material, which they had to develop before placing their orders. Hopefully, they would order "double" the usual amount. In the second part, the retailers were sent a second disposable camera and were invited to take pictures of their display material in situ. The retailer with the best display won a trip to Orlando, Florida.

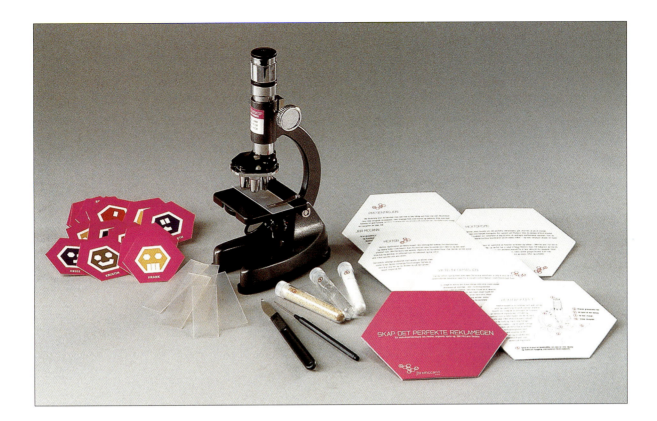

Agency:	JBR McCann Direkte, Oslo		
Creative Director:	Jan Petter Ågren		
Copywriter:	Frank Nystuen		
Art Director:	Jan Willy Skjølberg		
Client:	JBR McCann Self-Promotion		

The mailing to clients and prospects invited them to "search for the perfect advertising gene" using a microscope and slides printed with tiny writing. Those who participated in the competition were sent life-like doctor's diplomas.

Agencies:	Cayenne, Vienna
Creative Director:	Markus Huber
Copywriter:	Petra M. Schenk
Art Director:	Karin Kutsam
Client:	Innovest Financial Services

The different materials in the box each represented the wisdom offered by the company to its clients. For instance, the print on the grass reads: "Make sure that even your thoughts have the power to grow", while on the foam rubber it says: "Hard analysis makes for a good cushion." Finally, the wooden block suggests: "We have a good foundation to grow on."

Publications

Agency: Jung von Matt, Hamburg	This tactile cube enabled recipients to examine the features of the new Mini.
Creative Director: Mathias Jahn	
Copywriter: Martin Fuchs	
Art Director: Peter Harasim	
Photographer: Heribert Schindler	
Client: BMW Mini Cube	

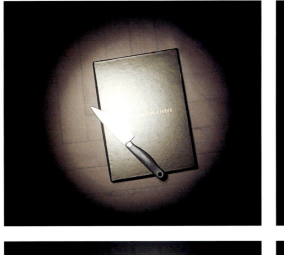

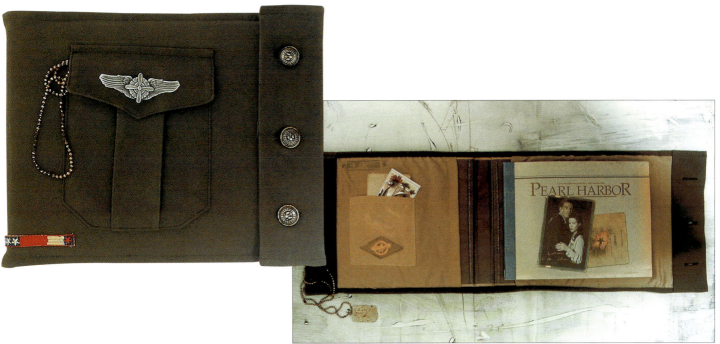

Agency:	Zapping, Madrid	Recipients literally had to cut through the "skin" of the book, drawing blood, in order to see the material inside.	Agency: Zapping, Madrid
Creative Directors:	Uschi Henkes Urs Frick		Creative Directors: Uschi Henkes Urs Frick
Art Directors:	Victor Gômez Marcos Fernandez Edmundo Irujo		Art Director: Kiko Argomaniz
Client:	"School Killer" Press Book		Client: "Pearl Harbour" Press Book

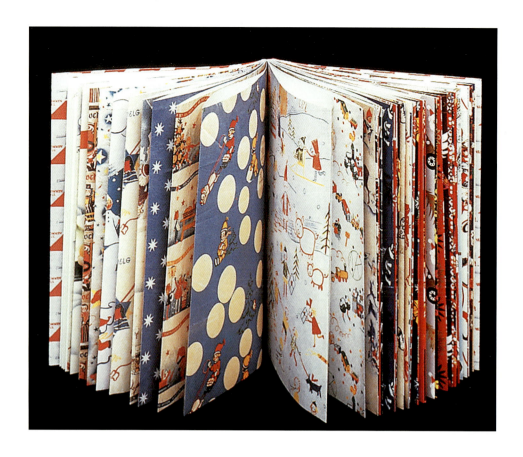

Agency:	Garbergs Annonsbyrå, Stockholm	
Copywriter:	Lotta Lundgren	
Art Director:	Karin Ahlgren	
Client:	Södra Cell Pulp & Paper, "Christmas Wrapping Paper Book"	

Agency:	Romson Seidefors, Stockholm
Creative Director:	Jan Lindforss
Copywriters:	Jacob Nelson
	Martin Bartholf
	Mikael Ström
Art Director:	Anna Romson
Designers:	Mussi Rosander
	Patric Leo
Client:	Swedish Bible Society

The very first publication of the Bible as a magazine, aimed at those who find the traditional format too overwhelming. This is book one: Luke. The plan is to publish all 77 books in the Bible at a rate of four a year – over a period of 19 years!

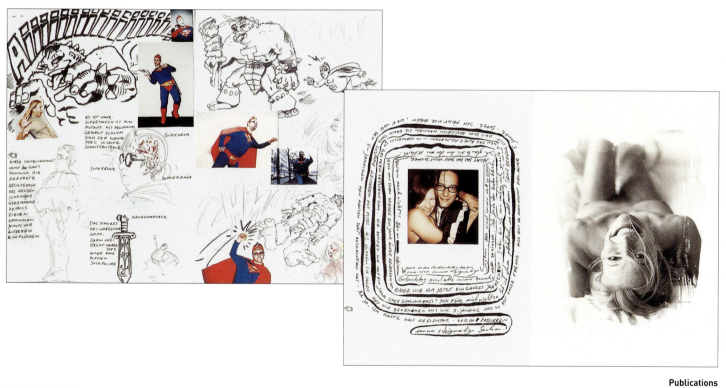

Agency:	Area Strategic Design, Rome
Client:	Universal Studios

The pay-TV movie channel published this "tactile" calendar dedicated to monster movies, providing a unique opportunity to spill Dracula's blood or stroke The Wolf Man! Other classic movies treated in 3D included The Mummy, Creature of the Black Lagoon, The Invisible Man and Frankenstein.

Agency:	FCBi Deutschland, Hamburg
Creative Director:	Stefan Schwarz
Copywriter:	Uli Lion
Art Director:	Thore Evers
Photographer:	Chon Choi
Client:	Igepa Paper

To draw attention to the qualities of fine paper, 11 different types of paper were combined in a "creative" diary.

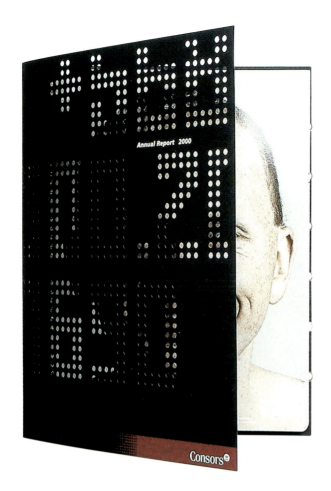
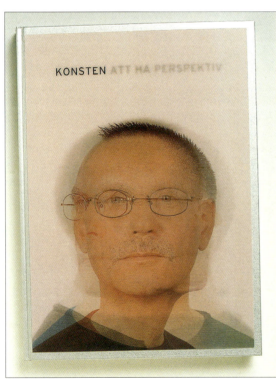
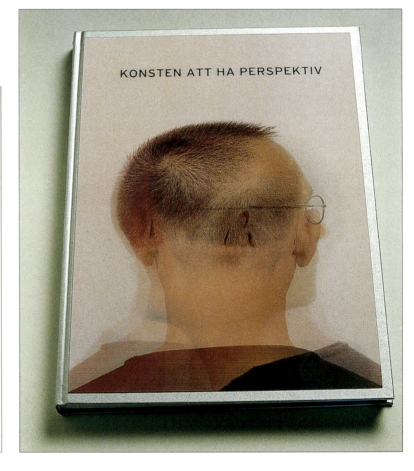

362 Publications

Agency:	Scholz & Friends, Berlin	Agency:	Sandberg Trygg, Malmö
Creative Director:	Stephan Ganser	Creative Director:	Peer Eriksson
Copywriter:	Petra Rothbart	Copywriters:	Mikael Roos
Art Director:	Antje Wolf		Sören Blanking
Photographer:	Caroline Otteni		Dan Wolgers
Client:	Consors Discount-Broker Annual Report 2000	Art Director:	Peer Eriksson
		Photographers:	Peer Eriksson
		Client:	Malmö Konst Museum

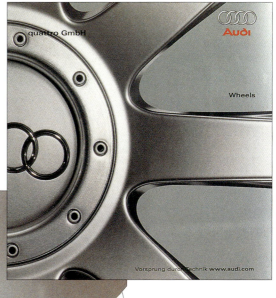

Agency:	W.A.F, Berlin	The book, Ten Years of Jenoptik, captures the history of the company and some of the personalities behind it.	**Agency:**	Philipp und Keuntje, Hamburg	A catalogue detailing the different wheels available for the Audi quattro, using turntables that enable the Audi owner to see what every possible combination looks like on his car.
Creative Director:	Klaus Fehsenfeld		**Creative Director:**	Hartwig Keuntje	
Art Director:	Heike Lichte		**Copywriter:**	Florian Baron	
Illustrators:	Paola Piglia		**Art Director:**	Bernd Westphal	
	Steff Jotzo		**Photographers:**	Thomas Jupa	
	Marcus Langer			Andreas Burz	
Client:	Jenoptik,			Eberhardt Sauer	
	10 Years of Jenoptik		**Client:**	Audi Quattro Wheels.	

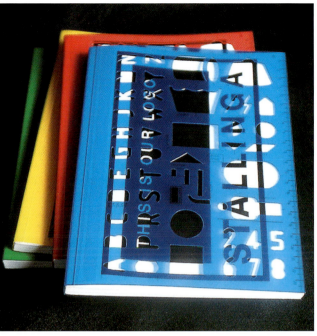

Publications

Agency: Lava, Amsterdam
Art Director: Hans Wolbers
Client: Henk Stallinga, Designer

Henk Stallinga designs, produces and distributes a wide range of products, from furniture and lighting to fashion accessories. The book's cover is a hard plastic stencil that was used to produce the interior typography and illustrations.

Agency: Zapping, Madrid
Creative Directors: Uschi Henkes
Urs Frick
Art Directors: Uschi Henkes
Edmundo Irujo
Client: C de C Magazine

C de C is the Creative Club of Spain, which publishes a news bulletin every six months. This time, it came in the form of a paper tablecloth!

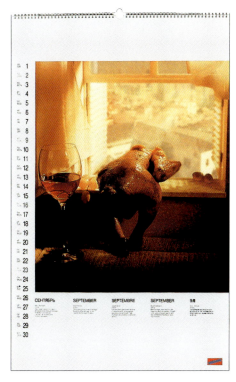

Agency:	Premier SV, Moscow
Creative Director:	Juri Bokser
Copywriter:	Juri Matis
Art Director:	Juri Bokser
Client:	Mosselprom Chickens Calendar

"Hot girls of the year". Produced for caterers and retailers, this calendar suggested that Mosselprom's chickens are the supermodels of the poultry world! Each month featured an international star like Miss Rio, Miss Dresden, Miss Kyoto, etc. with comments by each beauty in five languages.

366 Packaging Design

Agency:	Intellecta Corporate, Stockholm	Intellecta's regular Barsquare in-house event is held on November 6, a day of remembrance for Swedish King Gustav Adolf II, who was known for his wild parties. Bottles bearing these labels were served at the event, but perhaps only those who remained sober noticed the gradual change.
Creative Director:	Anders Schmidt	
Client:	Intellecta Corporate, Barsquare Wine Labels	

Agency:	\Brand Company, Paris	**Agency:**	Ytterborn & Fuentes, Stockholm
Creative Director:	Chris Brun-Vargas	**Creative Director:**	Oscar Fuentes
Art Directors:	Laurence Sicard Emeric Semin Sophie Lucas	**Copywriters:**	Jonas Andersson Stina Holmgren
		Art Director:	Elisabeth Årbrandt
Client:	France Telecom Mobile Phones	**Illustrator:**	Stina Wirsén
		Graphic Designer:	Elionora Bergendal
		Client:	Läskfabriken i Vimmerby, Soft Drinks

NB: These children's drinks come from the town of Vimmerby, home of Astrid Lindgren, whose fairytales are used to illustrate the labels.

Packaging Design

Agency:	Futura DDB, Ljubljana	**Agency:**	Locomotiv Action Marketing, Stockholm
Creative Director:	Žare Kerin	**Creative Director:**	Staffan Schager
Copywriter:	Janez Filak	**Art Directors:**	Linus Berglund
Art Director:	Žare Kerin		John Lagerqvist
Client:	Totter Natural Fruit Spirit	**Client:**	M/52 Tactical Beer

Packaging Design 369

Agency:	VBAT Enterprise, Schiphol Oost	Agency:	Jaxvall Design, Stockholm
Creative Director:	Teun Anders	Creative Director:	Nils Jensen
Art Director:	Allard Boterenbrood	Art Director:	Henrik Hallberg
Illustrator:	Allard Boterenbrood	Client:	Frost Beer
Client:	Etos Day Cures		

370 Packaging Design

Agency:	Lowe Brindfors, Stockholm	**Agency:**	SJWE, Stockholm
Creative Director:	Johan Nilsson	**Creative Director:**	Greger Ulf Nilson
Art Director:	Mitte Blomqvist	**Copywriters:**	Lars Torstensson
Photographer:	Lasse Kärkkäinen		Mattias Jersild
Client:	Arla, Yoggi Yoghurt	**Art Director:**	Greger Ulf Nilson
		Client:	Rabiega Rouge Wine Bottles

Packaging Design 371

Agency:	Clara, Karlstad	Agency:	Lewis Moberly, London
Copywriter:	Mats Åstrand	Art Director:	Mary Lewis
Art Director:	Olle Olsson	Designers:	Suze Klingholz
Illustrator:	Björn Nilsson		Ann Marshall
Client:	Katapult Coffee Drink	Client:	Waitrose, Diva Sanitary Towels

372 Illustration & Graphics

Agency:	Rose Design Associates, London
Creative Director:	Simon Elliott
Art Director:	Simon Elliott
Photographer:	Nick Knight
Client:	Royal Mail Stamps

The 'Fabulous Hats' range, which featured the best of British millinery, also neatly got around the fact that the Queen is the only living person traditionally shown on UK postage stamps.

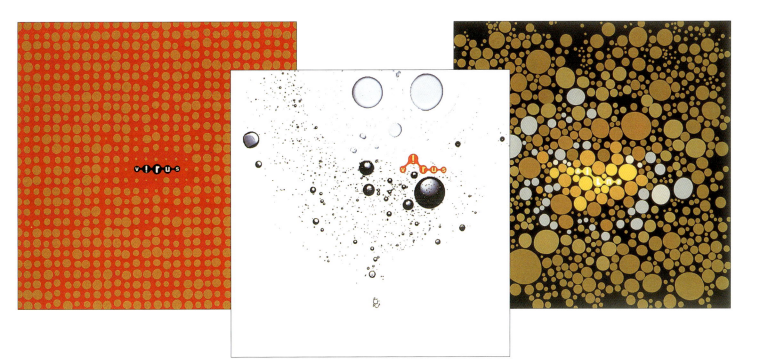

Agency:	Virus, Paris	The agency believes that brands, like viruses, must adjust to their environments to survive. And so it designed its own corporate identity as a series of mutations.	Agency:	Happy F&B, Gothenburg
Art Directors:	Jocelyne Fracheboud		Art Directors:	Anders Kornestedt
	K-mee Chung			Louise Lindgren
Client:	Virus Self-Promotion		Illustrator:	Fredrik Persson
			Client:	The Polar Music Prize

Illustration & Graphics

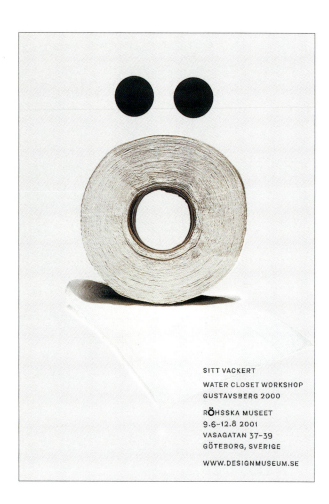

SITT VACKERT
WATER CLOSET WORKSHOP
GUSTAVSBERG 2000

RÖHSSKA MUSEET
9 JUNI–12 AUGUSTI 2001

Stolen av idag.

Trettioåtta stolar från de senaste fem åren.
15 februari–11 mars 2001

RÖhsska museet
Vasagatan 37–39, Göteborg
www.designmuseum.se

Agency:	Happy F&B, Gothenburg	Posters from the Röhsska Museum never show the exhibit – that's what the exhibition is there to do. And so this poster for "Sit Beautiful!" – an exhibition themed around water closet design – expresses the idea in another way, while retaining the bold "ö" of the museum's logo.
Art Director:	Andreas Kittel	
Photographer:	Jesper Sundelin	
Client:	Röhsska Museum, "Sit Beautiful" Exhibition	

Agency:	Happy F&B, Gothenburg	Poster for the "Chairs of Today" exhibition, featuring work from top furniture designers. Volunteers from the agency made the imprints.
Art Directors:	Andreas Kittel Helena Redman	
Client:	Röhsska Museum, "Chairs of Today" Exhibition	

Agency:	Springer & Jacoby, Hamburg	Agency:	Michael Conrad & Leo Burnett, Frankfurt	The evolution of the business card into product advertising. Furniture designer Holger Jahn can fold his perforated cards into pretty designer chairs when handing them to contacts.
Creative Directors:	Thomas Walmrath Peter Jooss Paul Holcmann	Creative Directors:	Uwe Marquardt Kerrin Nausch	
Copywriter:	Ben Clapp	Copywriter:	Jens Sabri	
Art Director:	Stephen Reed	Art Directors:	Michael Schacht Mariko Neumeister	
Illustrator:	Stephen Reed			
Client:	Fisherman's Friend	Client:	Jahn Furniture Design	

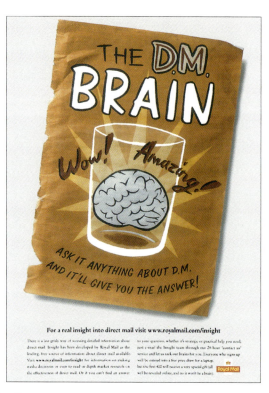

376 Illustration & Graphics

Agency:	Heye & Partner, Unterhaching	Agency:	OgilvyOne Worldwide, London
Art Director:	Alexander Emil Möller	Creative Directors:	Harvey Lee
Client:	Su Bühler Costume Designer		Colin Nimick
		Copywriter:	Rae Stones
		Art Director:	Fiona Sanday
		Illustrator:	Nicola Slater
		Client:	Royal Mail

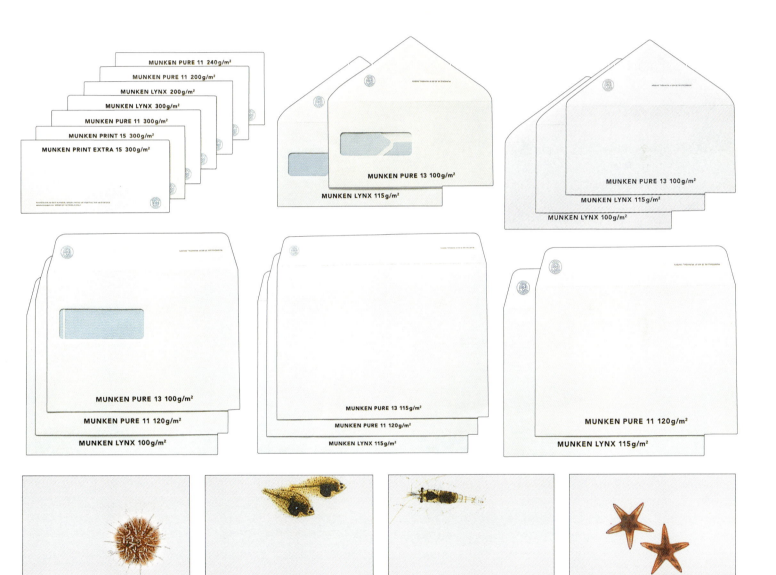

Agency:	Lewis Moberly, London	Agency:	Happy F&B, Gothenburg	Munkedals' correspondence material is effectively also a marketing tool, as each item is an example of its own paper.
Art Director:	Mary Lewis	Creative Director:	Anders Kornestedt	
Designer:	Bryan Clark	Art Director:	Andreas Kittel	
Client:	La Grande Epicerie De Paris, Luxury Food Store	Client:	Munkedals Papermill	

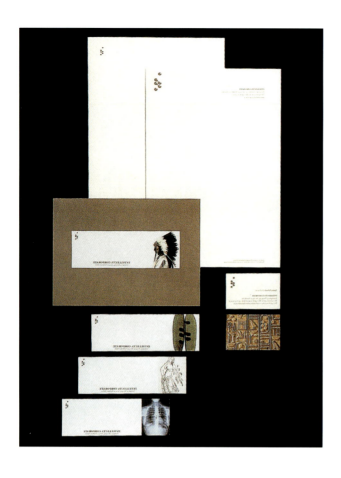

378 Illustration & Graphics

Agency:	Intellecta Corporate, Stockholm	The agency's new graphic design programme featured a 'hidden logo' printed in the designs on all its correspondence material.
Creative Director:	Anders Schmidt	
Client:	Intellecta Corporate Self-Promotion	

Agency:	Happy F&B, Gothenburg	The selection of picture frames is printed on Munken Print Extra to convey the quality of the paper, which is good enough to frame even when blank. The ads appeared in magazines that were printed on Munkedals paper.
Creative Director:	Anders Kornestedt	
Art Director:	Andreas Kittel	
Client:	Munkedals Papermill	

Agency:	Attila, Milan	Agency:	McCann-Erickson, Milan
Creative Director:	Betti Bongiasca	Creative Director:	Dario Neglia
Copywriter:	Silva Castellani	Copywriter:	Dario Villa
Art Director:	Nuria Martin	Art Director:	Matteo Civaschi
Illustrator:	Anja Kroencke	Illustrator:	Matteo Civaschi
Client:	PierAntonioGaspari Clothing	Client:	Martini

AA ROADSIDE ASSISTANCE 346
AAD, Kuijper 44
AAPOLA, Henna 132
AASHEIM Paal Tarjei 141, 217, 294
AASTRAND, Calle 294
ABBA SEAFOOD 30
ABBY NORM, Stockholm 307
ABEL, Marc 252
ABSOLUT VODKA 56
ACADEMY, London 223
ACCENTURE 116
ACE SOFT DRINK 74
ACNE, London 28, 111, 114
ACQUATI, Silvia 179
ADDV EURO RSCG, Bucharest 206
ADECCO EMPLOYMENT AGENCY 260
ADHAMI, Sadry 224
ADIA EMPLOYMENT AGENCY 264
ADIDAS 102, 286
ADP, SKIN CANCER PREVENTION 149
ADVICO YOUNG & RUBICAM, Zürich 51, 89,190, 211, 343
AEBI Jean Etienne 83, 110, 341
AER LINGUS 81
AFA ADVERTISING, Dublin 345
AFTENPOSTEN NEWSPAPER 302
AGAH, Manu 178
AGENCE .V., Paris 242
AGH & FRIENDS, 'S-Hertogenbosch 251, 330
AGI, Stuttgart 333
AGNETUN, Lisa 169, 344
ÅGREN, Jan Petter 347, 353, 357
AGUADO, Mikel 170
AGUAYO, Lay 206
AGUSTSDOTTIR, Anna 52, 141
AHLERS, Susanne 22, 275
AHLGREN, Karin 360
AHMED, Sam 226
AHMED, Shahir 226
AHRENS, Tobias 230
AIDES, ANTI-AIDS ASSOCIATION 154
AIMAQ RAPP STOLLE, Berlin 285
AIMAQ, André 285
AIR FRANCE 20, 85
AIRBUS 269
AIWA PORTABLE CD PLAYERS 203
AKEHURST, John 289
ALAKARI, Nono 243
ALARCON, Mauricio 291
ALBANESE, Luca 175
ALBEROLA, Jose Luis 202
ALBERT NOLTEN SHOES 16, 282
ALBERT, Thierry 267
ALBINUS, Marietta 317
ALBROW, Victor 266
ALCARRIA, Miquel 170
ALCOHOLICS ANONYMOUS 150
ALDORF, Frank 231
ALENDAHL, Peter 272
ALFA ROMEO 147 223
ALFARO, Juan Ramon 106
ALLANSSON, Christer 278, 354
ALLEGRI 275
ALPHA RECRUITMENT 262
ALTMANN, Olivier 99, 163, 167, 172, 208, 210, 252, 261, 267
ALVAREZ, Javier 263
ALVES, Jarbas Teixeira 192
ALZEN, Niels 319
AMBRO, Mette 158
AMERLYNCK, Georges 112, 222
AMLINSKY, Andrey 179, 186
AMMANATH, Manoj 215
AMNESTY INTERNATIONAL 133, 134, 135
AMROP JENEWEIN GROUP, EXECUTIVE SEARCH 266
AMSTERDAM CITY COUNCIL 338
AMV/BBDO, London 47
ANAGNOSTARA, Aliki 25
ANAHORY, Diogo 240
ANDER, Anna 334
ANDERS, Teun 369
ANDERSEN, Espen Lie 90
ANDERSEN, Torben 276
ANDERSON, Paul 307
ANDERSSON, Christer 57
ANDERSSON, Jonas 367
ANDERSSON, Mimmi 200
ANDERSSON, Patrik 218, 272, 274
ANDREASSON, Hans-Erik 278, 354
ANR BBDO, Gothenburg 278, 354
ANTILA, Marko 30
ANTON, Rafa 196, 263
ANTTILA, Petteri 310
APERS, Olivier 224, 227
APG BILLBOARDS 337
APPEL, Dodo 239
ARAMBURU, Javier 170
ÄRBRANDT, Elisabeth 367
ARDEN SUTHERLAND-DODD, London 245
ARDEN, Paul 245
AREA STRATEGIC DESIGN, Rome 361
ARGELICH, Nuria 231, 233, 236
ARGOMANIZ, Kiko 359
ARIEL LIQUITABS 195
ARIH ADVERTISING AGENCY, Ljubljana 202, 214, 351
ARIH, Igor 202, 214, 351
ARIOLA, Dante 237
ARISTOC TIGHTS 276
ARLA YOGGI YOGHURT 48, 370
ARMANDO TESTA, Milan 275
ARMANDO TESTA, Rome 184
ARNAL, Guilhem 167
ARNAUD, Christophe 44
ARNOLD, Radovan 161
ARTICULATE GAME 329
ASICS SPORT SHOES 284
ASKELÖF, Oscar 72
ASSADIAN, Chermine 269
ASSUR, Jens 300
ASTORGA, Alberto 231, 233, 236
ÅSTRAND, Mats 371
ATHAYDE, Edson 48, 192, 294, 295, 337
ATMOSFÄR, Stockholm 30, 260
ATTILA, Milan 379
AUDI 221, 222, 231, 232, 233, 236, 363
AUDITOIRE EVENTS AGENCY 267
AUMANN, Oliver 331
AUTODISCO, FIRESTONE/BRIDGESTONE TYRES 249
AUTOTRADER, ANTI-DRINK-DRIVING CAMPAIGN 156
AVETTI, Anna Paula 142
AWDRY, Will 232
AXA INSURANCE 112
AXE DEODORANTS 215
AXION BANK 114
B&W FILM, Copenhagen 100, 101
BABINET, Rémi 166
BABST, Mathias 51
BACARDI BREEZER 58
BACH, Lone Tvedergaard 100, 101
BADEN-WÜRTTEMBERG 352
BAGOLA, Aljoša 161
BAGUR, Jean-Luc 224, 225, 227
BAILIE, Julie Anne 157
BAISTER, Michael 318
BALDERDASH GAME 328
BALESTRERI, Paola 275
BALL, Alex 57
BALLANTINE'S SCOTCH WHISKY 57
BALTRUSCHAT, Silke 145
BANASZUK, Bruno 269
BANCO PRIVADO PORTUGUES 113
BANCOS DE ALIMENTOS 146
BANNÖHR, Frank 230
BARBOU, Jean-Pierre 84, 112
BARDOU-JACQUET, Antoine 185
BARFOED, Kasper 276
BARIPOGLU, Mustafa 187
BARNARDOS 24
BARNES, Phil 318
BARON, Alexander 153, 283
BARON, Florian 363
BARRAUD, Martin 307
BARROTE, Jorge 192
BARRY, Tony 61, 273
BARTER, Andy 67
BARTH, Christoph 204, 255
BARTHOLF, Martin 164, 360
BARTHUEL, Antoine 20, 71, 85, 240
BARTLE BOGLE HEGARTY, London 24, 232, 278
BARUSSAUD, Hervé 44, 50
BARY, Koert 74
BARZ, Fabian 145
BASTHOLM, Lars 327, 333
BASTIDA, Aline 86
BASTIMAN, Pete 22, 156, 304
BATES HEALTHWORLD, London 267
BATES FRANCE, Paris 135
BATES NORWAY, Oslo 33
BATES PORTUGAL, Lisbon 147
BATTAGLIA, Roberto 57, 239, 246
BATTISTEL, Hugo 109
BAUDINE, Brigitte 55
BAUGHEN, Mark 28, 114
BAUMEISTER, Anke 193
BAUMGARTEN, Mickaël 135
BAYALA, Carlos 34
BAYERISCHES NATIONAL MUSEUM 320
BAYGON INSECT REPELLENT 208
BBDO INTERONE, Munich 332
BBDO PORTUGAL, Lisbon 113, 240
BBDO, Düsseldorf 45, 108
BBDO, Moscow 179, 186
BDDP & FILS, Paris 19, 99, 163, 167, 172, 208, 210, 252, 261, 267
BDH\TBWA, Manchester 342
BEATES HUNDESALON, DOG GROOMING PARLOR 108
BEATTIE, Trevor 317
BEAUREGARD, Xavier 252
BECK, Miro 352
BECKER, Flavie 167
BEDESCHI, Michele 50, 121
BEHAEGHEL, Vincent 37, 185
BEHRENDT, Sebastian 189
BEKA MATTRESSES 185
BEKO WASHING MACHINES 187
BELAYA KARONA, Minsk 130
BELETIC, Brian 177
BELGIAN OLYMPIC COMMITTEE 323
BELLON, Damien 19, 208, 210
BELTRAMI, Carla 223
BENGTSSON, Bisse 78
BERECIARTUA, Ricardo 170
BERENDS, Joost 297
BERG, Matthias 303
BERGEN, Jeannette 231
BERGENDAL, Elionora 367
BERGER, Frank 284
BERGER, Kathrin 280
BERGER, Nahuel 86
BERGLUND & WEISS 100, 101
BERGLUND, Lena 129
BERGLUND, Linus 368
BERGLUND, Pelle 307
BERGMANN, Georges 185
BERLANDER, Elisabeth 351
BERTS, Jean-Michel 201
BERVELL, Katrine 80
BERVILLE, Pierre 21, 176, 207
BESL, Martin 246
BESSAGUET, Anne 88
BETC EURO RSCG, Paris 20, 71, 85, 164, 166, 240
BETTS, Gary 155, 302
BETTS, James 266, 356
BEVITT, Paul 178
BFI 116
BGS D'ARCY, Milan 179, 223
BIAGINI, Mauro 229
BIANCO FOOTWEAR 287
BIASIA HANDBAGS 288
BIDARRA, Pedro 113, 240
BIDDLE, Paul 290
BIERNACKA, Teresa 105
BIG FOOD CATERING 106
BIG PRODUCTION, Paris 44
BIJL, Miranda 58
BILLY & HELLS 76
BINDER, Christian 99
BIONDI, Marco 246
BISHREY, Neil 46
BIZOT, France 42, 46
BJØLBAKK, Stig 165
BJØRKLØF, Jan 130
BJÖRN BORG 274
BJORNSSON, Sverrir 52, 141
BLACK PENCIL, Milan 50, 121
BLANKING, Sören 362
BLASCO, Rafa 216
BLM FILMPRODUKTION, Hamburg 104
BLOMQVIST, Mitte 27, 28, 298, 299, 370
BLOOD, SWEAT & TEARS LTD., Zürich 128
BLUM-HEUSER, Christine 350
BMW 234, 235
BMW C1 MOTORBIKE 245, 246
BMW FINANCIAL SERVICES 235
BMW MINI 237, 358
BODEGAS MIGUEL TORRES WINE 63
BODENSTEDT, Stefanie 263
BODIN, Frank 128, 316, 352
BODSON, Laurent 87
BOEBEL, Michael 148
BÖGEL, Malin 284
BOGNER JEANS 279
BOIJE, Johan 225
BOIL, Santiago 196
BOILLOT, Jean-Marie 56
BOKSER, Juri 365
BOLDT, Jens 149
BOMTEMPO, José 113, 240
BONAVIA, Fulvio 175
BONE MARROW TRANSPLANT FOUNDATION 154
BONFIM, Fabiano 295
BONGIASCA, Betti 379
BONNEAU, Chrystel 37
BONTSCHEFF, Nadja 187
BONUX DETERGENT 197
BONZO DOGFOOD 336
BOONMAN, Linda 58
BORCHARDT, Philip 250
BORCHERDING, Rolf 332
BORGIONS, Mark 323
BORISENKO, Andrés 39
BORN, Mick 138
BØRSEN DAILY BUSINESS NEWSPAPER 305
BOSCH, Pep 236
BOSIO, Sascha 332
BOSTOFTE, Christina 322
BOSTRÖM, Peter 300
BOTERENBROOD, Allard 369
BOTSCHKA, Andreas 209
BÖTTCHER, Philipp 18, 132, 136
BOTTERELL, David 232
BOUCHET, Jean-François 84
BOUFFORT, Christine 99, 163, 172
BOULET, Cécile 88
BOULLET, Albert 33, 217
BOUNTY 42, 46
BOUTIE, Philippe 258
BOZZA, Francesco 179
BRANDT, Jesper 211, 243
BRANKO 270
BRANNING, Matthew 250
BRAUN, Claus-Steffen 143
BRECHBUEHL, Juerg 89
BRIGINSHAW, Paul 276
BRIM, Richard 355
BRINK, Johan 314, 348, 349
BRINKENBERG, Joakim 278
BRITISH AIRWAYS 353
BROCKMAN, Didde 334
BROCKMANN, Heike 325, 331
BROENNIMANN, Peter 51, 89
BRONSTEIN, Paula 131
BROOKE-TAYLOR, Danny 342
BROSSMANN, Igor 66
BROVELLI, Fabrice 240
BROWN, Rob 184
BRUCKNER, Patrik 108
BRÜGGE, Alex 138
BRUGGE, Sabine 320
BRUKETA & ZINIC, Zagreb 304
BRUN, Mats 354
BRUN, Thomas 90
BRUNSWICK, Margrit 89, 190
BRUN-VARGAS, Chris 367
BRW, Milan 125
BRYDE, Petter 260
BUDGEN, Frank 64, 273, 278
BUGDAHN, Dirk 148
BULLDOG ENERGY DRINK 74
BULLEIT BOURBON 58
BULLET PRODUCTION, Copenhagen 93, 94, 158
BÜLLOW, Henrik 107
BULTMANN, Holger 239, 306
BUMBÁLEK, František 171
BURDIN, Laurent 228
BUREAU, Bernard 75
BURGAUD, Pierre-Dominique 289
BURGER, Peter 172
BURKARD, Alfred 226
BURZ, Andreas 363
BUSCH, Bettina 40
BUTTERFIELD, Richard 226
BUXRUD, Bjørnar 294
BYRAMJEE, Ghislaine 112
BYRNE, Noel 81
C DE C MAGAZINE 364
CA'N ROSES HOTEL 333
CAFIERO, Stephen 154, 234, 235, 238
CAKE FILMS, Paris 207
CALLEGARI BERVILLE GREY, Paris 21, 176, 207
CAMERINI, Mario 125
CAMPBELL, Steve 43
CAMPORA, Stefano 127, 210
CANALE, Alessandro 127
CANSADO, Ricardo 240
CANZIO, Stefano 179
CARAZO, Fabrice 228
CARAZO, Rachel 228
CARDONA, Marc 216
CARLING BEER 62
CARLSBERG BEER 59
CAROW & WRONO 99
CARRASCO, Julia 236
CARRAU, Emma 106
CARRENO, Jorge 261, 313
CARROL, Stephen 318
CARTY, Tom 296
CASPARI FILM, Düsseldorf 250
CASPARI, Thomas 250
CASTAY, Bertrand 109
CASTELL, Giovanni 183
CASTELLANI, Silva 379
CATALA, Gabriel 350
CATSKY, Claude 120, 123, 150, 158, 259
CAUSSE, Jean-Gabriel 252
CAVALLONE, Carlo 50, 121
CAYENNE, Vienna 357
CERKEZ, Robert 287
ČESENKOVÁ, Věra 62
ČESKÝ MOBIL 171
CHALKLEY, Jules 181
CHANTIER, Thierry 76
CHANTREL, Sébastien 163
CHAOUAT, Audrey 32
CHARAL MEAT 32
CHARHON, David 37, 312
CHARLESWORTH, Jo 181
CHARVÁT, Martin 154
CHATELAIN, Patrice 264
CHAUVIN, Nicolas 277
CHESTERMAN, Catharine 317
CHIO CHIPS 26
CHIUMINO, Thierry 75
CHOI, Chon 361
CHRIS & LEE 62, 73, 79, 328, 329
CHRONOPOST INTERNATIONAL 164
CHUDALLA, Thomas 262
CHUNG, K-mee 373
CIMMERBECK, Magnus 314
CINEMAXX CINEMAS 319
CINOTTI, Nini 270
CINZANO 57
CIPRAMIL ANTIDEPRESSANT 219
CITIGATE ALBERT FRANK, London 307
CIVASCHI, Matteo 127, 379
CLAN CAMPBELL 19
CLANG, John 166
CLAPP, Ben 375
CLARA, Karlstad 371
CLARK, Bryan 377
CLASSIC GARDEN OUTDOOR FURNITURE 348
CLAVIÈRE, Frédéric 77
CLAYDONHEELEYJONESMASON, London 76, 353
CLEMENTSON, Sara 205
CLIFF, Anthony 346
CLM/BBDO, Paris 18, 37, 42, 46, 68, 185, 208, 250, 274
COATES, Christina 280
COBBLESTONE PICTURES, Hamburg 229, 296
CODINA, Fernando 231, 233, 236
COFFIN, Pierre 209
COFFRE, Alexandre 34
COFFRE, Christophe 29, 32, 34, 306
COGGINS, Justine 322
COI, SEX INFORMATION FOR TEENAGERS 155
COLE, RUSSELL & PRYCE, Stockholm 138
COLLABORATE, Stockholm 111
COLLARD, Jean-Luc 247
COLLINS, Damon 61
COLLINS, Joe 345
COLLINS, Lis 85
COLLOMBET, Marc 71
COLNAGHI & MANCIANI-SPRINGER & JACOBY, Milan 229
COLOMBO, Stefano 127
COMMISSAIRE, Aude 135, 228
COMSTAR 165
COMTESSE, Bruno 87
CONERGY SOLAR TECHNOLOGY 187
CONSORS DISCOUNT-BROKER 362
CONTINENTAL TYRES 248
COOP PRIX SUPERMARKET 96
COOPER, Nathan 334
COPELAND, Mary Lee 243, 260
COPPENS, Willy 59
COPPERTONE 213
CORDOVIL, Vasco 256
CORNARA, Guido 125
CORNELIS, Herlinde 37
CORNU, Caroline 71
CORSAND, Christophe 71
CORTSEN, Lars 333
COSENTINO, Sonia 275
COSGROVE, Adrian 81
COSMETICS OY SKIN CREAMS 213
COTIER, James 88
COURADJUT, Olivier 99, 167, 172
COURLANDER, Toby 47
COX, Paul 226
CP HART BATHROOM FITTINGS 184
CRAMER, Kim 192, 211, 326
CRAVENS ADVERTISING, Newcastle Upon Tyne 318
CREATIVE CENTER CARDEA, Sarajevo 22
CREDITANSTALT 122
CRISP, Charles 61, 273
CRZIB, Yvonne 82
CVETNIČ, Andrej 343
CZESCHNER, Olaf 332
D'ADDA, LORENZINI, VIGORELLI, BBDO,
Milan 57, 235, 239, 246, 288
D'ADDA, Maurizio 235
D'AGUILAR, Jonathan 58
D'ARCY MASIUS BENTON & BOWLES, Hamburg 35, 40
D'ARCY, Amsterdam 341
D'ARCY, London 43
D'ARCY, Paris 71
D'EPENOUX, François 88
DACHS, Muntsa 291
DAGBLADET NEWSPAPER 294
DAGENS NYHETER NEWSPAPER 309
DAHNKE, Sandra 104
DALLEY, David 219
DÂMBOVICEANU, Vlad 206
DAMMANN, Felix 109
DANGERFIELD, Richard 98
DÁNIEL, Csákvári 45
DANIEL, Stephane 109
DANISH LOTTERY 311, 322
DANISH RAILROADS 86
DANKELMANN, Andy 280
DANSKE BANK 117
DANTAS, Liliana 48, 337
DANZKA VODKA 59
DARLING MAGAZINE 334
DAS WERK, Frankfurt 127
DAS WERK, Hamburg 283
DAUL, Christian 209
DAUM, Jens 319
DAVOR, Bruketa 304
DAWID 257
DAWSON, Prague 62
DDB, Brussels 112, 222
DE AMSTERDAMSE SCHOOL, Amsterdam 101
DE ANTONIO, Alejandro 249
DE BOISMENU, Geoffroy 277
DE CEUSTER, Philippe 114, 118, 323
DE JONG, Elise 31
DE LAUW, Michel 112, 222
DE LESTRADE, Robin 112
DE MARCILLAC, Jacques 238
DE MAUPEOU, Anne 18, 250, 274
DE MELO, Albano Homem 191, 285, 314, 316
DE MICO, Domenico 290
DE PIERREFEU, Roland 34
DE RITA, Lorenzo 286
DE SOUZA, Joe 308
DE STANDAARD NEWSPAPER 297
DE STREEKKRANT FREE NEWSPAPER 330
DE VIÑALS, Jose Maria Roca 106

DE VOS, Kees 330
DE VRIES AMBULANCES 251
DE ZEEUW, Patrick 214
DEBOEY, Yves-Eric 68, 208
DEC, Barcelona 350
DEGRYSE, Mathieu 68, 208
DEISS, Sophie 71
DELANEY LUND KNOX WARREN & PARTNERS, London 155, 302
DELEHAG, Hjalmar 180
DELHOMME, Bruno 208, 210
DE-MARTINI, Carlo 307
DEMNER, MERLICEK & BERGMANN, Vienna 120, 122
DEMSCHIK, Mirko 199
DEPILSOAP 206
DERESE, Michel 55
DERMAUX, Olivier 18, 274
DESCALS, Tomás 106, 159, 194, 238
DESSO, CARPET TILES CD ROM 330
DEUTSCH BAHN 90
DEUTSCHE KREBSHILFE, GERMAN CANCER SOCIETY 148
DEUTSCHE TELEKOM 162, 173, 339
DEUTSCHES THEATER BERLIN 320
DEVARRIEUXVILLARET, Paris 289
DEVAUX, Jocelyn 224, 227
DEZSO, Nagy 45
DI BERARDINO, Angelo 59
DIAS, Marco 113
DÍAZ, Antonio 292
DIE MOBILIAR INSURANCE 110
DIE WELT NEWSPAPER 296
DIECKERT, Kurt Georg 65, 230, 262
DIESEL JEANS & WORKWEAR 23, 272
DIET TIZER 342
DIETSCH, Andrée 284
DIMENSION, San Sebastian 170
DINAMO REKLAMEBYRÅ, Lysaker 302
DIOT, Marie-Thérèse 207
DIRECT HOLIDAYS 91
DISKO BISCUITS 38
DIWADKAR, Nirmal 215
DIXON, Vincent 75, 208, 263
DMA CHICAGO 347
DUAN, Minh Khai 29
DOKTOROW, Kjell 78, 274
DOLDING, Nick 147
DOLLEY, Calvin 244
DOM & NIC 181
DONALD, Alex 58
DORIS, John 317
DORIZZA, Enrico 142
DOVIDAT, Frank 239
DOWIE, Claus 132
DR. PEPPER 69, 70
DRAVET, Laurent 29
DRESDNER BANK 350
DREYER, Eric 88
DROBNITZA, Sven 348
DRUSCHEL, Sebastian 108
DU PREEZ, Warren 281
DUBOIS, Michel 56
DUBOIS, Pauline 201
DUDAR, Galina 165
DUFFAUT, Laurent 330
DUFFY, Malcolm 276
DUFFY, Sean 271
DUNKELZIFFER 140
DUNMORE, Lawrence 286
DUPUIS, Yves 290
DURACELL BATTERIES 202
DURBAN, Mike 47
DUREX CONDOMS 205, 209, 210
DURSTON, Tony 73
DUTKIEWICZ, Józef 142
DÜTTMANN, Uwe 231, 255, 271, 280, 320
DUVAL GUILLAUME, Brussels 114, 118, 323
DYMECKA, Agnieszka 142
DYRUP PAINT 191
EAST CENTER MALL 97
EASTPAK BACKPACKS 290
EDET WIPE & CLEAN 192
EDF ELECTRICITY SUPPLIER 185
EDFELDT, Fredrik 48, 114
EDIN, Marcus 326
EDITORIAL NOTÍCIAS, PUBLISHER 294
EDSON FCB, Lisbon 48, 192, 294, 295, 337
E-FACT, London
EFTI, Stockholm 27, 278
EGHAMMER, Johan 30
EHRENSTRÅHLE & CO., Stockholm 354
EHRLER, Stefan 89, 211
EICHHOEFER, Sandra 82
EICK, Collin 141
EIDE, Øivind 130
EILOLA, Kari 174
EINIÖ, Antti 243, 260
EISELE, Gertrud 339
EKENSTAM, Felix af 334
EKLIND, Anders 180, 182, 243
EKONEN, Jani 143
EL ALJ, Medhi 238
EL LEÓN BLEACH 194
ELÁSTICA, Lisbon 222
ELDORAUTO AUTOMOTIVE RETAILER 247
ELIAS, Eric 261
ELLIOT, Yan 36, 69, 70
ELLIOTT, Simon 372
ELSOM, Jon 155
ELVESTEDT, Sofie 191
ENGART, Lisa 309
ENGEL, Sebastian 35
ENGELBRECHT, Michael 229
ENGELHARDT, Klaus 239
ENGHAGE, Jonas 72, 211, 326
ENGLER, Håkan 138
ENGLUND, Jens 218
ENGSTRÖM, Björn 300, 301
ENPA, ANIMAL PROTECTION ORGANISATION 142
ENTEROGERMINA 207
ENTROPIE, Paris 172, 269
EPA INTERNATIONAL, Stockholm 96, 164, 294, 311
ERAM SHOES 289
ERBEŽNIK, Gal 214, 351
ERICSSON BLUETOOTH TECHNOLOGY 257
ERIKSSON & GULLBERG, Stockholm 159
ERIKSSON, Lauri 132
ERIKSSON, Peer 257, 362
ESSLINGER, Angelika 296
ESTERMANN, Frank J. 128
ESTRELLA DAMM BEER 65
ETCHEBARNE, Pascal 56
ETOS DAY CURES 369
EURO RSCG CATAPULT, Zürich 352
EURO RSCG CORPORATE, Paris 269
EURO RSCG MAXIMA, Moscow 165
EURO RSCG MRT, Lisbon 49
EURO RSCG SWITZERLAND, Zürich 128
EURO RSCG WORKS, Paris 201, 247
EURO RSCG, Helsinki 33, 143
EUROPEAN STEEL ALLIANCE 271
EUROSTAR 87
EUSKALTEL METROPOLITAN PHONE CALLS 170
EUTHANASIA ASSOCIATION 160
EVERI, Timo 310
EVERS, Frank 26
EVERS, Thore 361
EVIAN MINERAL WATER 71
EXTRA FILM PHOTO DEVELOPING 200
EYRE, Mic 159
FABICKI, Slawomir 142
FAIRCHILD, Tenney 41
FAITH, Len 219
FAKTA SUPERMARKET 100, 101
FALUSI, Corinna 136
FAMO OFFICE CHAIRS 256
FANFANI, Luca 142
FARFAR, Stockholm 335
FARRELL, Gerry 62, 73, 79, 116, 324, 328, 329
FATHEUER, Kai 104
FAULDS ADVERTISING, Edinburgh 22, 156, 304
FAULI, Søren 322
FAULKNER, Ciska 296
FAUSSURIER, Pierre-Marie 213
FCB, Berlin 345
FCB, Brussels 290
FCB, Frankfurt 239
FCBI Deutschland, Hamburg 361
FEHSENFELD, Klaus 363
FELLENBERG, Dirk 193
FENDER GUITARS 198
FERNANDEZ, Kike 42, 213
FERNANDEZ, Marcos 119, 359
FERNANDEZ-MAÑES, Tony 249, 292
FERRARI, Pier Paolo 235, 239
FERREIRA, Pedro 147
FERRUA, David 57
FHV/BBDO CREATIVE MARKETING AGENCY, Amstelveen 41
FIAT DOBLÒ 223
FICHTEBERG, Gilles 195, 241
FIDO FILM, Stockholm 334
FILAK, Janez 368
FILM MASTER, Milan 229
FILMHAUS WIEN, Vienna 120
FILMITALLI, Helsinki 160
FILOSA, Antonello 142
FINAL TOUCH, Hamburg 187
FINANCIAL TIMES 302
FINNISH DEFENCE FORCES, RECRUITMENT 160
FINNISH FEDERATION OF VISUALLY IMPAIRED 143
FINNISH TRAFFIC SAFETY 157
FIONA BENNETT HATS 92
FISCHER, Lori 83
FISHERMAN'S FRIEND 43, 375
FITNESS COMPANY 340
FJÄLL, Peter 225
FLACH, Tim 88
FLETT, Mark 355
FLORHAUG, Geir 141
FOCUS BOOK OF DOCTORS 338
FOHR, Daniel 71, 85, 240
FÖRBUNDET DJURENS RÄTT, EXPERIMENTS ON ANIMALS 138
FORCE, FORSMAN & BODENFORS, Gothenburg 169, 344
FORH, Daniel 20
FORSBERG & CO., Stockholm 138
FORSMAN & BODENFORS, Gothenburg 30, 72, 151, 180, 182, 192, 211, 243, 300, 301, 326, 349
FORSMAN, Staffan 151, 300, 301, 349
FORSTER, Hélène 343
FOUQUET, Benoist 164
FOURNON, Jean-François 195
FRACHEBOUD, Jocelyne 373
FRAEFEL, Stefan 150, 259
FRAMFAB DENMARK, Copenhagen 327, 333
FRANCE TELECOM 167, 172, 367
FRANCHINI, Angela 352
FRANÇOIS, Thomas 235
FRANDSEN, Rasmus 327
FRANK, Björn Ole 43
FRANK, Jens 127, 209
FRANK, Oliver 285
FRANKFURTER ALLGEMEINE ZEITUNG 17
FRANSEN, Ferdinand 84
FRED&FARID 68, 208
FREDAG REKLAMEBYRÅ, Oslo 356
FREDLUND, Alexander 52
FREESTYLE HAIRDRESSERS 25
FREILAND, Heiko 65
FRENDBERG, Mattias 200
FRESK MINTS 42
FREULER, Matthias 98, 317
FRICK, Urs 119, 188, 359, 364
FRID, Emil 307
FRIDEHALL, Mats 318
FRIDNER, Martin 66
FRIED-JUNKINS, Claudia 180
FRISTADS WORKWEAR 278
FROESCHER, Jan 256
FROST BEER 369
FRUX FERTILIZER 193
FUCHS, Martin 358
FUDICKAR, Jörg 280, 285
FUENTES, Oscar 367
FUNDACIÓ ÈXIT 350
FUNDACION METIS 159
FUSZ, Marco 92, 352
FUTURA DDB, Ljubljana 74, 133, 368
G3, London 290
GABELLI, Michela 229
GABRIJAN, Zoran 74, 133
GAILLARD, Julie 164
GALLO, Joe 62
GALMARD, Eric 154, 167, 234
GANSER, Stephan 348, 362
GAP FILMS, Munich 158
GARBERGS ANNONSBYRÅ, Stockholm 134, 360
GARCIA, Cesar 53, 202
GARCIA, Marcos 146
GARRIGA, David 291
GASIA, Anne 55
GASPAR, Pedro 222
GASPAROTTO, Daniela 125
GATBY, Ola 225
GAULOISES CIGARETTES 283
GAUPP, Amselm 178
GEHRIG, Kim 69, 70, 212
GEHRKE, Andreas 153
GEHRKE, Peter 277
GEISER, Hadi 148
GEISER, Regula 98
GEORGE, David 184, 188, 205
GEORGEON, Olivier 67, 77
GEORGIOU, Alex 25
GEORGOPOULOS, Anastasia 25
GERARD-HUET, Jessica 84
GERHARD, Werner 104
GERMAN RED CROSS 127
GERRITS, Pim 336
GESSEL, Ron 58
GEYER, Andreas 145, 152, 162, 339
GHEWY, Christophe 185, 330
GHIDOTTI, Angelo 207, 218
GHOUSSOUB, Cédric 72
GIATRA, Katerina 168
GIBLIN & JAMES 22, 46, 304
GIDÉN, Thomas 174
GIL, Marielo 42, 213
GILBERT, Christophe 185, 290
GILL, David 195
GILL, Nick 232
GINES, Guillermo 56
GINI 76
GIOTAKI, Ioanna 168
GIPPENREITER, Makar 105
GIRALT, Jordi 42
GIRAUDY OUTDOOR ADVERTISING 261
GITTO, Vicky 235, 239, 246
GJENSIDIGE NOR SAVINGS BANK 353
GKM WERBEAGENTUR, Berlin 104
GLAGE, Sven Ulrich 103
GLEY, Ove 90
GMX INTERNET PROVIDER 174
GOEDE, Eva 88, 234
GOETTERT, Benedikt 352
GOGUET, Olivier 264
GOIRAND, Paul 50
GOJOBSITE 262
GOLD FISCHLI 45
GOLDMAN, Paul 81
GÔMEZ, Victor 188, 359
GONZÁLEZ, Lidia 39
GONZÁLEZ, Montserrat 86
GORGEOUS ENTERPRISES, London 61, 64, 273, 276, 278, 296
GORINI, Paolo 179
GOSS REKLAMBYRÅ, Gothenburg 200
GÖTEBORGS-POSTEN NEWSPAPER 300, 301
GOTHENBURG HOMELESS SHELTER 354
GOTHENBURG INTERNATIONAL BOOK FAIR 314, 349
GOUBY, Marc 19
GOZZINI, Libero 50
GRABARZ & PARTNER, Hamburg 178, 182
GRABARZ, Andreas 182
GRÅBØL, Niels 100, 101
GRANDJEAN, François 96, 276
GRANDT, Oliver 57
GRASSO, Michela 223
GRAU, Christian 96
GRAVESEN, Christian 115
GREEK YELLOW PAGES 168
GREEN, John 267
GREEN, Malcolm 155, 302
GREGG, Colin 62
GRÉGOIRE, Pascal 177, 264
GRETHER, Daniel 231
GREY & TRACE, Barcelona 39
GREY & TRACE, Madrid 86
GREY, Århus 100, 101
GREY, Warsaw 54
GRIEGST, Noam 117
GRIFFIN, Kevin 84, 164
GRIMM, Florian 102, 231
GRISCHEK, Robert 306
GROEN, Mart 16, 282
GROSJEAN, France 256
GROUSSET, Sébastien 146, 229, 296
GRUNENBERG, Julia 332
GRÜTZMACHER, Kai 35
GSTF, FREE TIBET 128
GUAIS, Cécile 87
GUANY, Jean 131
GUDBJARTSDOTTIR, Kristin Thora 52, 141
GUEIRARD, Nathalie 312
GUIDE, Benoît 201
GUILLEMAND, Charles 163, 267
GUILLON, Romain 166
GUILMIN, Paul-Henri 109
GUIMARAES, David 63
GUIOL, Catherine 32, 34
GULBRANSON, Johan 64
GULLI, Petter 147, 217
GULLIMAN, Andy 232, 278
GUNNING, Gary 257
GÜNTER, Pascal 136
GÜRTLER, Uli 124, 271, 277
GUSTAF FILM, Ljubljana 74
GUSTAFSSON, Jens 309
GUT, Markus 97, 279, 308, 337
GUYOMARD, Sylvain 224, 227
GUYON, Sophie 56
GYLFADOTTIR, Sigrun 141
HAAPALEHTO, Markku 118
HAGELSTEEN, Henrik 33
HAGEN, Espen D. 302
HAK VEGETABLES 37
HÅKANSON, Staffan 151, 300, 301, 349
HAKLE SENSITIVE TOILET PAPER 211
HAKUHODO UK, London 201, 347
HALDER, Ralph 308, 337
HALLBERG, Göran 27
HALLBERG, Henrik 369
HALLER, Ueli 226
HALLETT, Sarah 64
HALVARSSON, Henrik 72, 298, 299
HAMBURGER, Lawrence 250
HAMMAR, Lukas 111
HAMMERSCHMIDT, Claudia 22, 275
HAMSTER PUBLICITÉ, Paris 99
HANDLOS, Oliver 139, 153
HANKE, Sascha 265
HANSEN, Hans 37
HANUSA, Deborah 35, 40
HAOZIOMERSPAHIC, Anur 22
HAPPY F&B, Gothenburg 270, 373, 374, 377, 378
HARASIM, Peter 358
HARCQ, Xavier 109
HARDIECK, Sebastian 187, 306
HARLE, Pete 76, 353
HARLEY DAVIDSON 101
HAROUTIOUNIAN, Cédric 42
HARRIS, Neil 32
HARRISON TROUGHTON WUNDERMAN, London 346
HARRY DOUGLAS, Stockholm 243
HART, Erik 140, 153, 283
HARTMANN, Barbara 98
HARTMANN, Urs 128
HARTOG, Marcel 315
HARTOG, Peer 321
HARTZ, Daniel M. 237
HASAN & PARTNERS, Helsinki 97, 174, 243, 260, 310
HASLE, Andreas 114
HASSELVALL, Musse 243
HASTINGS, Hamburg 283
HASTINGS, Nick 43
HAUG, Joachim A. 147, 217, 294
HAUS KONSTRUKTIV, ART MUSEUM 317
HÄUSERMANN, Dirk 230
HAUSSMAN, Michael 223
HAVSTAD, Charlotte 347
HAWES, Simon 65
HAYDEN, Helen 81
HAZELHURST, Simon 76
HECTOR, Tony 262
HEDDE, Antje 231
HEFFELS, Guido 149
HEGERFORS, Anders 200
HEIDORN, Oliver 145, 162
HEIL, Alexander 323
HEIMAT WERBEAGENTUR, Berlin 149
HEINDORF, Maik 92
HEINEKEN 61, 66, 67
HEINEMANN, Gerald 250
HEINEMANN, Mirjam 254
HEINTZSCH, Carsten 221
HEINZ 29, 34, 35
HEINZE, Pawel 64
HEISHOLT, Erik 82, 104, 130
HEITMANN, Matthias 173
HEITOR, José 113
HELDENS, Axel 229
HELIAS, Eric 313
HELL PRODUCTIONS, Warsaw 64
HELLE, Heinz 246
HELSINKI, EUROPEAN CITY OF CULTURE 150
HENKE, Karolina 180, 182
HENKEL, Mathias 338
HENKES, Uschi 119, 188, 359, 364
HENNØY, Odd Einar104
HENRIQUES, Sérgio 240
HEPLEVENT, Burak 82
HERBRICH, Thomas 284
HERMAN, Robert 250
HERMÈS, Carli 214, 241
HERNGREN, Felix 27, 278
HERRERA, María Jesús 292
HERSOUG, Erik 82
HERVÉ, Alexandre 225, 227
HERZOG, Alex 315
HESS, Alexander 132
HESS, Christoph 203, 262
HEUTER, Karen 23
HEWI HOME ACCESSORIES 189
HEYE & PARTNER, Unterhaching 376
HEYMACH, Kerstin 122
HEYN, Katharina 140
HICKS, William 48
HIELCKERT, Esther 286
HILARIUS, Camilla 274
HILDEBRAND, Christoph 344
HILL, Natalie 237
HILLER, Jost 45
HILSON, Benoît 185
HILTL VEGETARIAN RESTAURANT 98
HIRSCH, Pascal 29
HITACHI TELEVISIONS 201
HJALMAR, Björn 114, 298, 299
HJALTESTED, Fridrik Orn 141
HLA, London 227
HOESCHELER, Vera 280
HOFBECK, Thomas 18, 127, 132, 136, 200, 209
HOFFMANN, Alice 234
HOFFMANN, Andreas 187
HOFFMANN, Jörg 340
HOFFMANN, Thomas 100, 101, 117, 287
HOFMANN, Johannes 65, 230
HOFMANN, Wolfgang 332
HOHMANN, Till 234, 245, 246
HOJČOVÁ, Táňa 152
HOLCMANN, Paul 355, 375
HOLDEN, Eric 87, 312
HOLDEN, Ruth 173
HOLE, Anneli 356
HOLLANDER, Nicolás 146
HOLLENGA, Gordon 355
HOLLINGWORTH, Frank 225
HOLLOWAY, Wayne 91
HOLM, Anders 96
HOLMGREN, Stina 367
HOLMQVIST, Hanna 159
HOLTSLAG, Jan 84, 115, 295
HOM, Marc 208
HOMBOE, Eivind 263
HONDA 243
HORN, Espen 82
HORRÉE, Bart-Jan 41
HORTS, Meritxell 78, 160
HORVAT, Suza 61
HOSKINSON, Dawn 184
HOURA.FR CYBERMARKET 98
HOUTSMA, Antoine 84, 115, 295
HOWELL, Benji 47
HOWELLS, Gareth 116
HR SKYLINE, FINANCIAL RADIO STATION 303
HUBER, Klaus 187
HUBER, Markus 357
HUBERT SPARKLING WINE 66
HUBL, Ondrej 171
HUDSON, Tom 232
HUEBNER, Norbert 303
HUESMANN, Bernd 140, 153, 283
HUNGER, Reinhard 35, 305
HUNNICUTT, Gabriela 314
HUNTER, Mark 278
HUTTER, Tibor 38

HVOSLET, Carl Christian 104
IAA & BASLER MEDIENGRUPPE GOLF CUP 352
IBM 18, 253, 264
ID RECRUITMENT CONSULTANTS 266, 356
IGEPA PAPER 361
IGLESIAS, Angel 56
IHM BUSINESS SCHOOL 351
IJSWATER COMMERCIALS, Amsterdam 74
IKEA 105, 177, 178, 179, 180, 181, 182
ILARIO, Danny 65, 231, 233, 236
ILLUM DEPARTMENT STORE 107
IMIGRAN PAIN RELIEVER 217
IMPACT/BBDO, Beirut 72
IMSENG, Dominik 109
INFONET 354
INGE, Charles 61, 64, 273
INGERSTEDT, Magnus 164, 335
INGVOLDSTAD, Erik 347
INNO DEPARTMENT STORE 109
INNOVEST FINANCIAL SERVICES 357
INSTITUTO NACIONAL DE CARDIOLOGIA PREVENTIVA 147
INTELLECTA CORPORATE, Stockholm 366, 378
INTERFLORA 93, 94
INVESTMENT WEEK 307
IODINE MEDIA 328
IRISH INTERNATIONAL GROUP, Dublin 81
IRN-BRU 73
IRUJO, Edmundo 359, 364
ISKRAEMECO ELECTRIC METERS 22
ITI FILM STUDIO, Warsaw 142
IVANCIC, Benjamin 74, 133
IVARSSON, Johannes 318
IWINSKI, Krzysztof 64
JACOBS, Richard 37
JACOBSSON, Karin 180, 182
JAGGY, Alexander 109, 203, 262
JAHN FURNITURE DESIGN 375
JAHN, Mathias 358
JANIŠ, Juraj 31
JANS, Annette 263
JANSON, Peter 334
JANSSON, Fredrik 180, 182
JARLSBERG RACE TRACK 321
JÄRNFELDT, Johanna 334
JAXVALL DESIGN, Stockholm 369
JAYNE, Cathryn 353
JBR McCANN DIREKTE, Oslo 347, 353, 357
JBR McCANN, Oslo 90, 141, 147, 217, 294
JEAN & MONTMARIN, Paris 44, 50, 76, 98, 213
JEAN, Gérard 44, 50, 76, 98, 213
JEAN, Sidonie 44, 50
JEAN BAPTISTE, Patrice 21, 176
JEDENBERG, Sara 169, 344
JEEP GRAND CHEROKEE 239
JEFFERY, Adrian 89, 91, 266, 356
JEFFRIES, James 329
JENOPTIK 363
JENSEN, Nils 369
JERLOV & KÖRBERG, Gothenburg 198, 314, 348, 349, 351
JERLOV, Fredrik 198, 351
JO! SCHMID, Berlin 221
JOBPILOT RECRUITMENT SITE 263
JOCHENS, Oliver 321
JOHANSEN, Jo 31, 38
JOHANSEN, Stian 96
JOHANSSON, Magnus 314
JOHN WEST CANNED FISH 31
JOHNSON, Tim 201, 347
JOKINEN, Antero 157
JONASON, Joakim 272
JONES, Kiri 91
JONES, Nick Thornton 281
JONSSON, Jen 236
JOOSS, Peter 355, 375
JORDAN, Greig 62
JORNAL DE NOTÍCIAS NEWSPAPER 295
JOST, Johnny 308
JOTZO, Steff 363
JULIUS, Oliver 250
JUNCTION 11 ADVERTISING, Weybridge 217
JUNG VON MATT, Berlin 303, 305
JUNG VON MATT, Hamburg 57, 82, 90, 136, 138, 140, 237, 254, 280, 319, 339, 358
JUNG VON MATT, Munich 88, 234, 245, 246
JUNG VON MATT, Zürich 109, 203, 262
JUPA, Thomas 363
JURAJ VACULÍK – CREATIVE STUDIO, Bratislava 340
JUUL-ANDERSEN, Kim 311, 322
JUVÉ, Rafael 78
KAÇAR, Suleyman 187, 194
KAČENKA, Peter 66
KADZ, Samuel 225, 227
KAISANIEMEN DYNAMO, Helsinki 132
KALOFF, Constantin 90
KAMOY, Magdalena 105
KANDER, Nadav 24
KANSALLIS NATIONAL MUSEUM 310
KAPUSTA, Oliver 57, 82
KARINIEMI FREE RANGE CHICKEN 33
KARKKAINEN, Lasse 108, 129, 134, 370
KARS, Edo 16, 282
KASSAEI, Amir 102, 231
KATAPULT COFFEE DRINK 371
KATBORG, Rikke 93, 94
KATER, David 315
KATHE, Michael 341
KATZSCHKE, Stefanie 333
KAUFMAN, Laura 223
KAUSSEN, Willy 140, 319
KAWASAKI NINJA ZX 6R 250
KD KAISER'S DRUGSTORE 104
KEILLOR, Michael 328
KEITEL, Sven 124, 144, 145, 271
KELLOGG, David 223
KEPIC, Simona 126
KERIN, Žare 368
KERMANI, Dawn 355
KERR, Graham 342
KESER, Michiel 315
KESSELS, Erik 23
KESSELSKRAMER, Amsterdam 23
KETTIGER, Christian 21, 176
KEUNTJE, Hartwig 363
KEY 103 FM 22, 304
KF FOODS 27, 28
KHAZEM, Jean-Pierre 23
KIEFER, Anna 149
KIER, Kai 174
KILLI, Lars 31, 38
KING, Stockholm 225
KISSELEV, Vassili 179
KITTEL, Andreas 270, 374, 377, 378
KIVILAHTI, Kimmo 97, 310
KLAAR KIMING, Hamburg 321
KLAGES, Matthias 182
KLAIPEDA CULTURAL CENTER 21
KLAZES, Reinoud 341
KLEIN, Andre 35, 40
KLEINFELD, Gerrit 108
KLEINMAN, Daniel 205, 232
KLENZENDORF, Christoph 322
KLEP, Maarten 242
KLEVER, Alexandra 43
KLINGHOLZ, Suze 371
KLINGLER, Christoph 250
KLOHK, Sven 344
KLUSZCZYŃSKA, Iwona 142
KNIGHT FRANK PROPERTY 188
KNIGHT, Nick 372
KNOBLOCH, Thomas 279
KNOX, Tim 253, 264
KOBOLT, Katja 161
KOCH, Alexander 113, 147
KODAK 199, 200
KOECHER, Michael 143
KOHL, Chris 331
KOLD, Mads 311, 322
KOLLE REBBE, Hamburg 140, 153, 183, 187, 193, 283, 306
KOLLE, Stefan 187, 193
KONDOMSHOP.ORG 209
KONIKA FILM 356
KONONENKO, Ksenia 105
KONOPKA, Waldemar 345
KOOKAÏ 18, 274
KOOSHMANIAN, Stephane 269
KORB, Françoise 167
KÖRBERG, Pelle 314, 348, 349
KORNESTEDT, Anders 270, 373, 377, 378
KOSLIK, Matthias 92, 153, 168
KOSTGELD, Ralf 341
KOTOULAS, Nikos 25
KOTTE, Anatol 22, 275
KOYLUCELI, Ergin 194
KRAFT TOMATO KETCHUP 29
KRAMER, Hanneke 44
KRAMMER, Johannes 120, 122
KRAPP, Martin 139, 153, 256
KRASTING, Guntram 209
KRATZ, Diederik 101
KRAUSE, Jan 339
KREJČÍ, Martin 62
KREMPL, Johannes 103, 320
KRIEG, Daniel 83, 91
KRIEGER, Jürgen 39
KRISTIANSEN, Morten 80, 82
KRISTLOVÁ, Monika 62
KROENCKE, Anja 379
KROESKAMP, Hans 24, 59, 291
KROGH, Katja 356
KROISS, Stefan 320
KRØJER, Kristel 107
KROLEWSKIE BEER 64
KROMBACHER, Leo 182
KRUG, Jenny 296
KUHN, Bastian 296
KUIJPER, Aad 44, 172, 214
KUJALA, Vesa 132
KUKULSKA, Ulrika Granlund 307
KUONI REISEN TRAVEL 343
KURBAŠA, Tvrtko 66
KURTTILA, Jukka 160
KURZWEG, Stefan 332
KUTSAM, Karin 357
KVICKLY 276
KWIATKOWSKI, Lechoslaw 64
KYRILLOS, Giselle 203
L'ILLA DIAGONAL SHOPPING CENTER 106
LA CITY 277
LA FOURMI, Paris 209
LA GLORIA, Barcelona 170
LA GRANDE ÉPICERIE DE PARIS 377
LA PAC, Paris 167
LA POSTE 163
LACORRE, Laurent 45
LAFLEUR, Georges 37, 297
LAGERCRANTZ, Henrik 164
LAGERQVIST, John 368
LÄHDESMÄKI, Markku 249
LAMMERS, Ben 336
LAMTAR, Paris 258
LANCASTER, Neil 188, 205
LAND ROVER 239
LANDESFEUERWEHR-VERBAND HESSEN 143
LANDMANN, Hinnerk 145
LANGAN, Eugene 345
LANGENBERG, Jaap 315
LANGER, Marcus 363
LANGEVAD, Hans-Henrik 311, 322
LANGPAUL, Jiří 154
LANGSETH, Tove 272
LÄNSFÖRSÄKRINGAR INSURANCE 111
LAPÁČKOVÁ, Nikola 62
LARRONDO, Valérie 250
LARSEN, Sigurd Gaston 356
LARSEN, Steen 59
LARSSON, Håkan 278, 354
LÅSKFABRIKEN I VIMMERBY 367
LÁSZLÓ, Mészáros 45
LATOUR, Susanne 35
LAU, Christian 199
LAUBSCHER, Axel 96
LAURELL, Philip 159
LAURITSEN, Stig 96, 276
LAVA, Amsterdam 364
LAVOLA, Minna 33
LAWACZECK, Axel 348
LAX, Ola 274
LE GOFF, Nicole 44
LE GUAY, Hélène Bremond 207
LEAF, LISBON EROTIC ADVERTISING FESTIVAL 316
LEAGAS DELANEY PARIS CENTRE 177, 264
LEAHY, Kevin 81
LEAR, Chris 342
LEE FILMS INT'L, Madrid 236
LEE, Harvey 376
LEHTINEN, Mikko 160
LEHTONEN, Markus 160
LEITES, Zeza 256
LENSVELT, Huub 172
LEO BURNETT, Amsterdam 31
LEO BURNETT, Athens 168
LEO BURNETT, Budapest 45
LEO BURNETT, Milan 142
LEO BURNETT, Oslo 80, 82, 96, 104, 130
LEO BURNETT, Paris 29, 32, 34, 306
LEO BURNETT, Prague 62, 154
LEO BURNETT, Warsaw 105, 197
LEO, Patric 360
LEO'S SPORTS CLUB 315
LEONETTI, Jean Baptiste 207
LEPPÄNEN, Mira 249
LES FRERES POIREAUD 269
LES TÉLÉCREATEURS, Paris 177
LESKO, Adrian 340
LESKOVAR, Saša 126
LETULE, Ulrike 279
LEUCH, Lisa 316
LEVI'S ENGINEERED JEANS 278
LEVIS PAINTS 25
LEWANDOWSKI, Hans-Jürgen 229
LEWIS MOBERLY, London 371, 377
LEWIS, Mary 371, 377
LEYCK, Axel 187, 283
LIBENS, GHEWY & FAUCONNIER, Brussels 185, 330
LIBENS, Luc 185, 330
LIBERO DIAPERS 211, 326
LICHTE, Heike 363
LIDZELL, Anders 78, 129
LIEBERATH, Fredrik 28
LIGA PROTI RAKOVINE, ANTI-SMOKING 152
LIGNE ROSET FURNISHINGS 21, 176
LIMA, Evandro 222
LIMA, Pedro 203, 316
LIMPINSEL, Stefanie 178, 182
LIND, Sesse 52
LINDAHL, Lars-Henrik 159
LINDEMANN, Arno 228, 277, 279
LINDFORSS, Jan 360
LINDGREN, Louise 373
LINDSTRØM, Annelie 96, 311
LINDSTRÖM, Axel 311
LINEHAN, Graham 293
LINTAS MIDDLE EAST NORTH AFRICA, Dubai 215
LION, Uli 361
LIPOWEC, Regina 193
LIPPERT, Susanne 350
LIPPO, Oliver 152
LIVSHITS, Gregory 130
LOBELLE, Vincent 154, 234, 235, 238
LOCKSTEIN, Bjoern 254
LOCOMOTION, Copenhagen 287
LOCOMOTIV ACTION MARKETING, Stockholm 368
LODGE, David 47
LÖFROTH, Jesper 334
LOGAN, George 76
LOMMEL, Benjamin 221
LOMMERS, Stan 214
LÖNN, Andreas 218
LÖÖF, Jörgen 30
LOPEZ, Antonio 136, 138
LOPEZ, José Luis 146
LORAN, Berta 350
LORETTI, David 281
LOUIS XIV DDB, Paris 224, 225, 227, 236, 277
LOVELIDGE, Craig 303, 305
LÖVKVIST, Jesper 326
LOVY, Robert 45
LOWE BRINDFORS, Stockholm 27, 28, 48, 114, 271, 298, 299, 309, 370
LOWE LINTAS & PARTNERS, Brussels 37, 297
LOWE LINTAS DIGITEL, Zagreb 66, 270
LOWE LINTAS GGK, Warsaw 64
LOWE LINTAS GGK, Zürich 226, 265
LOWE LINTAS, Amsterdam 44, 172, 214
LOWE LINTAS, Copenhagen 311, 322
LOWE LINTAS, London 61, 64, 273
LUANG CHINESE FOODS 37
LUCAS, Sophie 367
LUCKAS, Katja 45
LUCSUSOWA VODKA 54
LUDWIG GÖRTZ SHOES 102
LUKAS, Bernhard 88, 234, 245, 246, 254
LUKASIEWICZ, Tomasz 142
LUND, Johnny 158
LUNDBERG, Stein 65
LUNDGREN, Fredrik 334
LUNDGREN, Lotta 134, 360
LUNDH, Pelle 155
LUNDIN, Ola 314, 348, 349
LUTTI CRYPO CHOCOLATES 44
LUTTS, Igor 179, 186
LUVERDIS, Evelyne 112
LUXTON, Cressida 91
LUZZANI, Massimiliano 218
LYLE, David 157
LYNGBYE, Christian 167
LYSØ, Janne Brenda 96
LYUTSKOV, Timur 165
M&M'S 45
M/52 TACTICAL BEER 368
M-80 FILMS, Santa Monica 41
MAAF CAR INSURANCE 119
MABOTT, Peter 201
MACARTNEY, Syd 157
MACHARZ, Katarzyna 197
MACIA, Fernando 63
MACK, Bianca 283
MACKEN, Jan 24, 25, 291
MACRI, Ionut 206
MACZEY, Markus 88
MADABOUTWINE.COM 65
MADSEN, John 181
MAERSCHALCK, Eric 37
MAES, Kato 55, 112, 114
MAESTRI, Pietro 223
MAESTRO DESIGN & ADVERTISING, Amsterdam 338
MAFFI, Flora 173
MAGGINI, Alvaro 120, 123, 158
MAGREAN, Joe 56, 313
MAGRI, Filippo 142
MAHER BIRD ASSOCIATES, London 342
MAHESO FROZEN FOODS 39
MAHON, Alan 65
MAJEWSKI, Arek 197
MALCOLM MOORE DEAKIN BLAZYE, London 296
MALCOLM, Tony 296
MALLINSON TELEVISION PRODUCTIONS, Glasgow 73, 116, 329
MALLINSON, Simon 73, 116
MALLMANN, Nina
MALM, Andreas 72, 243
MALMÖ KONST MUSEUM 362
MALTESERS 43
MANGEMATIN, Yanis 225
MANIERI, Mauro 142
MANIX CONDOMS 210
MANIX GEL 208
MANSON, Lee 184
MANSUKOSKI, Jussi 33, 143
MANSUKOSKI, Maija 143
MANTHEY, Andreas 149
MANZARDO, Michael 341
MARA, John 191
MARCA SPORTS NEWSPAPER 292
MARCO, Paco 63
MARCUS, Pierre 37, 185, 250
MARIANI, Michele 275
MARIESTADS BEER 78
MARINUS, Frank 24, 25, 291
MARITHE & FRANÇOIS GIRBAUD 281
MARKENFILM, Berlin 285
MARKENFILM, Wedel 82, 145, 280
MARKKU RÖNKKÖ, Helsinki 150
MARKS, Fiona 276
MARQUARDT, Uwe 340, 375
MARS MINIATURES 40
MARSHALL, Ann 371
MARSILLY, Agathe 37
MARSILY, Jacques 247
MARTEL, Xavier 88
MÅRTENSSON, Kristofer 28, 309
MARTÍN, Alex 106, 159, 194, 238
MARTIN, Fernando 196
MARTIN, Nuria 379
MARTINI 379
MARTINS, Carlos 137
MARYON, Dean 286
MAS, Joan 39
MASER, Silke 193
MASSIS, Marie 177
MASSON, Guido 204, 255
MASTERS, Donnie 223
MATIS, Juri 365
MAWHINNEY, Billy 22, 156, 304
MAWHINNEY, Steve 22, 304
MAX MAGAZINE 303
MAYRHOFER, Chris 95, 315
McCANN-ERICKSON, Amstelveen 58, 74
McCANN-ERICKSON, Belfast 157
McCANN-ERICKSON, Brussels 55
McCANN-ERICKSON, Frankfurt 322
McCANN-ERICKSON, Geneva 316
McCANN-ERICKSON, Hamburg 209
McCANN-ERICKSON, Lisbon 131, 137
McCANN-ERICKSON, Madrid 146
McCANN-ERICKSON, Manchester 184, 188, 205
McCANN-ERICKSON, Milan 127, 210, 379
McCANN-ERICKSON, Prague 31, 38
McCANN-ERICKSON, Warsaw 142
McCANN-ERICKSON, Zürich 120, 123, 150, 158, 259
McCARTHY, Paul 267
McDONALD'S 96
McKAY, Darren 342
McKINSEY & COMPANY 265
McNAB, Maresi 120
McPHAIL, Allan 239
McPHEE, Jamie 327, 333
McTEAR, Tony 278
MEDIAMETRIE AUDIENCE MEASUREMENT 258
MEDIAMIX, Maribor 343
MEE, Aude 177
MEEK, Nick 79, 312
MEIER, Daniel 109, 203, 262
MEIER, Thorsten 187
MEIJER, Paul 223
MEIKLEJOHN 302
MEIMOOM, Christophe 71
MELENDEZ, Marcio Cortez 184
MELIK, Richard 290
MELLBERG, Richard 318
MELVIN, Trevor 120
MENDUIÑA, Hugo 160
MENTASTI, Pucho 228
MENTZOS, Dominik 18
MENZEL, Peter 45
MER FRUIT DRINK 72
MERCEDES-BENZ 228, 229, 230, 244, 250, 325, 331, 344
MERKEL, Moritz 245, 280
MERKISCH, Robin 108
MESKE, Stefan 228, 277, 279
MESSMER, Fredy 128
METRO NEWSPAPER 307
METSÄVAARA-MILDH, Merja 150
MEUNIER, Sébastien 167, 261, 267
MEUNIER, Thierry 98
MEY FINE BODYWEAR 280
MEYER, Michael 228, 231
MEYRAN, Julia 237
MGF 242
MI ADIDAS WORKOUT CAMP 332
MICHAEL CONRAD & LEO BURNETT, Frankfurt 35, 204, 255, 338, 340, 375
MICROSCOPE 236
MICROSOFT 252, 254
MIDAS 250
MIHÁLIK, Marián 152
MIKKELSEN, Jens 287
MIKKONEN-MANNILA, Sari 118, 310
MIKOLA, Erkki 118
MILA DAIRY PRODUCTS 50
MILANÉS, Antonio 249, 292
MILCZAREK, Raphael 319
MILES CALCRAFT BRIGINSHAW DUFFY, London 276
MILKO FRUIT YOGHURT 335
MILLER, Bertie 205
MILLIEX, François 290
MILLINGEN, David 54
MILLS HAVBRIS 33
MILLS, Graham 346
MIMOSA DAIRY PRODUCTS 49
MINCHAN, Amabel 53, 202
MINDER, Stefan 83, 120, 123, 128, 279
MINI BABYBEL 53
MINI MAX FILMS, Prague 38
MIRANDA, Ricardo 192, 337
MIRAVALLES, Eduardo 39
MITCHELL, Greg 355
MITCHELL, Robert 239
MITCHINSON, Adam 230
MITJANS, Jordi 63
MITSIS, Christina 353
MIXTURAS, Lisbon 222
MLADINA, REFUGEE AWARENESS IN THE EU 161
MODE, Patrick 258

MOGREN, Johan 334
MOHN, Anette Waage 353
MÖHRKE, Volker 122, 316
MOINE, Olivier 277
MOKITOWN 332
MOLAND FILM, Oslo 104
MOLAND, Hans Petter 104
MOLINDER, Carl 278
MOLINO, Roberto 223
MÖLLER, Alexander Emil 376
MONHEMIUS, Simon 47
MOÑINO, Vicky 236
MONKEWITZ, Nicolas 262
MONNET, France 37
MONSE, Sandra 283
MONTEIRO, César 48, 294
MONTENEGRO, Alexandre 48, 294
MONTERO, Nines 249
MOOGE, Ben 293
MOONWALK, Stockholm 334
MOORE, Alan 271
MOORE, Guy 296
MOORE, Nicholas 20
MOOS, Martin 115, 305
MORENO, Luis Felipe 146
MORIA, Arno 177
MORRIS, Sara 201
MORTAROLI, Mauro 184
MORTENSEN, Jens 271
MORTIER, Jens 114, 118, 323
MOSSELPROM CHICKENS CALENDAR 365
MOST, Charlotte 30
MOTA, Judite 147
MOTHER, London 34, 36, 69, 70, 212, 293, 308
MOTION BLUR, Santa Monica 165
MOTION PICTURE, Milan 179
MOULIERAC, Olivier 269
MOUTAUD, Cédric 234
MOVIE VENTURES, Amsterdam 172
MTV 125, 296
MUDROV, Andrey 186
MUELLER, Daniel 98
MÜHLING, André 88
MUIR, Chris 156
MUMMERY, Richard 71
MUNDHENKE, Sarah 316
MUNILL, Xavi 106, 159, 194, 238
MUNIZ, Celso 203
MUNKEDALS PAPERMILL 270, 377, 378
MUONA, Marko 160
MURRAY, Greg 345
MURRAY, Michael 342
MURZEAU, Christine 269
MUSCHALLA, Gudrun 245, 246
MUSEUMS OF FRANKFURT 323
MUSTANG JEANS 277
MUSTARD, London 317
MYLES, Euan 73
NABBEN, Roger 321
NACHTEY, James 131
NAGEL, Sven 234, 246
NANDORF, Helga 124
NARDI, Luciano 223
NASCIMENTO, Mário 49
NAUG, Thorbjørn 33
NAUMANN, Petersen 321
NAUSCH, Kerrin 340, 375
NAVARRO, Andre 316
NAVILLE, Bernard 37, 185
NAWROT REDUTA ACTING SCHOOL 321
NEGLIA, Dario 127, 379
NEIGE, Rose 264
NELSON, Jacob 108, 335, 360
NEMO PRODUCTIONS, Milan 142
NESI, Fabio 179
NET AGAINST NEO-NAZI VIOLENCE 152
NEUE DIGITALE, Frankfurt 332
NEUE SENTIMENTAL FILM, Frankfurt 132, 199
NEUE ZÜRCHER ZEITUNG NEWSPAPER 308
NEUMEISTER, Mariko 340, 375
NEW DEAL DDB, Oslo 165
NEWTON, Helmut 17
NEXCLUSIVE BATHROOM FITTINGS 186
NICKLASSON, Linus 334
NICOLSON, Don 219
NIEDERMAIR, Brigitte 275
NIELSEN, Joachim 93, 94, 107
NIFTY OXFORD, MADE-TO-MEASURE CLOTHING 279
NIKE 285, 327, 333
NIKOLA, Zinic 304
NILSON, Greger Ulf 370
NILSSON, Filip 180, 182, 243
NILSSON, Johan 27, 28, 48, 114, 298, 299, 309, 370
NILSSON, Sofia 334
NIMICK, Colin 376
NINETY NINE, Paris 225
NISSAN 238, 240
NOAH, ANIMAL RIGHTS 136, 138
NOEL, Rémi 87, 312
NOHKE, Deborah 140
NOKIAN TYRES 249
NOLAN, Jack 346
NONZIOLI, Juan 146
NORDISK FILM COMMERCIAL, Copenhagen 96, 276
NORDISKA KOMPANIET DEPARTMENT STORE 108
NORWEGIAN POSTAL SERVICE 165
NOURY, Gilbert 264
NUNES, Raul 48, 294
NYKREDIT ØSTIFTERNE FORSIKRING INSURANCE 115
NYQUIST, Mats 302
NYSTUEN, Frank 357
O'BRYAN TEAR, Nick 232
O'DONNELL, And 248
O'HARE, Fergus 253, 264
OBEID, Adham 215
OBERHÄNSLI, Bruno 265
OBERS, Carlos 22, 275
OBSERVATÓRIO DO AMBIENTE 137
OCCHIOMAGICO 218
OEHLSCHLAEGER, Lars 285
OGILVY & MATHER, Frankfurt 18, 29, 127, 132, 136, 199, 200, 209, 263, 323
OGILVY & MATHER, Paris 75, 253, 264
OGILVY ADVERTISING, Stockholm 318
OGILVY CANAVERAL, Paris 88
OGILVYONE WORLDWIDE, Frankfurt 350
OGILVYONE WORLDWIDE, London 376
OHANIAN, Michael 280
OHLSSON, Magnus 174, 260
OKRENT, Sarah 196
OKU & SOAP 199
OLANDER, Jessica 334
OLDIGS, Olaf 284
OLF, Bettina 124, 144, 145, 265, 271
OLIVER, Isahac 39
OLIVERO, Johan 243
OLSEN, Bjørnar 90
OLSEN, Tom 115
OLSSON, David 28, 111, 114
OLSSON, Mikael 354
OLSSON, Olle 371
ON-COMPUTING, APPLE SERVICE 256
ONDA SALUD HEALTHCARE WEBSITE 206
ONDREIČKA, Boris 152
OOSTERVELD, Evelien 58
OPAL, Porto 256
OPEL FOOTBALL TOURNAMENT 322
OPITZ, Cornelia 27, 278
OPPMANN, Simon 322
ORAMORPH PAIN RELIEVER 218
ORANGE 166
ORANGINA 79
ORGANICS SHAMPOO 212
ORLIAC, Axel 29
ORTIZ TUNA 39
OSIPIAN, Sergey 179
OSKY 202
OSSEWOLD, Jurrienne 335
OSTA- OG SMJORSALAN 52
ØSTBYE, Tonje 294
ØSTLIE, Jannicke 294
OTTAHALL, Tobias 326
OTTENI, Caroline 362
OUI FASHIONS 22, 275
OUTSIDER, London 47, 181
OVERKAMP, Denise 148
P&S CIGARETTES 284, 355
PAECH, Kati 345
PÄIVINEN, Jappe 150
PALACIOS, David 119, 188
PALMER HARGREAVES MINT, Leamington Spa 248
PALMER, Chris 61
PALM-JENSEN, Matias 335
PALOMBI, Stefano Maria 175
PALTEMAA HUTTUNEN SANTALA TBWA, Helsinki 30, 249
PALTEMAA, Unto 249
PALYEKAR, Anil 226
PANASONIC BATTERIES 203
PANIER DE YOPLAIT 50
PAPENBROOK, Frank 104
PARADIS, André 71
PARADISET DDB, Stockholm 78, 129, 218, 272, 274
PARADOX, Oslo 260
PARAFILM, Copenhagen 322
PARENTAL INITIATIVE FOR MISSING CHILDREN 144
PARMALAT MILK 48
PARPA 142
PARR, Adrian 267
PARTIZAN MIDI-MINUIT, Paris 185
PASCOA, António 147
PASCUCI, Dorian 206
PATERSON, Ian Scott 99
PATNI, Tejal 215
PATRAMANIS, Harry 158
PATTERSON, Richard 96
PATTERSON, Sarah 223
PAULI, Andreas 338
PAUSER, Diana 339
PAVLENKO, Marina 165
PAY, Caroline 69, 70, 212
PBH LIFE INSURANCE 118
PEARL HARBOUR PRESS BOOK 359
PECKETT, Tim 155
PEDERSEN, Hans Jan 100 , 101
PEJAS, Steffen 303
PELLETTIERI, Paola 129, 134
PENA, Joaquim 222
PENICAUD, Pierre 67
PEPE, Federico 210
PEPSI 68, 72
PEREIRA, Paulo 294
PEREZ, Alfonso 53
PEREZ-AGUA, Guillermo 86
PEREZ-PAREDES, Juanma 292
PEROCCO, Erminio 184
PERRIER MINERAL WATER 75
PERRUCHAS, Christophe 163
PERSSON, Anna 243
PERSSON, Björn 28, 309
PERSSON, Fredrik 373
PERSSON, Johan 164, 294
PERTSEVA, Marfa 179
PETERSEN NAUMANN FILM, Hamburg 322
PETITJEAN, Fréderic 290
PETTINARI, Letizia 179
PEUGEOT 240
PEZZINO, Guglielmo 210
PFEFFERMANNOVÁ, Roxana 38
PFIZER IMAGE CAMPAIGN 218
PHILIPP UND KEUNTJE, Hamburg 363
PHILIPS TELEVISIONS 201
PIANA, Dario 229
PICARD, Alain 112
PICARD, Caroline 77
PIEBENGA, Piebe 341
PIELTAIN, Luc 109
PIERANTONIOGASPARI CLOTHING 379
PIERENS, Ivan 238
PIGLIA, Paola 363
PILLET, Bianca 58
PINGUET, Hugues 224, 227
PINGUIN FILM, Stockholm 48
PINKSE, Bas 44
PINO, Rozzi 239
PIRSON, Benoît 112
PITSIAVA, Amalia 309
PITZOLU, Marco 206
PIX & MOTION, Brussels 55, 112, 114
PLANCHON, Frédéric 112, 240
PLANET INTERNET 172
PLEWNIA, Kirsa 344
PLUEMECKE, Lutz 139, 153, 256
PLUMET, Hervé 236
PMSvW/Y&R, Amsterdam 315
POCHET, Genevieve 109
POKON PLANT FOOD 315
POLCE, Elio 184
POLEC, Andrzey 142
POLTRONA FRAU, FURNITURE RETAILER 184
POMIKAL, Miroslav 171
POMPADOUR INTERIOR DESIGN 183
PONÁHLÝ, Přemysl 171
POOTJES, Frans 101
POPINGER, Thomas 189
POPPE, Erik 38
PORCHEZ, Cédric 77
PORTO 2001, HORROR FILM FESTIVAL 314
PORTO, Sandro 48
PORTSIDE SHOES 285
PORTZ, Vera 228
POTKA, Pekka 97
POWLETTE, Helen 232
PRATA, Francisco 203, 295
PREISLER, Frederik 158
PRELEC, Monika 122
PREMIER SV, Moscow 365
PREMIÈRE HEURE, Paris 112, 240
PRICE, Dave 188, 205
PRIL ALOE VERA DISHWASHING DETERGENT 194
PRINZ MYSHKIN VEGETARIAN RESTAURANT 95
PRISTOP, Ljubljana 126, 161
PRO FAMILIA MARRIAGE COUNSELLING 145
PROJECT FOUNDLING 339
PROPAGANDA FILM, London 237
PROPAGANDA, Copenhagen 158
PROSS, Martin 92, 168, 244, 250, 352
PUBLICIS CONSEIL, Paris 67, 77
PUBLICIS ESPAÑA, Madrid 249, 292
PUBLICIS, Amstelveen 336
PUBLICIS, Frankfurt 143, 148
PUBLICIS, Zürich 83, 91, 97, 110, 279, 308, 337, 341
PUENTE AÉREO, Barcelona 146
PUERTAS, Gonzalo 86
PUETTMANN, Raphael 139, 153
PUPELLA, Marco 45
PYTKA PRODUCTIONS, Venice, Ca. 253
PYTKA, Joe 253
Q MUSIC MAGAZINE 308
QTV MUSIC CHANNEL 293
QUAD, Paris 34
QUARTILHO, Claudio 314
QUESTER, Peter 250
RABIEGA ROUGE WINE BOTTLES 370
RADEGAST BEER 62
RADIO 101 304
RADIO B1 340
RAD-ISH 42
RAID INSECTICIDE 192, 337
RAMA MARGARINE 31
RAMALHO, Paulo 49
RAMIREZ, Guillermo 78, 160
RAMML, Dr. Wolfgang 120
RAMOS, João Silveira 191, 285
RAMSAY, Russell 278
RANDSTAD EMPLOYMENT AGENCY 259
RANKIN 18, 210, 274
RAWI MACARTNEY COLE, London 157
RAYMENT, Richard 217
RAYNERT, Benoît 195
READMAN, Paul 355
REBOLJ, Aljoša 202
RECIO, Angel 236
RED CELL, Milan 223
RED CROSS CHILD RELIEF 141
REDMAN, Helena 374
REEBOK 273
REED, Stephen 375
REGELL, Tobias 309
REHN, Michaela 339
REICHENBACH, Petra 17
REICH-RANICKI, Marcel 173
REID, David 89, 91, 266, 356
REID, Matt 219
REIDENBACH, Felix 319
REIDENBACH, Nicola 173
REIMER, Christian 319
REIMER, Jorgen 186
REIN, Alison 165
REIN, Michaela 99
REINHARD, Dietmar 322
REINIKKA, Jyrki 30
REISS, Alexander 285
REKLAMBYRÅN HJARTSJÖ 155
RENOMMÉ, Oslo 321
REPUBLICA, Albertslund 96, 276
RETTINGHAUSEN, Peter 343
REXHAUSEN, Jan 57, 82
REXONA DEODORANTS & BODYSPRAYS 214
REY, Franck 135, 228
REYNIER, François 173
RF, Klaipeda 21
RG WIESMEIER, Munich 22, 275
RHEINDORF, Oliver 313
RHODES, Kathy 253
RIAU, Carles 78, 160
RIBEIRO, João 285
RICCARDO CARTILLONE SHOES 103
RICCI, Daniele 223
RICHA, Dani 72
RICHARD, Stéphane 289
RICHARDS, Tom 156
RICHTER, Brigitte 333
RIEKEN, Torsten 230
RIELE, Josée 330
RIESS, Pierre 166
RIETZ, Björn 272
RIFFAULT, Hervé 195, 241
RIJKEN, Kees 58
RIMI GROCERY STORES 104
RINGQVIST, Martin 30, 151, 192, 300, 349
RIOCHE, Alcide 201
RIPPY, Anne 147
RISOOLO, Francesca 175
RITTER, Jan 230
RITTER, Tanja 339
ROBERT, Michael 93, 94, 107
ROBERT, Yann 242
ROBERT/BOISEN & LIKE MINDED, Copenhagen 93, 94, 107
ROBERTSON, Patrick 342
ROBINSON, Simon Chatter 240
RODRIGUEZ, Aurelio 263
RODRIGUEZ, Sergio 50, 121
ROELS, Hans 330
ROGÉ CAVAILLÈS INTIMATE SOAP 207
ROHNER, Patrik 89
ROHRBEIN, Robert 284
ROHRER, Hans Ruedi 98
RÖHSSKA MUSEUM 374
ROIG, Miguel 53, 202
RØKEBERG, Glen 302
RÖMER, Alex 303, 305
RÖMMELT, Peter 322
ROMSON SEIDEFORS, Stockholm 108, 360
ROMSON, Anna 360
ROMSON, Stockholm 164, 335
RONACHER, Nikolaus 187, 306
RÖNKKÖ, Markku 30, 150
RÖNNBERG McCANN, Stockholm 52
RÖNNBERG, Bo 111
RONSHAUGEN, Eric 76
ROOS, Mikael 362
ROSANDER, Mussi 360
ROSE DESIGN ASSOCIATES, London 372
ROSE, Marcel 104
ROSENSTAND, Joachim 96, 276
ROSET, Vigdis 82, 104
ROSSELLI, Stefano 246
ROSSI, Adrian 24
ROSSI, Davide 127
ROTÁ, Mark 82, 237
ROTHBART, Petra 362
ROTHWELL, Paul 64, 273, 276, 278
ROUTLEDGE, Helen 296
ROUWHORST, Margo 335
ROYAL MAIL 372, 376
ROZIER, Marc 240
ROZZI, Pino 57, 246, 288
RSA, London 286
RUBIN, Ilan 288
RUBY, Gary 296
RUDOLPH, Glenn 41
RUEHMANN, Bjoern 103
RUF, Markus 97, 279
RUFFERT, Thomas 338
RÜHMKORF, Nina 43, 145, 152
RUSSO, Luigi 207
RUUD, Thorbjørn 260
RŮŽIČKA, Janek 38
RYBERG, Staffan 27, 28
RYNE, Jarle 321
RYSMAN, André 24, 25, 291
S COMME SERVICES CYBERMARKET 99
SÁ COUTINHO, Isabel 222
SAATCHI & SAATCHI, Frankfurt 221
SAATCHI & SAATCHI, Madrid 53, 202
SAATCHI & SAATCHI, Milan 125
SAATCHI & SAATCHI, Paris 195, 241
SAATCHI & SAATCHI, Rome 175
SABRI, Jens 375
SACCO, Jean-François 195, 241
SAETIL PAIN RELIEVER 216
SAEVARSSON, Erling I. 52
SAHIN, Halil Oner 194
SAHORES, Benoît 42
SAIEGH, Santiago 196
SALA, Maurizio 275
SALA, Ramón 78, 160
SALAMEH, Fady 62
SALDANHA, Frederico 295
SALES, Miquel 106, 159, 194, 238
SALMINEN, Hanna 160
SALVADORI, Pierre 172
SALVATION ARMY 151, 349
SAMOT, Patrick 20
SAMSONITE 24, 291
SAMSUNG N100 MOBILE PHONE 167
SAN NICOLÁS, Vicens 42, 213
SAN VICENTE WATER 78
SANDAY, Fiona 376
SANDBERG TRYGG, Malmö 257, 362
SANDER, Henrik 165
SANDERS, Rob 227
SANGDHORE, Rajeev 226
SARA, Ken 155
SAS AIRLINES 80
SASHA WINTER COLLECTION 345
SAT 1 345
SATELLITE FILMS, Hollywood, Ca 177
SAUER, Eberhardt 363
SAURINA, Albert 216
SAUTER, Elisabeth 120
SAVE THE CHILDREN FOUNDATION 130
SAVILLE, Robert 34, 36, 69, 70, 212, 293, 308
SCALABRE, Aurélie 20, 85
SCARDACCIONE, Gabriela 34
SCHACHT, Michael 375
SCHACK, Peder 59, 115
SCHÄFER, Michael 193
SCHÄFERS, Holger 284, 355
SCHAGER, Staffan 368
SCHAUDER, Gabi 178
SCHENK, Petra M. 357
SCHEPER, Uli 145
SCHERZER, Florian 153, 283
SCHIERWATER, Tim 189
SCHILL, Alexander 229, 296, 344
SCHILLING, Sandra 250
SCHINDLER, Heribert 271, 358
SCHLACHTER, Melanie 183
SCHLICHT, Guenter 143
SCHLUNGS, Katharina 325
SCHLUPP, Uwe 91, 110
SCHMID, Lukas 226, 265
SCHMID, Martin 221
SCHMID, Michael 221
SCHMID-BURGK, Nico 174
SCHMIDER, Benoît 76
SCHMIDT, Anders 366, 378
SCHMIDT, Christine 350
SCHMIDT, Jesper 107
SCHMIDT, Julia 17
SCHMIDT, Matthias 244, 250
SCHMIDT, Stefan 65, 230, 262
SCHNABEL, Michael 57
SCHNAUDER, Gabi 178
SCHNEIDER, Günther 99
SCHNEIDER, Tim 149
SCHOBBERT, Sebastian 162, 339
SCHOELERMANN, Marc 82, 280
SCHOEPFER, Joachim 92, 168, 244, 352
SCHOLZ & FRIENDS, Berlin 17, 92, 103, 139, 153, 168, 189, 244, 250, 256, 320, 348, 352, 362
SCHOLZ & FRIENDS, Hamburg 26, 99
SCHOLZ & VOLKMER, Wiesbaden 325, 331
SCHOLZ, Anette 331
SCHOOL KILLER PRESS BOOK 359
SCHREGENBERGER, Felix 83, 120, 123, 279
SCHREPFER, Urs 211
SCHREYER, Benedict 174
SCHROD, Jörg 209
SCHRODERS INVESTMENT MANAGEMENT 121
SCHROLL, Jutta 221
SCHULTE, Helmut 303
SCHULTZ, Michael 200

SCHUSTER, Birgit 303
SCHWARM, Christian 333
SCHWARZ, Denis 190
SCHWARZ, Roland 303
SCHWARZ, Stefan 361
SCHWIEDRZIK, Boris 250
SCOTONI, Roland 211
SEBASTIA, Jordi 78, 160
SEIFERT, Christian 199
SEILAND, Alfred 17
SEK & GREY, Helsinki 157, 160
SELIGSON & CO. INVESTMENT BANK 118
SELTMANN, Oliver 256
SEMIN, Emeric 367
SENUYSAL, Engin 187
SEQUEIRA, Susana 316
SERIOUS PICTURES, London 223
SERRASQUEIRO, Rogério 113
SERRAT, Raul 91
SERVAES, Paul 185
SERVICEPLAN, Munich 320
SETZKORN, Stefan 26
SF SNOWBOARD SCHOOL 91
SHAVE, Matthew 267
SHENOUDA, Rene 45
SHOUKAIR, Alexandre 72
SHOW OFF, Lisbon 48, 294
SICARD, Laurence 367
SIEBENHAAR, Dirk 178
SIEVERS, Marek 178, 182
SIGNY, Claire 73
SIIRILÄ, Vesa 118
SILBURN, Paul 64
SILZ, Dirk 57
SIMPL HAIRSTYLING SALONS 214
SINDICATO DOS JORNALISTAS 131
SIXPACK, Düsseldorf 284
SIXT CAR RENTAL 88
SIXT ONLINE SERVICES 82
SJÖDÉN, Olle 138
SJÖNELL, Calle 334
SJÖVALL, Jonas 192
SJWE, Stockholm 370
SKA, Porto 203
SKANDAALI, Helsinki 118
SKARBYE, Anne 276
SKARLAND, Gunnar 200
SKJØLBERG, Jan Willy 357
SKODA OCTAVIA 242
SKOGING, Tomas 28
SKOPA, Vasso 168
SKOVBOOLLING, Jesper 86
SKRÅMESTØ, Børge 353
SKROBLIES, Markus 209
SKRONSKI, Mariusz 287
SKWRNA, Daniela 35
SLAGARE, Alex 191
SLANICEANU, Ioana 206
SLATER, Nicola 376
SLIVKA, Vlado 66, 266
SLOVENIAN RED CROSS 126
SMART MICRO-CARS 231
SMITH, Chris Frazer 262
SMITH, Tony 116
SMITSMAN, Hanro 74
SNICKERS 41
SOBOTKOVÁ, Lenka 171
SÖDRA CELL PULP & PAPER 360
SOHO SHORT FILM FESTIVAL 342
SOLBERG, Eivind 90, 147
SOLE, Xavier 65
SOLIN, Vanja 304
SONY HANDICAM 202
SONY PLAYSTATION 312, 313, 317
SORIA & GREY, Bratislava 152
SORRISO, Alexandre 222
SOSNIERZ, Kasia 54
SOTO, Valentín 350
SPÅNG, Patrik 198
SPECTRE, London 205, 232
SPEEDY TOMATO 334
SPEKTRUM PAINT & WALLPAPER 191
SPENCER, Linda 307
SPENGLER-AHRENS, Doerte 280
SPIESSL, Thomas 320
SPILLMANN, Martin 51, 190, 211, 343
SPILLSBURY, Simon 155
SPINK, Yves 128
SPORTPLAUSCH WIDER RACING BIKES 97
SPRING, Roy 317
SPRINGER & JACOBY, Barcelona 216
SPRINGER & JACOBY, Hamburg 43, 102, 124, 144, 145, 152, 162, 173, 228, 229, 230, 231, 265, 271, 277, 279, 284, 296, 339, 344, 355, 375
SPRINGER & JACOBY, London 65, 262
SPRINGER & JACOBY, Paris 228
SPRINGFELDT, Adam 28
SQUIBB, Vince 64, 273
SROKA, Jassna 145
ST. FLORIAN, Ilaria 41
ST. LEGER, Tony 317
ST. LUKES, London 181
ST. LUKES, Stockholm 334
STAHEL, Mark 226, 265
STALLINGA, Henk 364
STAM, Robin 74
STANČIK, Petr 171
STANGERTZ, Mia 351
STARCOM MEDIA PLANNING 263
STARK FILMS, London 62, 91
STAUB, Simon 262
STAUDINGER & FRANKE 203
STEFFEN, Nicole 40
STEFFENS, Annette 296
STEIGER, Nina 250
STEINER, Beate 168
STEINHILBER, Jan 143
STELLA ARTOIS 64
STELLATOS, Athanassios 250
STERRENBURG, Kees 242
STEVENSON, Mal 81
STIGAMOT, AGAINST DOMESTIC VIOLENCE 141
ŠTIMAC, Goran 66, 270
STINK, London 236, 250
STJERNSTRÖM, Anders 48
STOCKHOLM PRIDE FESTIVAL 318
STOCKHOLM VATTEN, WATER UTILITY 159
STOJANOVIĆ, Slavimir 202, 214, 351
STOLL, Christian 303
STOLTZ, Calle 274, 318
STONE, Bill 154
STONES, Rae 376
STORA ENSO, PAPER PRODUCTS 271
STORBRÅTEN, Bjarte A. 302
STRASSER, Sebastian 145
STRAT, Lisbon 222
STRAUGHAN, Peter 318
STRÄULI, Philipp 226, 265
STRAUSS, Ruck 157
STREULI, Felix 337
STRIDBECK, Mattias 326
STROGALSKI, Thomas 29, 230, 246
STRÖM, Mikael 360
STRONG, Tony 47
STROTMANN, Marc 315
STRZESZEWSKI, Maciek 64
STUB, Totte 111
STUCCHI, Bruno 207, 218
STUESSEL, Therese 320
STUTZNÄCKER, Tobias 279
SU BÜHLER COSTUME DESIGNER 376
SUBRAMANIAN, Suresh 226
SUDLER & HENNESSEY, Milan 207, 218
SUMMERS, Kevin 190, 234
SUNDBERG, Carl 311
SUNDELIN, Jesper 198, 374
SUNDQVIST, Cathrine 162, 339
SUNTINGER, Francy 27
SUOMI 24 FI, INTERNET PORTAL 174
SUPERNOODLES 34, 36
SUTCLIFFE, John 302
SUTHERLAND-DODD, Nick 245
SUVA INSURANCE 120, 123, 158
SVANVIK, Arvid 111
SVILPA, Raimundas 21
SWATCH SCUBA COLLECTION 291
SWEDBANK 114
SWEDISH BIBLE SOCIETY 360
SWISS MILK PRODUCERS 51
SWR TV, ANTI-TV VIOLENCE INITIATIVE 132
SYLVIN, Mika 30
TAČEVSKI, Nikola 31
TADDEUCCI, Francesco 175
TALLGÅRD, Åsa 191
TAMANDER, Maria 28
TAMBAY, Derya 187, 194
TANDEM CAMPMANY GUASCH DDB, Barcelona 63, 65, 106, 231, 233, 236
TANGERINA AZUL, Lisbon 240
TAPPERT, Johan 260
TASSRE, Amanda 286
TATARKO, Raffo 66, 266
TAUBES, Nicolas 29, 32, 34, 306
TAVIO, Joanna 157
TAXI PLUS 343
TAYLOR, Sam 317
TBWA\Athens 25
TBWA\Barcelona 42, 78, 106, 159, 160, 194, 213, 238
TBWA\Berlin 248
TBWA\Brussels 24, 25, 291
TBWA\E-Company, Amsterdam 335
TBWA\ESPAÑA, Madrid 56, 206
TBWA\Istanbul 187, 194
TBWA\London 317
TBWA\Paris 56, 84, 87, 112, 154, 167, 234, 235, 238, 312, 313
TEAM/YOUNG & RUBICAM, Dubai 226
TEIDLER, Natascha 228, 229
TEIXEIRA, Jorge 49
TEIXEIRA, Manuel 240
TEKO FILMS, Moscow 179
TELA PAPER TABLEWARE 190
TELLERUP, Dorte 93, 94
TEMIN, Frédéric 247
TEMPOMEDIA, Hamburg 228
TEN HEUVEL, Ismaël 172
TENGBY, Magnus 198
TERREEHORST, Paula 330
TESAURO, Madrid 146
TETLEY EARL GREY TEA 71
TETRA PAK, PACKAGING 270
TÉTU MAGAZINE 306
TEUNISSEN, Bert 31
TGV 84
THALYS 84, 88
THE BRIDGE, Glasgow 58
THE CHURCH OF SWEDEN 129
THE GANG FILMS, Paris 228
THE HAGUE PUBLIC TRANSPORT SERVICE 341
THE LEITH AGENCY, Edinburgh 62, 73, 79, 116, 324, 328, 329
THE MACALLAN SINGLE MALT SCOTCH WHISKY 355
THE MINISTRY OF ENVIRONMENT, RECYCLING CENTER 158
THE POLAR MUSIC PRIZE 373
THE SHACK, Hamburg 209
THE SWEDISH POST OFFICE 164, 169, 344
THE WHITE HOUSE, Reykjavik 52, 141
THEO FENNELL JEWELLERY 290
THERAPY FILMS, London 232
THEUNISSE, Ewald 31
THEY, Patrick 199, 263
THIACHE, Sylvain 177
THIEDE, Patrick 345
THITO, Philippe 55
THOMAZ, Lourenço 285, 316
THOMSEN, Axel 229, 296, 344
THÖRN & TÄCKENSTRÖM, Stockholm 191
THÖRN, Johan 191
THORNTON, Jim 293
THORNTON, Pete 328
THWAITES, Peter 276
TIELEMANS, Frank 251
TIELMAN, Roland 242
TIERSCHUTZVEREIN BERLIN, ANIMAL RIGHTS 139
TIETOENATOR IT SERVICES 260
TILLY, Berit 30, 260
TIMAN, Bertil 354
TIMMERMANN, Martin 213
TIMMS, Stephen 346
TIMNEY, John 217
TIMONEN, Mikko 72, 243
TIP LADY SHAVER 204
TODD, Daniel 232
TÖDT, Claudia 124, 144, 145, 271
TOMAŠEK, Toni 343
TORRE LAZUR McCANN, London 219
TORSTENSSON, Lars 370
TORTAJADA, Jose Miguel 39
TORTOSA, Luis Enrique González 202
TOSCANA, Agostino 125
TOTH, John 41
TOTTER NATURAL FRUIT SPIRIT 368
TOYOTA RAV4 TURBO DIESEL 241
TRAMONI, Jean-Marc 240
TRÄNKLE, Markus 110, 337
TRAVELPRICE 86
TREBELJAHR, Caroline 35
TREND MICRO ANTI-VIRUS SOFTWARE 255
TREURNIET, Maarten 44
TRICOT, Rémy 99, 167, 172
TRILL BIRD FOOD 35
TRISTÃO, Nuno 147
TRIZIVIR HIV THERAPY 217
TROLDAHL, Hans 96
TROMP, Peter 101
TROUVÉ-DUGENY, Christophe 98
TRUGEON, Corinne Assuerus 207
TRY ADVERTISING, Oslo 260
TRY, Kjetil 260
TRY-LEINER, Øyvind 321
TSM-PALMARÈS, Brussels 109
TULINIUS, Tomas 88, 234
TUOHIMAA, Teemu 143
TURCHETTI, Federico 125
TURHALA, Jussi 97, 174
TURNER, Sebastian 17, 103, 153, 352
TURQUET, Etienne 20, 85
TUURI, Jarkko 157
TV LICENCE INSPECTION 132
TWENFM 306
UBACHS WISBRUN, Amsterdam 242
UBACHS, Wim 242
UENAL, Gabriella 138
UHLE, Astrid 104
ULLAKKO, Jari 271
ULMER, Goetz 136, 138, 237
UMWELT, Copenhagen 86, 305
UNICEF 124, 145, 155
UNIVERSAL STUDIOS 361
UNIVERSITY OF NORTHUMBRIA 318
UPC CABLE TV 298, 299
URMETZER, Eric 348
USTINOVICH, Oleg 130
UTBERG, Mats 169, 344
UTTERLY BUTTERLY 47
UTURN, Paris 163
UYTTENHOVE, Frank 25, 297, 323
VAASAN BREAD 30
VACULÍK, Juraj 340
VA-H 142
VALENCIANO, Dani 42
VALERO, Xavier 63, 65
VALETTE, Eric 99
VALPAS, Kalle 33
VAN DE VIJVER, Frank 59
VAN DEN BRANDT, Willem 172
VAN DEN BROECK, Joeri 297
VAN DEN HEUVEL, Robert 31
VAN DER AA, Wieke 251
VAN DER HEIJDEN, Patrick 251
VAN DER HELM, Peter 74
VAN DER LECQ, Dick 115
VAN DER PLAS, Leendert 58
VAN DER STRAATEN, Violet 44
VAN DER VEN, Martijn 330
VAN DER VLUGT, Sylvester 336
VAN DIJK, Darre 341
VAN GELDER, Anne 58
VAN GILBERGEN, Dominique 297
VAN GOGH MUSEUM, LIGHT EXHIBITION 335
VAN HARREWIJEN, Willem 84, 115, 295
VAN HEEL, Tom 279
VAN MEEL, Jan 108
VAN SCHAIK, Raymond 115, 295
VAN SOMMERS, Jenny 247
VAN SONSBEEK, Martijn 31
VAN TRAN, Tho 281
VAN VELSEN, Pieter 44, 172, 214
VAN WALBEEK ETCETERA, Amsterdam 84, 115, 295
VAN ZACHTEN, Jurgen 330
VAN ZWAM, Jeroen 315
VANDEPUTTE, Anne-Marie 112
VAQUERO, Agustín 39, 86
VARELA, Miguel 240
VATTULAINEN, Marja 30
VAUGHN, Leslie 253
VAZQUEZ, Samuel 53
VBAT ENTERPRISE, Schiphol Oost 369
VBZ PUBLIC TRANSPORT 89
VEGA, David R. 249
VEIGUELA, Carmen 86
VENTURINI, Olivier 55
VENVILLE, Malcolm 232
VERDUYCKT, Brigitte 112
VERNER, Martin 158
VERONICA MAGAZINE 295
VESEL, Grega 74
VIDAL, Quico 206
VIGLIONE, Guillermo 170
VIGORELLI, Gian Pietro 235, 288
VILEDA ULTRA-MOP 196
VILLA, Dario 379
VILLIERS, Jean 228
VILLOUTREIX, Mathieu 34
VINCE, Christian 242
VINCE, Dario 270
VINCIGUERRA, Mathieu 18, 274
VING TRAVEL AGENCY 90
VINILE.COM 175
VINIZIUS YOUNG & RUBICAM, Barcelona 291
VIRANT, Franci 133
VIRANT, Iztok 343
VIRUS, Paris 373
VISIT SCOTLAND 89
VITRUVIO LEO BURNETT, Madrid 196, 263
VITTEL MINERAL WATER 77
VÍZNEROVÁ, Tereza 31, 38
VLIEGENTHART, Jaap 242
VOGEL, Dr. Stephan 18, 127, 132, 136, 200, 209
VOLKMER, Michael 325, 331
VOLKSWAGEN BEETLE 222, 224, 225, 226, 227
VOLVO C70 CONVERTIBLE 243
VÖLZOW, Stephanie 26
VON BÜREN, Thilo 315
VON REIS, Christoffer 294
VON RICHTOFEN, Ossi 158
VON SCHEVEN Burkhart 254
VON STEYERN, Patrik Vult 314, 348, 349
VON UNWERTH, Ellen 272
VON WELTZIEN, Deneke 237, 339
VONIER, Julien 51, 89, 211
VOSS, Oliver 237
VOSSEN, Jürgen 149, 305
VUCIC, Ivana 270
VULCAN FILMS, Helsinki 30
VVL/BBDO, Brussels 59
W.A.F, Berlin 363
WAEBER, Jürg 128
WAGNER, Thim 319
WAITES, Mark 34, 36, 69, 70, 212, 293, 308
WAITROSE, DIVA SANITARY TOWELS 371
WALICZEK, Grzegorz 54
WALKER, Cora 323
WALKER, Pius 189, 320
WALKER, Sam 308
WALMRATH, Thomas 43, 145, 152, 162, 284, 339, 355, 375
WALRAFF, Jean-Luc 55
WAPPENSCHMIDT, Manfred 35
WARD, Ash 73
WARREN, Richard 302
WASSNER, Nicola 255
WATERKAMP, Hermann 140
WATERS, Patrick 48, 114, 309
WATSON, Chris 58
WATT, Les 62, 116
WATTION, Raf 114
WEBB, Trevor 43
WEBER, Alexander 296
WEBER, Marco 18, 132, 136, 200
WEBER, Timm 124, 144, 145, 265, 271
WECOVER CAR INSURANCE 112
WECZEREK, Alexandra 237
WEDDERBURN, Martin 73
WEDDERBURN, Rufus 89, 266, 356
WEDENDAHL, Kasper 93, 94, 260
WEEKS, Randy 248
WEISHAEUPL, Hans 319
WEISS, Lee 253
WELLENS, Antoine 330
WELLERMANN, Martin 231
WELSH, Al 232
WENDLER, Marcus 140
WENGENMAYR, Ralf 331
WENTZ, Jan 285
WESTMEN, Jacob 334
WESTPHAL, Bernd 363
WESTRE, Susan 253, 264
WESTUM, Paul 104
WETZEL, Matthias 95
WHY US?, Paris 224
WIDGREN, Kalle 52
WIENER STÄDTISCHE 120
WIEWIÓRSKI, Jaroslaw 142
WIKERBERG, Malin 155
WIKTOR/LEO BURNETT, Bratislava 66, 266
WILDBERGER, Thomas 136, 138, 237
WILHELM, Alexander 183
WILHELM, Steven 321
WILLIAM LAWSON'S 55
WILLIAMS, Helen 286
WILLIAMS, Jody 248
WILLIAMSON, Luke 36, 69, 70
WILLIAMSON, Nick 296
WILLIAUME, Jean 236
WILMES, Ralph 16, 282
WILSON, Dougal 116, 324, 329
WING, Bob 217
WINTERHAGEN, Michael 168
WINTERHALDER, Katja 90
WIRSÉN, Stina 367
WIRTSCHAFTSWOCHE MAGAZINE 305
WIRZ & FRAEFEL PRODUCTIONS, Zürich 150, 259
WIRZ WERBUNG, Zürich 98, 317
WIRZ, Dana 51, 89
WIRZ, Ernst 150
WITTE, Carsten 152
WITTIG, Harald 221
WLODARSKA, Malgorzata 142
WOERNER, Rüdiger 332
WOKOWSKI, Jacek 54
WOLBERS, Hans 364
WOLF, André 218
WOLF, Antje 362
WOLGERS, Dan 362
WOLOSZ, Magda 64
WÖLTJE, Gregor 174
WOODPECKER FILM, Helsinki 150
WOODS, Dave 76, 353
WORLDWIDE FUND FOR NATURE 127, 136
WRENN, Trevor 172
WRIGHT, Chris 181
WROBEL, Torben 345
WUCHNER, Heinz 200
WURSTER, Stefan 57
WÜTHRICH, Hanspeter 352
WWAV RAPP COLLINS, Edinburgh 355
WYSNY, Regina 140, 265
XIBERRAS, Stephane 164
XMASTREESDIRECT.CO.UK 188
XYNIAS, WETZEL, VON BÜREN, Munich 95, 315
YARDEN FUNERAL INSURANCE 115
YELLOW PAGES 341
YEO, Jonathan 290
YES CHOCOLATE CAKE 44
YOKYOR, Amsterdam 16, 282
YOPLAIT PETITS FILOUS 52
YOUNG & RUBICAM, Copenhagen 59, 115
YOUNG & RUBICAM, Frankfurt 303
YOUNG & RUBICAM, Lisbon 191, 285, 314, 316
YOUNG & RUBICAM, Prague 171
YTTERBORN & FUENTES, Stockholm 367
ZABALA, Rodrigo 263
ZÁLEŽÁK, Rast'o 66, 266
ZAMBELLI, Max 22
ZANINI, Sébastien 213
ZAPATER, Sergi 106
ZAPPING, Madrid 119, 188, 359, 364
ZATORSKI, Darek 105, 197
ZAVRL, Mateja D. 126
ZELO HAIRDRESSERS 109
ZIMMERER, Wolfgang 173
ZIMMERMANN, Stefanie 26
ZINKE, Gerrit 102
ZLATAR, Ajna 22
ZOO, Les 44
ZORNROT, ORGANISATION FOR SEXUALLY ABUSED CHILDREN 140
ZU INNHAUSEN UND KNYPHAUSEN, Ysabel 334
ZUERCHER, Hansjoerg 51
ZÜNKELER, Ulrich 145, 152, 162, 339
ZÜRICH BALLET 316
ZVV VERKEHRSVERBUND 83
ZWART, Harald 82, 165
&CO., Copenhagen 117, 287
.START, Munich 174
\BRAND COMPANY, Paris 367
1/33 PRODUCTIONS, Paris 32, 37, 312
11840 AG, TELEPHONE ENQUIRY SERVICE 168
1576 ADVERTISING, Edinburgh 89, 91, 266, 356
180 COMMUNICATIONS, Amsterdam 286
25 FPS, Amsterdam 44
2AM FILMS, London, 81
4½, Oslo 82
7 UP 76